KENNETH BURKE + THE POSTHUMAN

RSA·STR

THE RSA SERIES IN TRANSDISCIPLINARY RHETORIC

The RSA Series in Transdisciplinary Rhetoric is a collaboration with the Rhetoric Society of America to publish innovative and rigorously argued scholarship on the tremendous disciplinary breadth of rhetoric. Books in the series take a variety of approaches, including theoretical, historical, interpretive, critical, or ethnographic, and examine rhetorical action in a way that appeals, first, to scholars in communication studies and English or writing and, second, to at least one other discipline or subject area.

*Edited by Chris Mays, Nathaniel A. Rivers,
and Kellie Sharp-Hoskins*

KENNETH BURKE +
THE POSTHUMAN

THE PENNSYLVANIA STATE UNIVERSITY PRESS
UNIVERSITY PARK, PENNSYLVANIA

Library of Congress Cataloging-in-Publication Data

Names: Mays, Chris, 1976– , editor. | Rivers, Nathaniel A.,
   editor. | Sharp-Hoskins, Kellie, 1982– , editor.
Title: Kenneth Burke + the posthuman / edited by Chris
   Mays, Nathaniel A. Rivers, and Kellie Sharp-Hoskins.
Other titles: Kenneth Burke and the posthuman | RSA series
   in transdisciplinary rhetoric.
Description: University Park, Pennsylvania : The Pennsylvania
   State University Press, [2017] | Series: The RSA series in
   transdisciplinary rhetoric | Includes bibliographical references
   and index.
Summary: "A transdisciplinary exploration of the work of
   Kenneth Burke and posthumanist rhetorics. In considering
   questions of power and persuasion, as well as of ethics,
   responsibility, the contributors to this volume imagine the
   contradictions among Burke's writings and posthumanism
   as opportunities for knowledge making"—Provided by
   publisher.
Identifiers: LCCN 2017029196| ISBN 9780271079080
   (cloth : alk. paper) |
ISBN 9780271079097 (pbk. : alk. paper)
Subjects: LCSH: Burke, Kenneth, 1897–1993—Criticism and
   interpretation. | Rhetoric—Philosophy. | Humanism.
Classification: LCC P85.B85 K455 2017 | DDC 801/.95092—
   dc23
LC record available at https://lccn.loc.gov/2017029196

The Pennsylvania State University Press is a member of the
Association of American University Presses.

Contents

Acknowledgments

Edited collections such as this one invariably have both concrete and ephemeral beginnings. It can be accurately said that this collection emerged from the Ninth Triennial Conference of the Kenneth Burke Society, organized by Paul Lynch and Nathaniel A. Rivers, which took place in the summer of 2014 at Saint Louis University. More specifically, it began to emerge in a seminar on Kenneth Burke and New Materialisms led by Steven Katz. It was this conference and this seminar that brought us together as editors, surfacing the shared curiosities and commitments that ground this collection. But the collection's emergence also took place across the range of scholars who ultimately came to compose it. As the depth and dexterity of the chapters demonstrate, each contributor brought with them a range of expertise and experience that coalesced into some rather stunning scholarship. Additionally, we are indebted to series editors Leah Ceccarelli and Michael Bernard-Donals, and to our two reviewers, who offered precise and patient readings. And, finally, we owe no small measure of gratitude to our own editor, Kendra Boileau, who generously shepherded this project from beginning to end.

As editors, too, we each came to the collection assembled by networks of experiences, institutions, and individual relationships, which we, in turn, acknowledge here:

Chris

Acknowledgments are always lacking, never complete. Here, though, is the tip of the iceberg of people and experiences that contributed to my work on this collection: my coeditors, who provided support, collegiality, and brilliance, and in general made this an amazing and thoroughly enjoyable collaboration; Julie Jung, whose mentorship and encouragement played a significant role in creating the conditions for the emergence of this collection, and who continues to provide indispensable and inimitable perspective; *JAC: A Journal of Rhetoric, Culture, and Politics*, the journal that gave me years of editorial-assistant experience and helped me begin to understand what exactly this field is about (and, of course, begin to understand the job of editing); and my partner, Sam, who has contributed more than anyone else to who I am, what I write, and how I think.

Nathaniel

I would like to acknowledge the support of my friend and colleague Paul Lynch, with whom I organized the Ninth Triennial Conference of the Kenneth Burke Society. The framework we developed for that conference continues to shape my thinking about Burke. And, as always, I am grateful for the love and support of my family: Jodi, Will, and little Scarlett Rose, who arrived as this collection came together. Finally, I want to thank Kellie and Chris for inviting me along: the lunch we shared in that mostly empty restaurant in Tampa inaugurated both this collection and a lasting friendship.

Kellie

I would like to thank my mentor and collaborator Julie Jung, who not only first suggested that Chris and I pursue this project but also trained us in how to imagine and tackle complex, worthwhile projects. I'd also like to thank the other mentors and colleagues who inspire and challenge me, especially Amy Robillard, Angela Haas, Erin Frost, Kyle Jensen, Lynn Worsham, and Marie Moeller. This project would not have been possible without my family, especially Mike—sounding board and support extraordinaire—and Frankie, who slept through the whole thing. And finally, thank you to my two amazing coeditors. Go Team.

Introduction | Articulating Ambiguous Compatibilities

Chris Mays, Nathaniel A. Rivers, and Kellie Sharp-Hoskins

Posthumanism first appears as antithetical, nearly impossible, for rhetoric. In place of the polis and politics, it offers microbes and machines; instead of symbol-using animals, it foregrounds cells and cybernetics. Rhetoric concerns itself with human affairs; *post*humanism seems concerned with leaving the human behind. The prospect of a posthuman rhetoric thus seems to signify, at best, a paradox, a contradiction in terms. At its worst, it suggests the end of our discipline. And yet, in the past decade, as scholars (re)map and (re)imagine previously taken-for-granted categories that organize rhetorical inquiry—language, bodies, materiality, agency, responsibility, ethics—they increasingly draw on posthumanist theories to do so (Brooke; Muckelbauer and Hawhee; Mara and Hawk; Dobrin; Gries; Lynch and Rivers; Barnett and Boyle; Boyle). Posthumanism might be said to be collated by "a refusal to take humanism for granted" (Badmington 10). Rosi Braidotti explains, almost as a caveat, that "to be posthuman does not mean to be indifferent to humans, or to be de-humanized" (190). It offers, instead, both a "thematics of the decentering of the human in relation to either evolutionary, ecological, or technological coordinates" as well as an investigation into "how thinking confronts that thematics, what thought has to become in the face of those challenges" (Wolfe xvi). Posthumanism opens up the human, and it does so first and foremost by unpacking previous definitions of the human, particularly those humanist definitions that privilege the human as some hermetically sealed, ontologically discrete entity in the world.

Perhaps the posthuman turn in rhetoric, then, spins from the propensity of posthumanist terminologies to unpack and reexamine the *human*. This work strikes us as rhetorical. The question of what constitutes *the rhetoric of the human* moves in two compelling directions. This first, epistemological question pursues how the concept of the human is deployed and composed as a trope. What is the history of *human*, how has it been employed, and to what ends? What ways of seeing and not seeing does it enable? In this posthuman move, we see a disciplinary affinity. The second, ontological line of thought drives toward the heart of (the) matter. What is the nature of *being* in rhetoric? What constitutes the boundaries and features of *human beings engaged in rhetoric*? So much of rhetoric is predicated upon both epistemological and ontological understandings of the human. A rhetoric presumes an anthropology, so to speak. To speak of rhetoric, then, is to have already decided something about *the human*. We see this at work in rhetoric with none other than Kenneth Burke, whose dramatism (a way of rhetorically engaging the thorny question of motive) is paired with and grounded in his "Definition of Man." Burke's definition of humans as symbol-using and symbol-misusing animals is at the heart of his rhetorical project. Treating human *beings* as defined and distinguished as symbol-using animals sets the stage for Burke's rhetorical project (as many of the chapters in this collection demonstrate). This grounding move, in whichever direction, inheres across rhetorical studies writ large. Burke is the figure with whom this collection engages the posthuman, which is, again, a renewed thinking of the human.

A move toward Burke in the context of posthumanism, however, is not without complications. It is Burke, after all, who sees humans as a fundamentally distinct kind of being: "regardless of man's biological origins, his specific aptitude for symbol-systems marks *the passing of a critical point* (as with the steps that divide water from ice or steam)" ("Revival" 488; emphasis added). Burke here challenges the distinction between humans and other animals as merely one of degree. Contra Charles Darwin, Burke sees the human/nonhuman distinction as one of kind:

> In all decency, and lest we dishonor the many non-human species that are trying to eke out an honest living, we should at least *categorically* distinguish between all those other poor devils and the kind of symbol-wielding animal that can produce Isms, Madison Avenue, Wall Street, yellow journals, a Hitler, a Birchite, an occasional soft-spoken, cross-burning Southerner, and exalted calls to wage thermonuclear, chemical, and bacteriological war in the name of progress and freedom. Mr. Darwin, it was not nice of you to play down the fact that *we are something special*, endowed with the ability to be the unkindest kind of all. (488; emphasis added)

Not only are humans a distinct *kind* of animal—a line of thought that posthumanism brings in for some serious questioning—but it appears to be *rhetoric* itself that distinguishes the human. If rhetoric and the posthuman seem an unlikely fit, then using Burke to join them appears to be a fool's errand.

Despite rhetoric's turn to the posthuman, however, Burke—humanist par excellence—remains a towering figure in rhetorical studies. As suggested as early as 1966, one reason "for looking carefully at the work of Kenneth Burke when considering the future of rhetoric is that he is truly concerned with something that can still be called rhetoric within the historical meaning of that term" (Swartz 210). His body of work still anchors many of our field's most basic precepts: extended or challenged, dismissed or developed, coopted or simply copied, Burke is a figure with whom we feel we must commune. And yet, Burke's body of work is multiple. There are, Burke scholars never tire of pronouncing, many Kenneth Burkes: "There are as many Burkes as there are books and essays by him and probably more Burkes than there are books because there are often many Burkes in one book" (Rueckert 3). It is this very multiplicity, we suggest, that offers one way in which posthumanism can commune with Burkeology, which is itself already transdisciplinary. Scholars who work with Burke, that is, do so by necessarily thinking beyond disciplinary walls. These Burkeans may study rhetoric, generally, but they hail from—and speak to—a number of disparate disciplines: communication, English, composition, American studies, sociology, and philosophy, among others. Not coincidentally, the same transdisciplinary ethos is a characteristic of scholars who study posthumanism, even those who ostensibly do not study rhetoric; their work can be found in English, communication, technology studies, media theory, philosophy, theology and religious studies, and American studies, among many other examples.

Despite the theoretical and practical difficulty posed by this multiplicity, we posit that it allows both posthumanism and Burke studies to thrive in the form that Gilles Deleuze and Felix Guattari call a rhizome, which suggests possibilities but also takes the form of a chaotic web of interconnections in which any point "can be connected to anything other" (7). As Deleuze and Guattari remind us, despite its seeming tangle, from this multiple can always be subtracted the one; as they put it, a person must begin mapping, or must find a point at which to engage, via "subtraction" (6–7). In short, to deal with the multiple, as we do with this project, a person has to start somewhere.

And so, Burke. But why Burke? Why this *somewhere*? In brief, we argue that Burke is *compatible* with posthumanism. Not prescient. Not anticipatory. Not nascent. *We are decidedly not arguing that Burke was a posthumanist: he certainly wasn't.* Then again, we do not think that posthuman impulses within rhetoric arrive *sui generis*. As someone who articulated a rhetoric while also ever writing about bodies and technology (which, as the chapters here collected evidence, he did often), Burke's work can be made to connect to or fit within contemporary posthumanism. Of the many twentieth-century rhetoricians one could draw upon, Burke's work is perhaps most intensely populated by bodies and technologies. The work of Debra Hawhee in particular makes plain that Burke was a rhetorician particularly focused, if not fixated, upon the body. Burke as well, in letters and in essays, was most vocal in his anxiety about the place and influence on human life specifically and the broader ecology generally. As rhetoric continues to grapple with the disciplinary implications of the posthuman and the Anthropocene, we find that the sprawling work of Burke contains more than a few resources. In a rhizome, as a bramble, more than a few thorns catch.

And so, *compatibility*. *Compatibility* is a word of French origin, and it provides, more or less, the ethos of this collection's engagement with Burke in the context of the posthuman. The etymology of *compatibility* is suggestive in this regard. It encompasses the emotional, the social, and the technological. *Compatible* connotes the capacity for mutual suffering and/or sympathy as well as mutual tolerance (or of being admitted together). The word also has (more recent) scientific and technical uses with respect to chemistry and biology as well as colors in painting, specifically with paints that one can use together "without producing undesirable effects" ("Compatibility"). More recently, the term shows up in computing contexts to refer to a piece of technology that can work with another, a sense that even better serves our purposes here. Admittedly, the word somewhat falls short because typically it means "usable without adaptation or modification," which seems to be the required meaning if we are to fit Burke with the posthuman. Of course there's a tension here, as we often speak of something being *made compatible*. Adaptors are sometimes needed. At its simplest, *compatibility* marks a relationship made possible by an available means of connection.

Compatibility, then, is a function of *ambiguity*, which itself has a compelling etymology. Karen Pinkus argues, in the context of environmental studies, that

> we can learn, for example, something useful about our attitudes to climate science by examining the Latin prefix *amb(i)*, which is the basis of terms

such as *ambiguous*, *ambient* (or *ambiance* or *ambience*), and *ambivalence*. Etymologically and formally related to the Greek prefix *amph(i)*, *ambi* actually traces its cultural and philosophical development from the Greek *peri*. We may begin with *ambiguous*, which is, perhaps, the least ambiguous of the three terms we are concerned with here. *Ambiguous* is a direct incorporation into medieval French and English of the Latin *ambiguus* (movable, in doubt) from the verbs *ambire* or *ambagere* (to go around, wander, doubt). (89)

To be compatible requires a certain dexterity, an ambidextrousness. We are also drawn to *ambiguity* for the same reason that Burke was: it is a rich resource for intellectual work. Terminologies are where "ambiguities necessarily arise," and, Burke argues, we need terms that clearly reveal these spots rather than terms that avoid them (*Grammar* xviii). But we also want to push Burke's usage of ambiguity in a mode that is similar to Victor Vitanza's mode of reading and intensifying Burke. "What we need and desire," Vitanza writes, "is not just terms that reveal the strategic spots at which ambiguities necessarily arise, but terms that create, detonate, and exploit these ambiguities" (55). This is the ambiguity that posthumanism provokes. For example, Braidotti, in her explanation of the posthuman, writes of the need for "pragmatic experimentation" (45). And this experimentation entails transdisciplinary flexibility.

This collection thus elides theoretical and methodological uniformity, premised, as it is, on wandering among the complexities of ambiguous interanimation. In response to these complexities, the chapters in this collection take shape under the rubric of two concepts—boundaries and futures—that also organize the collection itself. Such an organization (1) acknowledges the importance of such terms within Burke and posthuman studies; (2) contributes to scholarship about boundaries and futures within both Burkean and posthuman studies; (3) expands the appeal of the collection by focusing on concepts with broad circulation; and (4) models careful, thoughtful, transdisciplinary work. Indeed, terministically screened through boundaries and futures, this collection responds to such questions as: How can we account for the complex relationships between boundaries and futures? How do such accounts (acting as boundaries) produce or limit potential futures? How can we affirm human(e) ethics without reinscribing the troubling legacies of humanism? How can our disciplinary (and) epistemological commitments inform a new transdisciplinary spirit of inquiry that can challenge—and even "undo," as Jasbir Puar puts it—traditionally held and "taken-for-granted knowledge formations" (xv)? Finally, how might rhetoric contribute to an emerging sense of a "posthuman humanities" (Braidotti 143)?

Amid the rhizome introduced in this collection, then, we articulate a *somewhere* grounded in "true irony, humble irony" (Burke, *Grammar* 514). That is, in drawing together not only multiplicities but seeming antitheses, this collection is motivated by "a sense of fundamental kinship with the enemy, as one needs him, is indebted to him, is not merely outside of him as an observer but contains him within, being consubstantial with him" (514). Following Burke's definition, such consubstance does not conflate Burke (studies, attitudes, grammars, rhetorics) with posthumanism, but imagines the contradictions among Burke's body of work and posthumanism as generative, as opportunities for invention, revision, and, importantly, transdisciplinary knowledge-making. In short, compatibility activated by ambiguity. Such work also follows Braidotti's call for posthuman ethics, which, she argues, "have to be generated affirmatively and created by efforts geared to creating possible futures, by mobilizing resources and visions that have been left untapped" (191). Rather than merely map posthumanist rhetorics onto Burke's body of work or conduct Burkean analyses of posthumanist projects, then, the contributions to this collection purposefully interanimate Burke and posthumanist rhetorics across disciplines, allowing us to imagine rhetorical futures otherwise unthinkable, impossible.

Compatibility, then, both thematically describes the collection and anticipates its emergent organization. It suggests movements across boundaries and the building of relationships. *Compatibility* promises that we might, going forward, get along in some fashion. It means not just any match but a match that works to some end. *Compatibility* is a good posthuman term because it transcends human/nonhuman bounds. Technologies can be compatible; so, too, can people. The term does not discriminate. *Compatibility* is necessarily ambiguous in this respect. It also has a temporal quality (or expresses temporal conditions), as when one speaks of backwards compatibility. When thinking in terms of compatibility, one must think through time. What will (have) be(come) compatible? Compatibility, or a focus on or attention to it, is about the building *of and for* relationships. To make some*thing* compatible is to cross boundaries with an eye toward the future. The remainder of this introduction, then, attends to boundaries and futures.

Boundaries

If the posthuman entails possibilities of compatibility amid multiplicity and complexity, then boundaries may be the preeminent posthuman tool. As posthumanism delineates a multifaceted and rhizomatic epistemological landscape, boundaries allow us to carve that landscape into discrete and manageable chunks. N. Katherine Hayles argues that drawing boundaries, which she calls "making a cut," is a (perhaps *the*) key move in a posthuman epistemological paradigm: "The observer," she writes, in creating meaning "reduces the unfathomable complexity of undifferentiated reality into something she can understand" ("Making" 160). Such "cuts" create workable knowledge; they create a *somewhere* where we can make better sense of our complex environments. By repeatedly drawing and being drawn to different boundaries, we build our ability to understand how different knowledges fit together—how they might be compatible. As Karen Barad notes in her articulation of a "posthumanist performative approach" (135), when boundaries are reworked, they bring about different "exclusions" as to what is "intelligible," and these exclusions "open a space for the agential reconfiguring of boundaries" (181). Barad argues that we are in fact ethically *obligated* to "contest and rework what matters and what is excluded from mattering" (178). Boundaries create manageable space as a beginning, and so they allow us to understand and manage better the complexity that is an inescapable aspect of our engagement with a posthuman world.

That boundaries are necessary features of posthumanism may seem counterintuitive; after all, blurring and breaking down boundaries is a major feature of much posthuman work. Braidotti argues, for example, that the "shared starting point" for posthuman theory is a "non-dualistic understanding" of the "nature-culture continuum"—that is, we begin posthumanism by blurring the boundaries between these two realms (2–3). Posthumanism conspicuously posits a dynamic and indeterminate world: what was distinctly human becomes cyborg; what was distinctly animal becomes invested with consciousness and human-equivalent subjectivity; what were distinctly inanimate machines become animate and, perhaps, sentient. This boundary-blurring extends beyond the humanities (a term itself that recalls a time pre-posthumanism), as in the sciences, too, previously paradigmatic boundary lines are now in a state of transition. The boundaries of thought and consciousness, for example, are more and more being blurred and called into question. Andy Clark describes this new view of cognition in the sciences as that which takes into account "inextricable tangles of feedback, feed-forward, and feed-around loops . . . that promiscuously criss-cross the boundaries of brain, body, and world" (xxviii).

Concordant with this posthumanist blurring of boundaries is the rise of transdisciplinarity. Transdisciplinary inquiry erases the boundaries of more "traditional" disciplinary inquiry and brings together, as Melissa M. Littlefield and Jenell M. Johnson write, incongruous "vocabularies, methods, and epistemologies that might seem to be mutually exclusive" (87). As such, transdisciplinarity is a thoroughly posthuman mode(l) of inquiry. This transdisciplinary boundary-blurring has spread to a wide variety of fields, resulting in several unique and innovative collaborations, and inter- or transdisciplinary work is quickly becoming a respected model in the contemporary university. Interdisciplinary teaching, as well, is on the rise. Terumi Taylor argues that this kind of teaching is potentially transformative, as it can help scholars "participate actively with [their] students in their journey of alternating, integrating and understanding different viewpoints." As Burke himself remarked in 1941, "The new alignment will outrage in particular those persons who take the division of the faculties in our universities to be an exact replica of the way in which God himself divided up the universe. We have had the Philosophy of the Being; and we have had the Philosophy of the Becoming. In contemporary specialization, we have been getting the Philosophy of the Bin" (*Philosophy* 303). In short, as Glen Mazis puts it, traditional disciplinary inquiries have uncovered "realms" of knowledge that, rather than neatly separated parcels amenable to a crisp and ordered separation, are a "fluid, evolving, and problematic coming together of differing perspectives that cross-fertilize and also break off in differing vectors, only to rejoin again at some later point" (8). Such a complex picture, he continues, evokes "a nonlinear equation's graph with its myriad branches and discontinuities, rather than the incremental, straight-line and consistently predictable Cartesian graphs that the old philosophies and sciences sought as companion models and emblems of their thought" (8).

Understanding posthumanism as this branched network of interconnected and overlapping categories of thought—understanding it as transdisciplinary— brings into relief many related theoretical formulations ascendant in contemporary scholarship. Recent systems and complexity theories, for example, exemplify posthumanist precepts in their holistic and interconnected visions of world-as-complex-system, where no event or element is ever independent from the rest of the system. Posthuman systems theory arises in part from mid twentieth-century cybernetics, an early transdisciplinary framework where, as Hayles writes, disciplinary "concepts that began with narrow definitions" were able to "spread out" into interdisciplinary networks of "broader significance" (*How* 51). This posthumanist "systems-thinking" also arises from long traditions of indigenous knowledges. These traditions, as Daniel Wildcat writes, hold that "human tribal identities, and the largest part of all human cultures until very recently, were literally emergent from the complex systems, the environment and ecologies, where we lived" (127).

Emerging from these theoretical frameworks, posthumanism pushes past the notion that the boundaries that define our world simply need to be redrawn in order to be set right; rather, posthumanist thought suggests that the very act of categorization is untenable. Lynn Worsham summarizes this point well, explaining that we humans "are the kind of creatures who habitually wield conceptual categories as if they were descriptions of reality when in fact they are deeply interested interpretations of reality" ("From" 408). For posthumanists, the boundaries that define our world are determined in endlessly dynamic and infinitely complex contexts, and thus, through a posthuman lens, any transcendent-seeming basis for our boundary-drawing is revealed as a product of our own situated and partial perspective—a "deeply interested" fiction. No matter how we draw them, our boundary lines will *always* be imperfect, subject to critique.

In this sense, posthumanism's challenge to boundaries seems thoroughgoing. Here, though, lies the paradox. While posthumanism involves breaking down boundaries, as Hayles (and others) remind us, posthumanism *needs* boundaries. Boundaries wither in the face of posthuman complexity, but they also allow us to deal with complexity in the first place. The famous line of Deleuze and Guattari—"Never believe that a smooth space will suffice to save us" (500)—cautions us that to assume the world exists without boundaries—to assume that all is "smooth space"—neglects the "striated" space, or the "holey" spaces, that alternately score and puncture the seeming smoothness, giving our world order, hierarchy, and gradation.

Such negligence of boundaries is particularly tempting for a version of posthumanism that would posit none, just as for a version of transdisciplinarity that would eliminate disciplinary lines altogether. However, even with the most radical erasure, the boundary lines of our world are always being redrawn. Deleuze and Guattari's warning highlights that even as we break down boundaries, new ones are forming. Hierarchies are and will always be a significant feature of even the flattest network, and unequal power distributions will never vanish into the smoothness of complexity. Moreover, *we* are often the ones who provide the boundary lines that then organize our newfound, ostensibly "smooth" world, even as we strive to erase them.

In many cases, these new boundaries are drawn as a defense mechanism. Just as Wendy Brown argues that the erosion of national power can result in a "frenzy" of wall-building to protect national borders (24), the threat of post-humanism and of transdisciplinarity to break down boundaries can result in a defensive redrawing or even a reinscription of the old lines. In either case, as we confront what seems to be dazzling and expansive complexity with no limit to its potential to be explored, we do in fact set limits—often as a defense mechanism, as a way to cling to the certainty of familiar hierarchies, or simply to prevent ourselves from being overwhelmed by the very complexity we confront.

Such a recognition of boundaries where none are purported to be is precisely where the compatibility of Burke and posthumanism becomes evident. Burke's work lies squarely in the realm of hierarchy, of categories, and of division(s). Burke theorizes boundaries, but he also gives us tools with which to negotiate relationships between boundaries unrecognized, undertheorized, or unthought. Burke frames a world of order, but he also allows us to widen what he calls the "circumference" of a situation. "Altering the scenic scope affects the interpretation of the act," he writes, a remark pithy but expansive in its implication (*Grammar* 79). While Burke may posit a world beset by circumscriptions, in a compatible juxtaposition with the posthuman, he exemplifies the notion Wolfe calls "openness from closure" (167–68). "Closure," in this sense, *opens* a situation to new possibilities, creating the condition upon which we can move ahead to new formulations and new ways of thinking about transdisciplinary rhetoric. A Burkean/posthumanist mashup, then, provokes us to take a step back from the boundaries we draw in our work—even our transdisciplinary work—and to recognize what was left out of our theories and our thinking. Moreover, while transdisciplinary rhetorics may break down boundaries, Burke reminds us that rhetoric is in many ways the study of the persuasiveness of those boundaries and a study of their tendency to re-form. It is from the relations between Burke and posthumanism that frameworks of inquiry emerge that can intervene, reframe, and thus disrupt stable transdisciplinary imaginations of our boundaries. Even while these acts end up relying on new perspectives that themselves entail new boundaries, we can always start the process again. Situating Burke in compatible relation to posthumanism, we find ways to multiply the possibilities of transdisciplinary rhetorical inquiry.

Futures

Such multiplication is not merely an academic exercise, it not only offers rhetoricians new horizons to acknowledge, moves to make, boundaries to cross. Rather, the boundary work made possible by drawing together Burke studies and posthumanism participates in multiplying (rhetorical) futures. From his earliest work, Burke insisted on the necessary connection between boundaries and futures, positing boundaries—the terms and frames we use to *select* reality—as a way to *act* in the present with the goal of intervening in the future. Such thinking, as Worsham argues, radically reformulated the project of rhetorical inquiry itself. According to Worsham, "whereas classical theorists viewed rhetoric as an alternative to violence, Burke reconceived rhetoric as both the disease and the cure, to use his terms, by which he meant that violence or victimage—the disease—arises from the same source as the cure: from the very terms in which we categorize and frame a given situation as a problem, terms that train us to look in one direction rather than another for possible solutions" ("Moving" 30–31). Burke advocated responding to this terministic training (elsewhere characterized by Burke as "trained incapacity") with "hortatory, poetic naming" or "language as symbolic action." As M. Elizabeth Weiser explains in *Burke, War, Words*, poetic naming was, for Burke, a means for "evincing change," or more specifically, a means for how "poets and activists could exhort and how sociologists and semanticists could more accurately measure the present to predict future actions" (36–37). This poetic naming served as a direct rejoinder to "descriptive semantic naming," which Burke appraised as merely promissory—holding, according to Weiser, "the promise of some future action without pointing toward what that action might be" (36). Indicting the promise of the future as insufficient to address the conditions from which it arose (the conditions of the present), Burke asks, "might we, rather than living wholly by a future that threatens so strongly to refute us, do rather what we can to live in a present that may in good time spread into the future?" (*Philosophy* 162). For Burke, then, boundaries not only create the conditions of possibility for imagining action (as explained by his theory of poetic naming or dramatism), but underwrite the actions that will authorize or foreclose future action.

In short, as he suggests in *The Rhetoric of Religion*, "The future will inevitably be what the particular combination of all men's [*sic*] efforts and counter-efforts and virtues and vices, along with the nature of things in general, inevitably adds up to" (272).

With a similar goal for creating change, Braidotti argues for posthuman ethics predicated on "conceptual creativity" (54). As in Burke's rationale for poetic naming, Braidotti likewise correlates action and futures: "The future as an active object of desire propels us forth and motivates us to be active in the here and now of a continuous present that calls for both resistance and the counter-actualization of alternatives. The yearning for sustainable futures can construct a livable present. This is not a leap of faith, but an active transposition, a transformation at the in-depth level" (192). Of course, Braidotti articulates just one of many posthuman conceptualizations of time (past, present, and/or future). She is quick to disarticulate her own approach—"engaging affirmatively with the present" (5)—from other posthuman perspectives. Such perspectives include, for example, Hayles's review of early thinking on posthuman futures, which, she suggests "differ in degree and kind of interfaces they imagine [but] . . . concur that the posthuman implies not only a coupling with intelligent machines but a coupling so intense and multifaceted that it is no longer possible to distinguish meaningfully between the biological organism and the information circuits in which it is enmeshed" (*How* 35). According to Hayles, while posthuman thinkers hypothesize a range of possibilities for imagining futures, such possibilities cohere around the idea of boundaries among human and nonhuman losing their significance, their ability to signify meaningful difference. From this perspective, a posthuman future is not signified by tense (what comes after human?) or definition (what does it mean to be human or posthuman?) but by difference, by what and how differences matter.

Posthumanist engagement with futures is complicated even further in systems theory, which rejects temporal thinking per se but retains a distinction between the *actual* and the *possible*. For Wolfe interpreting Luhmann, this is "systems theory's version of what Derrida calls the dynamic force of *différance* as 'temporization' and 'spacing,' as 'protention' and 'retention,' a process that 'is possible only if each so-called element . . . is related to something other than itself, thereby keeping within itself the mark of the past element' while at the same time being 'vitiated by the mark of its relation to the future element,' thus 'constituting what is called the present by means of this very relation to what it is not'" (16–17). Although markedly different from Braidotti's engagement with present and future, systems theory, too, posits futures always already in relation to boundaries: both the present and future emerge *in relation to* and *different from* one another.

Collated rather than collapsed, these posthumanist perspectives shift attention from the *when* of the future to the *what*, contravening humanist interpretations of cause and effect that rely on discrete, stable articulations of before and after, past and future. That is, whereas a human cause-and-effect conceptualization of time can allow for multiple causes and complicated effects, it does not account for its own chronotopic selections and thus remains always already wed to successive chronology, in which time moves and people act (Gries). A posthumanist perspective of the future, by contrast, suggests that rather than the future merely following the present, both present and future emerge and become recognizable as bounded selections. Moreover, posthumanisms multiply possibilities for how we account for the future (and present) and what might count in the future (and present) regarding not only Anthroposcenic cause and effect, for example, but the Anthroposcenic consequences of generations of ecological terror, and regarding not only advances in technology that extend (human) life but the interrelated accumulation of e-waste that pollutes (human) drinking water.

Compatible Methodologies

Importantly, this collection attests to the shifts in rhetorical attention made possible at the intersections of Burke studies *and* posthumanisms, collectively and self-consciously pushing our rhetorical imagination with respect to how we conceptualize, rethink, and potentially intervene in emerging boundaries and futures. Far from being *methodically* similar, each chapter shares a methodological premise: the commitment to "reduce the unfathomable complexity," as Hayles puts it, by making methodological selections that contribute to an emergent project. As individual experiments, each chapter mobilizes specific Burkean texts or concepts posthumanistically, taking "account of the constitutive (and constitutively paradoxical) nature of its own forms, distinctions and procedures and tak[ing] account of them in ways that may be distinguished from the reflection and introspection associated with the critical subject of humanism" (Wolfe 122). In the collection as a whole, each chapter acts as "a relay point between different moments in space and time, as well as different levels, degrees, forms, and configurations of the thinking process" (Braidotti 166). The collection thus allows readers to consider, for example, how the specific, committed, perspectival work of Burke might intercede in the material becoming of our rhetorical futures. It allows us to question how decentering humans in rhetorical inquiry enables and constrains our imagination of ethical cause and effect. Drawing together Burke and posthumanism—in specific, circumscribed, even idiosyncratic ways—induces us to affirm the present and name the promissory future without peremptorily pointing toward what that future could be. Such a compatible methodology, then, prevents our denying an insistent, unfolding becoming.

The Assembled Body

As we've indicated, we see this collection of chapters as organized into two mutually constitutive parts: *boundaries* and *futures*. The chapters in the *Boundaries* section account for, question, and contest a diversity of ostensibly discrete epistemic and ontological categories found in both Burkean and posthuman studies. These chapters are not simply a recognition of different—or more—boundaries, however; they are also recognitions of the elements and ideas marginalized and excluded by these boundaries. The work in this section reveals boundaries as continually in relation and so opens up new avenues of understanding and interaction both within and across the complex subjects of Burkean and posthuman inquiry.

Continuing to grapple with and perform the complicated boundaries among Burke and posthuman inquiry, the chapters in the latter half of the collection cohere under the rubric of *Futures*. Careful to resist collapsing Burkean and posthuman perspectives, each chapter traverses disciplinary boundaries to complicate *both* extant representations of Burkean concepts *and* posthuman theory not necessarily against the grain of Burke but rather intensifying the admittedly strange strains within Burke: his compulsions, his drives. The result is a section bound by theoretical and methodological complexity adequate for exploring Burkean, posthuman, rhetorical futures. It is the futurity of these chapters that lends itself to speculative readings of Burke.

Boundaries

Deftly performing boundary work in her chapter, "Minding Mind: Kenneth Burke, Gregory Bateson, and Posthuman Rhetoric," Kristie S. Fleckenstein explores the "accords" and "discords" of Burke's engagement with cybernetics, and in particular with Gregory Bateson's notion of "ecology of Mind." Fleckenstein sketches "a vision of the posthuman rhetor as both individuated and networked," and so complicates our understanding of the shifting boundaries of the individual subject. Fleckenstein's work here entails a rethinking of traditional categories of material and symbolic, human and posthuman, and even rhetor and rhetoric.

Jeff Pruchnic's contribution, "The Cyburke Manifesto, or, Two Lessons from Burke on the Rhetoric and Ethics of Posthumanism," exemplifies the way the chapters in this section compel us to rethink our interactions with posthumanism's boundaries. In his chapter, Pruchnic maps the historical trajectory of the seemingly opposed notions of "traditional humanism" and "postmodern theory," and in so doing delineates posthumanism not as belonging to either tradition but rather as fundamentally refocusing ethics and ontology. Pruchnic advocates Burke's work as a way of directing inquiries about what posthumanism is, as well as about what motivates these conclusions. Pruchnic's theoretical interweaving here illustrates how Burke's work can create lines of inquiry that cut across posthumanism's well-worn theoretical and disciplinary boundaries.

While these two chapters exemplify the theme of "boundaries" that sustains this section, those that follow continue to push on this concept in unique and unexpected ways, each sustaining a multifaceted examination of how boundaries come to be drawn, how they evolve, and how they can become hardened into dogma and accepted thinking. The next chapter in the collection, "Revision as Heresy: Posthuman Writing Systems and Kenneth Burke's 'Piety,'" by Chris Mays, combines Burke's concept of piety—the way that perspectives tend "to crystallize once they become established"—with posthuman systems-thinking to complicate and refigure the humanist boundaries that sponsor discourses of writing and revision. Whereas humanist articulations of revision implicate individual authors in intentional piety (attached, as they are, to specific perspectives), Mays advocates a systems rendering of piety capable of calling attention to our "involuntary participation in systems" that themselves provoke revision.

Thereafter, Robert Wess argues in his chapter, "Burke's Counter-Nature: Posthumanism in the Anthropocene," for a rethinking of the divide between posthumanism and the ostensibly humanist notion of "the Anthropocene" via a rethinking (and reformulation) of the divide between Burke and posthumanism. Tracking Burke's revisions of his own concept of counter-nature through multiple editions of *Attitudes Toward History* and *Permanence and Change*, Wess shows how counter-nature can become a "framework for reorienting post-humanism."

In the final chapter of this section, "Technique–Technology–Transcendence: Machination and *Amechania* in Burke, Nietzsche, and Parmenides," Thomas Rickert explores "the posthuman as a capacity or trajectory already implicit in the question of the human," explicitly resisting the idea that posthumanism represents a recent, temporal shift heralded by emerging technology. In so doing, Rickert circles back to the fundamental boundary questions posed by the section as a whole, using a diversity of thinkers, as he puts it, to "offer insight into how new perspectives can be achieved."

In these chapters, it is clear that a rethinking of the boundaries instantiated by contemporary posthumanism(s) is not only useful but necessary. By looking to Burke and others typically considered outside the boundaries of posthuman thinking, the authors here allow us to consider alternate configurations of post-human knowledge that are both practically and disciplinarily capacious as well as theoretically and epistemically disruptive.

Futures

The move from *Boundaries* to *Futures* involves a shift in orientation both in the focus on the future and in the interface with Burke's work. It is in the *Futures* section that this collection Burkes Burke in developing resources for living in the posthuman. As a whole, these chapters are glued together by a considered *working through* of Burke's anxiety about technology in order to cobble together terministic resources for negotiating the increasing mergers among and between the analog, the digital, the nano, the semantic, the cultural, and the biological. As we suggested earlier in this introduction, wherever Burke himself landed with respect to the concerns that currently animate posthumanist thought, his ambiguous engagement with technology and the body, alongside his passionate commitment to rhetoric and the symbolic, makes exploring his work for compatible, posthuman equipment for living worthwhile.

The first chapter in this section is by Jodie Nicotra, who, in "The Uses of Compulsion: Recasting Burke's Technological Psychosis in a Comic Frame," complicates Burke's technological attitudes. In revisiting Burke's seeming anxiety about technology, she in fact mobilizes Burkean attitudes for posthuman futures. Specifically, Nicotra proposes mobilizing the compulsion evident in

Burkean satire as a posthuman strategy of affirmation capable of "thinking around the back door of . . . technological psychosis" and "remak[ing] the world."

Like Nicotra, Steven R. Katz and Nathaniel A. Rivers read across Burke's corpus, articulating "A Predestination for the Posthumanistic" that suggests Burke's concerns are posthumanism's concerns without positing Burkean predestination as a nascent posthumanism. Using the documentary film *Fixed* as a case study, the chapter argues that Burkean predestination can be understood as possible equipment for posthuman living cultivated by a thinker who moved around in the milieu of symbols, brains, bodies, and machines.

Julie Jung and Kellie Sharp-Hoskins also offer a kind of equipment for posthuman living—and, specifically, intervention—in their chapter, "Emergent Mattering: Building Rhetorical Ethics at the Limits of the Human." Bringing together Burke's concept of irony with new materialist articulations of emergences, they create a methodology capable of intervening in *how* matter comes to matter and how it can matter differently. More specifically, Jung and Sharp-Hoskins intervene in the materialization of gendered, racialized, and colonial bodies and logics that differentially allocate value to bodies and lives in a posthumanist world.

In their coauthored chapter "What Are Humans For?," Nathan Gale and Timothy Richardson more explicitly propose revising Burkean concepts, arguing that dramatism (as it stands) is inadequate to address contemporary mechanical/digital ubiquity, which has made it difficult to distinguish between the motion of machines and the action of bodies or even between machines and bodies. Specifically, Gale and Richardson work with pure persuasion in the context of wearables to suggest that technological devices, like literary ones, possess a motive force beyond the human deploying them.

Finally, in Casey Boyle and Steven LeMieux's "A Sustainable Dystopia," the authors sketch a theoretical frame, a design intervention, and a case study that productively reads Burke's fears of dystopia as something to embrace for a posthuman rhetoric. Their chapter takes an unconventional route to an engagement with posthuman futures, understanding our "posthuman predicament through Burke" as "as an opportunity to engage reversal as an affirmative mode of becoming." Perhaps "reversal" is a suitable metaframe for this collection, as all these authors articulate boundaries and futures of a transdisciplinary posthumanism that turns around and askance our ways of making meaning, and makes unconventional juxtapositions compatible, with unpredictable results.

Works Cited

Badmington, Neil. "Introduction: Approaching Posthumanism." *Posthumanism*, edited by Neil Badmington. London: Palgrave, 2000, 1–10. Print.

Barad, Karen. *Meeting the Universe Halfway: Quantum Physics and the Entanglement of Matter and Meaning*. Durham: Duke University Press, 2007. Print.

Barnett, Scot, and Casey Boyle, editors. *Rhetoric, Through Everyday Things*. Tuscaloosa: University of Alabama Press, 2016. Print.

Boyle, Casey. "Writing and Rhetoric and/as Posthuman Practice." *College English* 78, no. 6 (2016): 528–50. Print.

Braidotti, Rosi. *The Posthuman*. Cambridge: Polity Press, 2013. Print.

Brooke, Collin Gifford. "Forgetting to be (Post)Human: Media and Memory in a Kairotic Age." *JAC* 20, no. 4 (2000): 775–95. Print.

Brown, Wendy. *Walled States, Waning Sovereignty*. Brooklyn: Zone, 2010. Print.

Burke, Kenneth. *A Grammar of Motives*. Berkeley: University of California Press, 1969. Print.

———. *The Philosophy of Literary Form*. 1941. 3rd ed. Berkeley: University of California Press, 1973. Print.

———. "Revival of the Fittest." *Equipment for Living: The Literary Reviews of Kenneth Burke*, edited by Nathaniel A. Rivers and Ryan P. Weber. Anderson: Parlor Press, 2010, 486–89. Print.

———. *The Rhetoric of Religion: Studies in Logology*. Berkeley: University of California Press, 1961. Print.

Clark, Andy. *Supersizing the Mind: Embodiment, Action, and Cognitive Extension*. London: Oxford University Press, 2010. Print.

"Compatibility." *OED Online*. Oxford University Press, 2017. Web.

Deleuze, Gilles, and Felix Guattari. *A Thousand Plateaus: Capitalism and Schizophrenia*. Translated by Brian Massumi. London: Continuum, 1987. Print.

Dobrin, Sidney I., editor. *Writing Posthumanism, Posthuman Writing*. Columbia: Parlor Press, 2015. Print.

Gries, Laurie. *Still Life with Rhetoric: A New Materialist Approach for Visual Rhetorics*. Logan: Utah State University Press, 2015. Print.

Hawhee, Debra. *Moving Bodies: Kenneth Burke at the Edges of Language*. Columbia: University of South Carolina Press, 2009. Studies in Rhetoric/Communication. Print.

Hayles, N. Katherine. *How We Became Posthuman*. Chicago: University of Chicago Press, 1999. Print.

———. "Making the Cut: The Interplay of Narrative and System, or What Systems Theory Can't See." *Observing Complexity: Systems Theory and Postmodernity*, edited by William Rasch and Cary Wolfe. Minneapolis: University of Minnesota Press, 2000, 137–62. Print.

Littlefield, Melissa M., and Jenell M. Johnson, editors. *The Neuroscientific Turn: Transdisciplinarity in the Age of the Brain*. Ann Arbor: University of Michigan Press, 2012. Print.

Lynch, Paul, and Nathaniel A. Rivers, editors. *Thinking with Bruno Latour in Rhetoric and Composition*. Carbondale: Southern Illinois University Press, 2015. Print.

Mara, Andrew, and Byron Hawk. "Posthuman Rhetorics and Technical Communication." *Technical Communication Quarterly* 19, no. 1 (2010): 1–10. Print.

Mazis, Glen A. *Humans, Animals, Machines: Blurring Boundaries*. Albany: State University of New York Press, 2008. Print.

Muckelbauer, John, and Debra Hawhee. "Posthuman Rhetorics: 'It's the Future, Pikul.'" *JAC* 20, no. 4 (2000): 767–74. Print.

Pinkus, Karen. "Ambiguity, Ambience, Ambivalence, and the Environment." *Common Knowledge* 19, no. 1 (2013): 88–95. Print.

Puar, Jasbir. *Terrorist Assemblages: Homonationalism in Queer Times.* Durham: Duke University Press, 2007. Print.

Rueckert, William H. *Encounters with Kenneth Burke.* Urbana: University of Illinois Press, 1994. Print.

Swartz, Joseph. "Kenneth Burke, Aristotle, and the Future of Rhetoric." *College Composition and Communication* 17, no. 5 (1966): 210–16. Print.

Taylor, Terumi. "Navigating Interdisciplinary Awkwardness: Teaching and Learning at Effat University." *Impact* 5, no. 1 (2016). Web. 15 Dec. 2015.

Vitanza, Victor J. "Critical Sub/Versions of the History of Philosophical Rhetoric." *Rhetoric Review* 6, no. 1 (1987): 41–66. Print.

Weiser, M. Elizabeth. *Burke, War, Words: Rhetoricizing Dramatism.* Columbia: University of South Carolina Press, 2008. Print.

Wildcat, Daniel R. *Red Alert! Saving the Planet with Indigenous Knowledge.* Golden: Fulcrum, 2009. Print.

Wolfe, Cary. *What Is Posthumanism?* Minneapolis: University of Minnesota Press, 2009. Print. Posthumanities 8.

Worsham, Lynn. "From the Editor: Thinking with Cats (More, to Follow)." *JAC* 30, nos. 3–4 (2013): 407–33. Print.

———. "Moving Beyond the Logic of Sacrifice: Animal Studies, Trauma Studies, and the Path to Posthumanism." Dobrin 19–55. Print.

1 Boundaries

1

Minding Mind | Kenneth Burke, Gregory Bateson, and Posthuman Rhetoric

Kristie S. Fleckenstein

Frozen in the vintage 1949 black-and-white photograph, the arrangement of the ten men[1] participating in the Western Round Table on Modern Art suggests the oblique angle by which Kenneth Burke contributes to twenty-first-century posthumanism. Situated near the head of the table, surrounded by luminaries such as Frank Lloyd Wright, on his left, and Marcel Duchamp, on his right, Burke sits with a paper in one hand and a gesture in the other. Momentarily holding the floor in this gathering of self-described "prima donnas," Burke joins the three-day conversation exploring "questions about art today" (qtd. in Mac-Agy 26). Arriving on the West Coast on the cusp of publishing *A Rhetoric of Motives*, this "short man with a tall mind" tilts his body toward moderator George Boas, seeming to block the far end of the table from his attention (Rueckert, "Introduction" 7). Among those participants momentarily disregarded sits anthropologist Gregory Bateson in his characteristically hunched pose, trying to disguise his extraordinary height even while seated. Fresh from the Sixth Macy Cybernetics Conference—the collaborative series of post–World War II interdisciplinary meetings that yielded the foundation for cybernetic theory, a central component of posthumanism (Clarke; Wolfe)—this "papa" of cybernetics angles his body to intersect at a diagonal with Burke (Foerster 288).[2] Separated by table, training, and nationality, Burke and Bateson initiate at this 1949 round table a thirty-year dialogue on the skew in which others, but rarely themselves, link their thinking (Burke, *On Human* 341; Leeds-Hurwitz 63). Rather than a direct encounter, Burke approaches Bateson at a tangent, "an enduring aspect of his style and thought" (*On Human* 338). In so doing, he also approaches posthumanism at a tangent, offering an "incongruous" perspective from which to (re)view posthumanism.

The oblique intellectual trajectory between Burke and posthumanism mediated by the man he later refers to as "quite [a] gracious guy" forms the focus of this chapter (Rueckert, *Letters* 266). I argue that Burke's in/direct engagement with Bateson's work—especially the concept of an ecology of Mind—manifests an in/direct engagement with posthumanism via cybernetics. The convergences and divergences between Batesonian Mind and Burkeology illuminate not only Burke's intersection with posthumanism but also his contribution to formulating new questions for posthumanities and posthuman rhetoric. To explore such tangential but important connections, I examine both points of agreement and disagreement between the two giants, drawing particularly from the only essays—published in 1979—in which Burke explicitly addresses Bateson's thinking. I begin tracing Burke's posthumanist tangents by first addressing intersections between posthumanism and Bateson's version of cybernetics, attending especially to two concepts intrinsic to Mind: relationships and difference. Then I turn to sites of accord and discord between Burke and Mind, finding in the accord a Burkean reinforcement of posthumanism and finding in the discord a vision of the posthuman rhetor as both individuated and networked, one who is impelled to rhetorical action through dialectic.

Bateson's Mind: Through Cybernetics to Posthumanism

Man, Burke announces in his five-part definition of a human being, is a "symbol-using, symbol-making, symbol-misusing animal" (*Language* 6). By depicting humans as both corporeal and semiotic, Burke troubles the boundaries between the material and the symbolic, rehearsing a central claim of the "posthuman condition" a decade before Ihab Hasan first uses the term. But while the symbol-using/making/misusing animal adumbrates the posthuman animal, the congruencies between Burke and posthumanism arise less from any linear progression, by which idea A causes idea B in an orderly, measured movement, and more out of meandering paths whose conceptual wakes—like the turbulence created by two boats in parallel paths—ripple, traverse, and affect each other. Similar to the oblique spatial dynamic captured in a photographic moment at the Western Round Table, Burke's influence on posthumanism operates at a slant, mediated through cybernetics, especially Batesonian cybernetics. Following the intellectual trajectory whereby Burke and posthumanism intersect thus requires following that trajectory through cybernetics. Such an endeavor enriches not only our understanding of a cybernetic Burke but also our understanding of a posthuman Burke and, most important, a posthuman rhetor. In this section, I focus on those myriad connecting arcs—the pathways formed by the in/direct flow of ideas—by beginning with posthumanism itself. I define it cautiously, highlighting the contribution of Batesonian cybernetics to that definition. Then, focusing on Bateson's central metaphor of an ecology of the Mind, I set the stage for Burke's entrance into the drama of Mind.

To claim that Burke feeds into posthumanism—even at an angle—requires clarifying which posthumanism he nourishes. As Cary Wolfe concedes, the term "posthumanism" generates "different and even irreconcilable definitions" (xi), resulting in a confusing array of posthumanisms. I root my understanding of posthumanism in Donna J. Haraway's concept of the cyborg, sensitive to Haraway's reluctance to use the term "posthuman" (Braidotti 197) as well as to her later leap from cyborg to companion species. Haraway initially characterizes the posthuman through the "network ideological image" of the cyborg, an image—both real and metaphorical—replete with a profusion of permeable spaces and identities (170). The posthuman for Haraway ensues from the blurring of ecological, technocorporeal, and geopolitical boundaries, embracing at the same time the ethical and political accountability of the networked subject (Braidotti 197). Such a definition aligns with Wolfe's use of the term, which "opposes the fantasies of disembodiment and autonomy inherited from humanism itself" (xv). Wolfe distills his take on posthumanism into two key points that both complement and enrich Haraway's work. First, posthumanism "names the embodiment and embeddedness of the human being" in biological and technological worlds (xv). Wolfe describes this embeddedness as "a prosthetic coevolution of the human animal with the technicity of tools" (xv), echoing Burke's claim that humans are second-natured—are re-made—by the tools they create (*Language* 13). Second, extending the first point, Wolfe claims that posthumanism names the historical moment at which the human is decentered by its imbrication in "technical, medical, informatic, and economic networks" (xv), an imbrication that functions as an open system in which the whole exceeds the sum of its parts. What results from these key points, Wolfe contends, is a new way of thinking (xvi) necessary to understand and ameliorate twenty-first century ecological, political, and technological crises. That call for a new way of thinking, as well as the assertion that posthumanism provides this essential epistemological shift, resonates with a similar claim that Bateson forwards: that the systems thinking exemplified by the best of cybernetics offers a corrective to the epistemological[3] errors that are part and parcel of humanity's "descent into hell" ("Paradigmatic" 349).

The new thinking that characterizes posthumanism aligns itself with—if not anchors itself in—the new thinking that characterizes cybernetics. Bateson illuminates the nature of that new thinking and prefigures its contribution to posthumanism. As he argues, an epistemological error is no small matter; in fact, it can be "lethal" (Bateson and Bateson 24; Bateson, *Steps* 493). Guided by their currently erroneous epistemology—one steeped in Cartesian dualisms— human beings act and make decisions that jeopardize their survival as well as the survival of their natural environments, Bateson contends (*Steps* 468). However, he goes on, cybernetics, with its focus on transacting systems rather than discrete Cartesian isolates, offers a fresh approach to understanding and securing ecological—and human—(co)existence. Described by Bateson as the "biggest bite out of the fruit of the Tree of Knowledge that mankind has taken in the last 2000 years," cybernetics provides a remedy to the deadly mistake of configuring the world as a set of distinct entities that operate according to the mechanistic rules of Newtonian engagement (*Steps* 484). Such a reductive materialist epistemology, he warns, ratifies a pernicious dynamic. First, it encourages humans to think in terms of the individual, the individual family, or the individual community as the key unit of survival, thus setting these single actors "outside and against the things" around them (468). Second, those single units categorize everything beyond their circle as "mindless and therefore not entitled to moral or ethical consideration" (468). Consequently, they "arm" themselves against the "other social units, other races and the brutes and vegetables," treating the "other" as a resource to exploit rather than a mind to respect (468). The inevitable effect of such an epistemological error is the destruction of ecologies and peoples. Learning to think cybernetically, Bateson thus argues, "is the most important task today" because it counters the dangers of epistemological error (468). However, it is not just any form of cybernetics that Bateson advocates. It is second-order cybernetics, the particular configuration of systems theory that constitutes an integral element of posthumanism and an integral element in Burke's conjunction with posthumanism.

As Bruce Clarke explains, "of the many systems discourses taken up in the theory discourse of the posthumanities, the most refined and capacious line of thought is the second-order systems theory," a theory that he calls "neocybernetics" and grounds in Bateson's work (ix; see also, Wolfe xvii). Such a distinction between first- and second-order cybernetics is crucial for understanding Burke's intersection with posthumanism, for that intersection is mediated by the complexities of neocybernetics. As Jeff Pruchnic points out, Burke was "consistent and incessant about his disaffection with the emerging field of cybernetics" (103); however, that disaffection stemmed from what Bateson calls the dangers "latent" in first-order cybernetics, including a simplistic approach to technology, especially computerization (*Steps* 485). Burke rightly suspected the implications of first-order cybernetics, marked as it was by what R. L. Rutsky calls a "dialectic of control" (qtd. in Wolfe xvii; see also, Pruchnic 111–12). Perhaps best conceptualized by Norbert Weiner, the focus of first-order cybernetic theory consisted of "communication and control" (16), especially as applied to technology (15), culminating in a science of the *observed* system. An approach that separated information and communication from materiality, first-order cybernetics yielded what Haraway calls the C^3I mindset—command, control, communication, and information (150)—which placed the observer outside a system of information flow, detached from the circular chains of causality by which a system either self-corrects or tips into runaway (Bateson, *Sacred* 220). In contrast, second-order cybernetics embraces two correctives: first, it conceives of systems as recursive, and, second, it integrates the observer into a science of *observing* systems.

No longer solely tied to feedback *within* a system's circuits, a second-order system is recursive in that the information emerging from the dynamic activity of the system as a *whole* feeds back into the system. Bateson explains that "we live in a universe in which causal trains endure, survive through time, only if they are recursive"; therefore, "our logics must also be fundamentally recursive" (220). Second-order cybernetics emphasizes an epistemological shift from parts to wholes. Whereas first-order cybernetics emphasizes the feedback between the individual arcs of a circuit—a set of individual pathways by which information travels to constitute a system—second-order cybernetics emphasizes the importance of the transactivity among the totality of those arcs. The dynamism of the entire system in action is then communicated back into the full circuit of resonating arcs, a process that provides both identity and longevity to the system as a whole rather than to any individual element of it. Furthermore, recursiveness stipulates that the observer is always a component—an arc—embedded within the system. Never separate from the system, the observer is both product and producer of recursive feedback. To paraphrase Bateson, we are our own epistemology, an insight that destabilizes clear-cut boundaries separating inside-outside, subjective-objective, materiality-mind. Such innovative thinking,

Clarke argues, "has borne the widest and most promising dissemination beyond the home disciplines of cybernetics," especially in the work of the posthumanities (ix). Nowhere is that cybernetics of cybernetics more clearly articulated than in Bateson's concept of an ecology of Mind.

The pattern that connects Burke to posthumanism wends through Bateson's ecomental Mind, and that Mind situates itself in relationships formed through news of difference. Understanding Bateson's ecology of the Mind begins with understanding Bateson's reinterpretation of "a *Platonic* view," which celebrates that "in the beginning was the idea" (*Mind* 4; emphasis in original).[4] Concerned, as Burke was, with the dominating focus of science (or scientism) on a reductive materialism—or the "'Corporeal Universe' which our newspapers consider 'real'" (4)—Bateson aims to transfer attention from things to relationships from which the real "[spins off]" (4). Two elements are crucial to Bateson's complex ontological and epistemological shift: active relationships (pattern) and information (or difference that makes a difference). First, pattern exists of and through relationships, and relationships are not things. To illustrate, Bateson offers the mystery of the elephant's trunk, which might be identified as a "nose": a thing (15). However, that trunk is a nose only because it constitutes a single component in a set of relationships. For instance, it possesses a formal relationship in that the trunk is a nose because it possesses a particular spatial relationship to eyes and mouth. This formal relationship—not some intrinsic identity as a thing—guides the trunk's emergence in utero. Embryology possesses no pre-formed "nose" identity, only relationships. Furthermore, if we choose to classify a trunk as a nose because of its shared corporeal function—all mammalian noses help to detect scents—we would still be operating in the realm of relationships: that between the elephant and its environment (16). The nose's function does not operate outside of that relationship. Such is the world of pattern: relationships are primary, things secondary (*Steps* 154).

Second, that world of pattern is formed and maintained through the flow of information, a flow that unites and co-constitutes the transacting components comprising the whole. Bateson defines information as the "difference that makes a difference," an essential quality of relationships (*Mind* 99). A relationship between parts materializes only when a discontinuity or a change between those two parts (or between the same part at two different times) activates a perception (94). Furthermore, that difference gains traction only if it constitutes a *significant* difference: a difference that makes a difference. For instance, a fist-sized rock on the side of a path has no relevance—makes no difference—to me if all

I am doing is bird-watching. In fact, I might not even notice it. However, that rock becomes a difference that makes a difference if I am looking for something to anchor the edge of a picnic blanket. In both instances, two different systems, or patterns, are formed out of these differences that make—or do not make— a difference. Furthermore, both systems—the bird-watching and the rock-finding—exist as a "dance of interacting parts" (13) that are "pegged down by various sorts of physical limits" (17). Finally, the patterns co-constituted and maintained by news of difference yield minds, the ecomental systems that are positioned on the cusp between the corporeal universe and the realm of ideas. From elephant trunks to rocks, the flow of information integrating numerous parts into a whole constitutes a Batesonian mind. In turn, the *transaction* of minds yields an ecology of Mind, "the larger Mind of which the individual mind is only a subsystem" (*Steps* 467). As Bateson explains, the mental characteristics of the system are immanent, not in some part, but in the system—mind and Mind—as a whole (316).[5]

While this brief explanation only skims the richness and complexity of the Batesonian Mind, it does serve to highlight the reciprocity—the intersecting wakes—between second-order cybernetics and posthumanism. As the network of relationships formed by communication pathways between an organism and its environment, an ecology of Mind troubles the three "boundary breakdowns" that Haraway identifies as characteristic of the cyborg: the separations between human and animal, organism and machine, and physical and nonphysical (151– 54). In addition, an ecology of Mind emphasizes what Rosi Braidotti calls a "common dominator of the posthuman condition": the "vital, self-organizing and yet non-naturalistic structure of living matter itself" (2). The oblique logic by which Burke connects to posthumanism through minding Mind similarly highlights his status as a "common dominator of the posthuman condition," and, in 1979, Burke made that commonality explicit when he once again shared a table with Bateson.

Burke Minding Mind: Through Bateson to Posthumanism

If the spatial dynamic of the 1949 Western Round Table symbolizes the elliptical pathway by which Burke intersects with posthumanism through second-order cybernetics, then the spatial dynamic of the 1979 ICA-SCA Asilomar Conference[6] symbolizes a more direct convergence between Burke and posthumanism, a convergence mediated, again, by Bateson. As the keynoter invited, in part, to respond to Bateson's work, Burke publicly grappled for the first and last time with the alignments and misalignments between his thinking and Bateson's.[7] At a banquet marking the final evening of the conference, Burke sat not a table-length from Bateson but right next to him on the dais. Burke even commented on that arrangement, confessing to William H. Rueckert his suspicion that Bateson had requested "the Organizeress to put him next to his wife on one side and me on the other, whereas the Guvnr [Jerry Brown, one of Bateson's a former students] had wanted them on both sides of him" (Rueckert, *Letters* 266). Furthermore, as the last speaker of the evening,[8] Burke not only presented his talk but also brought "down the house" by singing a song he had written about "everywhere the double bind" (Burke, *On Human* 342). As a result, he and the conference honoree secured the designation of "the Bateson boys" (342).

In this section, I explore in two moves the ways in which Burke is and is not a Bateson boy, finding in those explicit convergences and divergences a Burkean posthumanism and a posthuman rhetor. I begin by identifying the cybernetic alignments—the pattern that connects—constituting Burke, through Bateson, as a "common denominator" of posthumanism. Then, I identify the cybernetic misalignments—the patterns that disconnect—where Burke the provocateur troubles posthumanism by troubling Mind. Such provocations, I contend, yield a vantage point for conceiving of a posthuman rhetor who, paradoxically, exists both as separate from and as part of Mind.

Perhaps the most important shared pattern that construes Burke as a "Bateson boy" consists of a joint appreciation for relationships. Burke opens his keynote with that exact acknowledgment, noting that "a tangle of individual organisms can be so interrelated that the lot can be viewed as an individual organism" ("Interactive" 331). He reinforces this point of congruence by quoting and confirming Bateson's insight from "Pathologies of Epistemology"[9] that the unit of evolutionary survival is the unit of mind (Burke, "Interactive" 332). Burke extols the "tangle" of human and ecological relationships for its laudable emphasis on "the environment as a necessary condition of our existence as biological organisms" and its contribution to "the cause of Environmentalist criticism now so badly needed" (333).[10] Thus, Burke signals from the outset his allegiance to relationships—to the tangle—an allegiance that circulates through Burke's thinking, as well as posthumanist thinking, on micro and macro levels.[11] Nowhere is that similarity more evident than in Burke's well-known concept of symbolic action, reliant as it is on the relationship between motion and action.

In his keynote, Burke underscores the correspondence between Bateson's Mind and the motion-action relationship. He affirms that Bateson's "ecology of weeds" (qtd. in Burke, "Interactive" 333) parallels Burke's own "realm of nonsymbolic action" (333) just as Bateson's "ecology of ideas" (qtd. in Burke, "Interactive" 333) corresponds to Burke's "realm of symbolic action'" (333).[12] As Burke elaborates elsewhere, motion consists of movement without intent; motion can, therefore, describe such movements as those made by a "sheerly physiological organism" ("(Non)Symbolic" 809) or an air conditioner as it adjusts to a room's increasing heat signature (834). Conversely, action involves movement with intent, or "modes of behavior made possible by the acquiring of a conventional, arbitrary symbol system" (809). While Burke configures motion-action as a "basic polarity" (809), he also interrelates them in complex ways, as his "first two Dramatistic axioms" indicate: "There can be motion without action" but "there can be no action without motion" (833–34; see also, 814). In other words, any symbolic action requires the world of motion to exist, while the world of motion exists in the absence of symbolic action. However, motion is not immune to symbolic action because, even though the ecology of weeds exists outside of the ecology of ideas, it cannot be known except through those ideas. The two are inextricably interrelated, for symbolic action joins symbol-using animals to the nonverbal (*Language* 5). Thus, while we do not need the word "breathe" to take a breath, we do need the word "breathe" to talk about what we are doing when we inhale and exhale—or to build a machine to help us when we cannot do either. As Pruchnic confirms, "Burke continually moves beneath the dance of words to the dance of bodies" (102), highlighting that, for Burke, as for Bateson, relationships are primary, things secondary.

This complex tangle of relationships is even more clearly evident in the constitution of the real, the realm of things. Again, echoing Bateson, Burke contends that the fabric of our reality is woven out of the dynamic—the dialectic—between motion and action. As a result, just as Bateson emphasizes that the real is a "spin-off" of pattern, so too does Burke assert that "overwhelmingly much of what we mean by 'reality'" is itself a "spin-off" of symbolic action, "built up for us through nothing but our symbol systems" (*Language* 5). He made that case to his audience on that February evening in 1979. Neither solely material nor solely symbolic, Burke states baldly, a human's sense of reality ensues from the dual realms of motion and action: "the conditions of the body as a physiological object" and "the responsiveness to the symbolic structures" serve "to define, rightly or wrongly, the nature of 'reality'" ("Interactive" 338). This codependent relationship between motion and action—the ecology of weeds and the ecology of ideas—is a crucial element linking Burke to Bateson and through Bateson to posthumanism.

The second point of convergence characterizing the "Bateson boys" concerns Burke's treatment of difference. For Bateson, difference is essential to forming the relationships that shape everything from an elephant's trunk to a morning greeting. It is at the heart of meaning and meaningfulness. So it is with Burke. While Burke is justly suspicious of the vocabulary of "information" and "information processing," which he associates with a reductive scientism (*Grammar* 447), he readily embraces the importance of difference, especially as captured by his concept of the negative. If anything, difference as the negative is at the core of Burkeology, just as difference that makes a difference is at the core of the Batesonian Mind. This reciprocity between Batesonian difference and Burkean negative is starkly manifested in Burke's second trait of a human being, who is inventor of the negative (or invented by the negative). Rather than existing in nature, the negative is a "function peculiar to symbol systems" (*Language* 9). To use any language, Burke points out, "we must know that they [words] are *not* the things they stand for" (12; emphasis in original). Analogous to Bateson's difference, Burke's negative is "but a *principle*, an *idea*, not a name for a *thing*" (10; emphasis in original). Burke highlights the necessity of the negative in meaning and Mind through his dissection of the term "substance," which he cites, along with *A Grammar of Motives*, in his Asilomar presentation. As he explains in *A Grammar of Motives*, the word "substance"—with the combination of *sub* and *stance*—contains within it a paradox. So, even as the word is used "to designate what a thing *is*," it does so by "designating something it *is not*" (23). More specifically, we know a word's meaning because that meaning is delineated by its difference from its context, its background. Without the context to "mark its boundaries," the meaning would not exist. It relies on the negative, the difference that makes a difference. Burke underscores the essential nature of difference through the negative: "Since determined things are 'positive,' we might point up the paradox as harshly as possible by translating it 'Every positive is negative'" (25). He brought this insight to the California conference, explaining that meaning and identity dissolve "into all sorts of *contextual* relationships," wherein those contextual relationships rely on—embody—what is not in order to assert what is ("Interactive" 334). Here, Burke reinforces Mind as a dance of relationships created by the negative: differences that make a difference.

Through a keynote address, an addendum, and a song, Burke minds Mind.[13] In the process, he deliberately, selectively, and idiosyncratically aligns himself with second-order cybernetics. As he does so, he also aligns himself at a slant with key elements of posthumanism, highlighting not only his identity as a Bateson boy—a (neo)cybernetic Burke—but also a posthumanist boy. However, Burke offers more to posthumanism than prevalidation, intriguing though that notion may be; he also offers a new perspective on posthumanism. For while there are patterns that connect Burke to Bateson and through Bateson to posthumanism, there are also patterns that disconnect, patterns by which Burke provokes Mind and, in the process, provokes posthumanism.[14] Burke identifies two differences that make a difference: the need for a "principle of individuation" and, through that principle, the need for "The Dialectic." Both points of misalignment coalesce to delineate a vision of the posthuman rhetor propelled to symbolic action through the torque of dialectic.

Burke opens up a space for the posthuman rhetor through his emphasis on the "principle of individuation." Burke posits that a weakness of the Batesonian Mind and, by association, of posthumanism stems from the constitution—or, more accurately, the effacement—of the rhetor. From a systems-theoretical view, the human agent—the rhetor—is inextricably formed by and coequal with the myriad components composing an ecomental system.[15] It is not separate from that system. Bateson's example of a man chopping down a tree, to which Burke gestures in his Saturday night performance, illuminates Burke's sticking point with Mind. To understand any human act, Bateson contends, we have to understand more than the human agent; we have to understand all pathways of information flowing past the boundaries of an individual's skin. Bateson uses the example of a man cutting down a tree to illustrate this distributed rather than isolated identity. For instance, when a man cuts down a tree, "he" is not the agent of the act. The system is. Within mind, man no longer has salience as a reified self, contained within a skin boundary. Instead, the man is drawn into information flow, "modified or corrected" with each stroke of the axe by differences in the tree, retina, brain, muscles, and axe. All those modifications and corrections conspire to cocreate an ecomental *system*, not a transcendent human agent, that cuts down the tree (*Steps* 317–18). Within mind and Mind, agency derives from—is spread across—the dynamic of the transacting system as a whole. However, Burke suggests that such distributed agency and embodiment, a central component of posthumanism, poses a key danger: if human agents are entangled in the dance of pattern to the extent that they have no self to express—only multiplicity and fluidity—how, then, can they act with any ethical authority or subjective responsibility? Burke tackles this problem and, in the process, provides the foundation for a posthuman rhetor, one that is both separated from and mortised within a part of mind.

Addressing what he calls his "only real disagreement" with Bateson, Burke begins fashioning the posthuman rhetor by disentangling the "organism-and-environment" in order to center, if only temporally, the decentered human ("Interactive" 332). Rather than conceiving of humans as only one component among many, all indistinguishable within the coevolving network of relationships, Burke argues that humans are by their constitution as symbol-using and as animals categorically different from their nonhuman compatriots. Humans are both a part of and apart from ecomental systems of minds. Focusing on bodies first, Burke argues that humans are apart from the Mind because they are isolated by their own constitution as animals, "the wordless body, in the realm of wordless motion" (338), which divides them from the organism-and-environment system even as they dwell in that system. Thus, the first principle of individuation results from the physiological nature of the human organism itself. It is here that Burke locates "an unstable but not random complexity of tendencies, attitudes, dispositions which differentiates one such motivated locus from another" (338). The human agent in the system is a knot of motivations that differs in degree from other human agents and differs in kind from other nonhumans. So, even as a Batesonian mind cuts down a tree, Burke insists on the inability of any human to become completely enchained within that ecomental system. While that individuated body might dissolve "into the complexities of *contextual* systems," it also paradoxically remains the obdurate "*ground* for a *unique* set of *personal equations*" (335; emphasis in original). What results is a posthuman rhetor, who, both individuated and networked, both apart from and a part of mind and Mind, finds the power to act with intent. That contradictory dynamic of networked individuation is further underscored by human symbolicity.

Just as human biology always and inevitably prevents the individual rhetor from becoming fully consubstantial with(in) an ecomental system, so, too, does human symbol-using prevent the same pure consubstantiality. A bridge to both unification and division, symbolicity, like biology, opens up "the *possibility* of an act . . . grounded in the 'will' of an agent" (*Language* 436), and it does so because human symbolic action is categorically different from the information that links an ecology of weeds. Unlike trees, bees, and fish, humans possess the "ability to learn verbal behavior" ("Interactive" 334), an ability at odds with the significant differences unifying an ecology of weeds. As Burke points out to his audience in California, human symbol-using operates according to a "reflexive principle" in that the symbolic medium possesses the power "to in some way set up the conditions for a second level of motives, as with words about words and tools for making tools" (339). Symbolic action is thus hierarchically higher—it is a different logical type—than the information that communicates retinal changes and muscle modification in the man-axe-tree ecosystem. This radical difference enables the posthuman rhetor to turn around and reflect on the nature of the mind within which he or she is integrated. Symbolicity separates and joins at the same time. "I need that one difference" (335)—that double-edged principle of individuation—Burke argues, because it ensures that posthuman rhetors can find a perspective from which to determine their agency in and responsibility to the ecomental system(s) that they are both a part of and apart from. That same paradoxical dynamic of individuation and unification powers forth the performance of posthuman rhetoric through the auspices of dialectic.

Just as the principle of individuation separates Burke from Bateson, so, too, does Burke's devotion to dialectic, which he refers to as a "difference with a difference . . . in a big way" (336). Whereas the principle of individuation opens up Mind to a posthuman rhetor, this second misalignment opens up Mind to posthuman rhetoric. The challenge of the Batesonian Mind for rhetoric derives from the compulsion of all components within an ecomental system to mutually adjust in ways that develop a collective identity for the system and maintain that identity across time. When bound by and to the feedback that fosters self-regulation and self-correction, how, then, can a posthuman rhetor find the impetus for rhetorical action or the motivation to induce change? Dialectic offers one response to this conundrum, and Burke emphasizes its importance in his Saturday night talk.

"In the light of things as being said these days," Burke tells his listeners, "I was surprised that in Bateson's pages there was no talk at all of 'dialectic'" (336). This is a serious omission, he protests, which he promises to rectify by sharing a few "transformations" that ensue from dialectic. For Burke, dialect refers to "the possibilities of linguistic transformation" (*Grammar* 402), by which one may "characterize the *dis*position and the *trans*position of terms" (402; emphasis in original). It is both a process of analysis—for instance, as manifested in the pentad—and a phenomenon that is characteristic of the intersection between the ecology of weeds and the ecology of ideas. Two elements of dialectic are essential for the emergence of a posthuman rhetoric within an ecomental system: contradiction and transformation.[16] Dialectic is rooted in contradiction, plunging humans into the constant play of ambiguity and paradox generated by oppositions. Dialectic entangles the posthuman rhetor in the very frictions with which Mind—as a product of differences that make a difference—contends. Timothy W. Crusius underscores the reciprocal chafing between the ecology of ideas and the ecology of weeds, arguing that "Burke strives to uncover tensions latent in natural language on the premise that they reflect paradoxes in the nature of the world itself" (25). Essential to dialectic, then, is the torque generated by opposing terms, for this opposition fosters conflicts from which rhetoric emerges. As Crusius explains, for Burke dialectic is the ground, the condition, for rhetoric (29). Confronted with contradictions that are inevitably a part of any mind, the rhetor is spurred to act rhetorically. Burke highlights this propulsive power in his Asilomar talk by returning to his trope of "a part of something" and "apart from it" ("Interactive" 336) He uses the example of God to illustrate the impossibility of any but the most transient balance, the most transient steady state, in an ecomental system. For while humans can be conceived as "a part of God," they are also not God; therefore, they are "apart from God" (336). They are both God and not God at the same time, a paradox without resolution. As Burke elaborates, "any *part of* a whole may become *apart from* the rest, any distinction may become a contrast" (336). As a result, the dialectic of contrasts in an ecomental system—the continuous and irresolvable oscillations between oppositions characteristic of dialectic—circulates through the entire Mind. In so doing, dialectic prods posthuman rhetors "to inquire about the relation between the symbolic and its nonsymbolic or extrasymbolic context" (*Language* 2), drawing them out of the self-regulation characteristic of Mind and thereby opening them up not only to the opportunity but to the need for rhetoric. Furthermore, that dialectical engagement offers posthuman rhetors the hope of rhetoric through transformation, or change in the system of constraints within which an ecomental system forms and sustains itself.

The hope and possibility of change are intrinsic to dialectic, Burke promises his Asilomar audience, illustrating both hope and possibility by transforming the double bind, a key formulation contributed by Bateson to psychotherapy. Simply put, a double bind ensues when an agent incapable of escaping a system (such as a child in the family unit) receives contradictory messages, and acting upon either message results in punishment of some kind. Via dialectic, Burke recasts the double bind "eulogistically" and "dyslogistically," offering the metaphor of two weights on a seesaw ("Interactive" 337–38). When the weights are balanced, "all is good," and we have an "interactive bind"; however, when the "balance of powers" is in conflict, we have a double bind that can drive the system crazy with deadly consequences (337). He illuminates those consequences with the ecomental system, consisting of humans-plus-technology. He contends that the human animal's "involvement in the motivation tangle" and "prowess with symbol-systems" have resulted in the "high development of technology" to the extent that the survival of the organism is threatened (339). Such is the dyslogistic double bind. However, "the vast complexity of interactions and double-binds" also offers the opportunity for transformation (339). Burke offers the example of prisoners within a penal system to demonstrate such a transformation. Some individuals, he claims, immersed within a demoralizing ecomental system—one that embodies the double bind in all its incipient insanity—have transformed that demoralization into a type of spiritual and moral resurrection (337). The dyslogistic double bind becomes the eulogistic interactive bind. Here, at the site of dialectic, is the potential for radical change in the ecomental system. Thus, Burke courts ambiguity and pursues paradox because transformation lurks in these moments of confusion. Rather than Mind as the pattern that connects, Burke concludes, dialectic is the pattern that articulates and disarticulates Mind: "The overall design *is* The Dialectic" (337). At the heart of The Dialectic, then, lies both the impetus for posthuman rhetoric and the hope of that rhetoric.

In *A Grammar of Motives*, Burke describes a mural at the Museum of Modern Art, one that consists of an aerial photograph of two launches moving side by side so that "their wakes crossed and recrossed each other in almost an infinity of lines" (xvi). Like those wakes, the conversation on the slant initiated by Bateson and Burke in 1949 crosses and recrosses over the duration of their thirty-year trajectory. Through that oblique angle, Burke also crosses and recrosses posthumanism. As he grapples explicitly with Batesonian Mind at Asilomar, he grapples implicitly with key pillars of posthumanism, offering, in his inimitable fashion, incongruous perspectives by which to (re)see posthumanism. Out of this turbulence of converging wakes emerges a vision of a posthuman rhetor and a posthuman rhetoric that is both individuated and networked. Neither the discrete self of Enlightenment humanism nor the effaced self of second-order cybernetics, the posthuman rhetor through a Burkean lens is one fully engaged with and within Mind and yet capable of reflecting on that engagement.

This transformation of Mind holds three key implications for the emergence of a Burkean posthuman rhetoric. While the rhetor abandons autonomous agency—and the fruitless blame game that all too frequently accompanies the myth of the discrete agent—the rhetor does not abandon accountability; rather, he or she embraces responsibility-with-intent, responsibility to and for the ecomental system within which he or she functions. As both individuated and mortised into Mind, as both mutually shaping and shaped by myriad human and nonhuman participants, the rhetor determines appropriate or ethical action on the basis of the obligations he or she owes to those participants. In addition, a Burkean posthuman rhetoric—posthuman symbolic action—derives its double motivation from its constitution as "a part of/apart from" the complex tangle of disparate life forces from which it emerges. Good rhetoric thus stems from a joint reflection on both the necessary differences (apart from) comprising an ecomental system and the need to protect the vulnerable shared futures of those necessary differences (a part of). From this perspective, posthuman rhetoric ceases to be the drive to identification but becomes the dance of disidentification with identification. Finally, the positioning of The Dialectic between the ecology of weeds and the ecology of ideas privileges a Burkean posthuman *kairos*. At the same time that the oscillation between materiality and symbolicity holds the potential for transformation, that oscillation also redefines *kairos* as something more than the opportune moment seized today; *kairos* becomes the opportune moment seized today for tomorrow. In other words, The Dialectic obligates a Burkean posthuman rhetor and rhetoric to inhabit simultaneously a short view and a long view. Posthuman *kairos* requires not only a canny assessment of the best time to speak but also a canny assessment of the cascading impact of a single symbolic action as it circulates not through a single system but through multiple transacting ecomental systems. If a rhetor acts today, he or she is ethically bound to grapple with what happens tomorrow, when the circular causality of an act wends its way throughout interlocking ecosystems, leaving in its path consequences both intended and unintended. Through The Dialectic, the posthuman rhetoric is poised between a favorable present and a possible tomorrow, reconstituting *kairos* as an element of survival as well as an element of transformation.

These, then, are the three implications of Burke's minding Mind: responsibility-with-intent, differences with a future, and a *kairos* of the long view. Individually and collectively, these three propositions underscore the value of revisiting Burke's conversation with Bateson begun more than six decades ago. Burke's effort to mind Mind yields a vision of posthuman rhetor and rhetoric that offers a hope not just for the future survival of Mind but for the future flourishing of Mind, a vision the "Bateson boys" would both endorse.

Notes

1. Eleven men actually participated in the round table, but one did so at a distance because of illness.

2. Bateson refers to cybernetics as a "significant historical event" of the twentieth century, stating that "we may call the aggregate of ideas cybernetics, or communication theory, or information theory, or systems theory" (*Steps* 482).

3. Bateson defines epistemology as the "net of premises that govern the adaptation (or maladaptation) to the human and physical environment" (*Steps* 314). Furthermore, when considering the biological world, Bateson believes that ontology and epistemology cannot be separated (314).

4. This is not to say that Bateson disparaged the "corporeal universe." Rather, for him, mind is immanent in matter and matter immanent in mind (*Sacred* 218), a point he states explicitly: "There is no mind separate from body, no god separate from his creation," he contends (Bateson and Bateson, *Angels* 12). Instead, "there is a combining or marriage between an objectivity that is *passive* to the outside world and a creative subjectivity neither pure solipsism nor its opposite" (*Sacred* 223).

5. Bateson identifies six characteristics of mind. In brief, they include (1) an aggregate of interacting parts, (2) difference as the key to aggregation, (3) a reliance on collateral energy (i.e., each part possesses energy that affects relationships), (4) a reliance on complex chains of determination, (5) a view of difference as a "transform" of previous events or information, (6) an emphasis on logical types as an organizing principle of all minds (*Mind* 92).

6. Jointly organized by the Speech Communication Association and the International Communication Association with support from San Francisco State University, the Asilomar Conference involved one hundred scholars from forty different institutions, all gathered to honor Bateson and explore the implications of his work for communication theory (see Wilder-Mott and Weakland xii; Wilder 2).

7. "Counter-Gridlock" (Burke, *On Human*)—a compilation of interviews with Burke conducted between 1980 and 1981—featured questions that invited Burke to explore potential connections and disconnections between his work and Bateson's in an ad hoc, rather than systematic, manner.

8. In "Counter-Gridlock," Burke is identified as the next-to-last speaker (*On Human* 342); however, the conference program lists him as the final speaker of the evening, following Bateson's address with a "response" (Wilder-Mott and Weakland 372).

9. Although Burke quotes extensively from Bateson's "Pathologies of Epistemology," an essay reprinted in Bateson's 1972 groundbreaking collection *Steps to an Ecology of the Mind*, he does not identify the essay in his conference presentation.

10. See Coupe on Burke and his interest in as well as commitment to environmental issues.

11. In fact, Pruchnic argues that Burke's dismissal of any easy distinctions between organism and environment, body and culture, human and machine echoes Bateson's similar dismissal in "Cybernetics of 'Self,'" a conceptual stance that Pruchnic calls an "often-neglected" aspect of "cybernetic work in the human sciences" (115).

12. It is important to note, however, that Burke and Bateson divide up the "ecology of weeds" and the "ecology of ideas" differently (which Burke would call a matter of symbolic action). For Burke, any biological entity exists within the realm of motion, within the ecology of weeds. For Bateson, all biological entities exist within the ecology of ideas, and, as with any ecology, those entities operate within material parameters. Thus, Bateson characterizes Lake Erie as ecomental (qtd. in Burke, "Interactive" 332) while Burke assigns it only the "eco side of the *mentalism*" (337).

13. The essay consists of a revision of Burke's keynote presentation; the "Addendum on Bateson" was written after Burke read Stephen Toulmin's review "The Charm of the Scout," originally published in the *New York Review of Books* in 1980 and republished as the concluding essay in *Rigor and Imagination: Essays from the Legacy of Gregory Bateson*, edited by Carol Wilder-Mott and John H. Weakland. The song was part of Burke's keynote, which he sang in the course of delivering his paper (*On Human* 342). Both essay and addendum were subsequently published in *Rigor and Imagination*. The recipient of the 1982 NCA Golden Anniversary Book Award, *Rigor and Imagination* was the only edited volume to receive this honor (Wilder 2).

14. In that spirit, it is, perhaps, no surprise that "Provocations" is the title of the section within which Burke's essay and addendum appear.

15. Bateson also notes the need for and continually works toward a "*Theory of Action* within large complex systems, where the active agent is himself a part of and a product of the system" (*Sacred* 254).

16. Bateson similarly embraces the inevitability of paradox within a system because of the contradictions inherent in the play of different hierarchical levels of communication required by even the most basic mind. He, too, finds in these paradoxes the impetus for transformation.

Works Cited

Bateson, Gregory. *Mind and Nature: A Necessary Unity*. New York: E. P. Dutton, 1979. Print.
———. "Paradigmatic Conservatism." Wilder-Mott and Weakland 347–55. Print.
———. *A Sacred Unity: Further Steps to an Ecology of Mind*. Edited by Rodney E. Donaldson. New York: HarperCollins, 1991. Print.
———. *Steps to an Ecology of the Mind: Collected Essays in Anthropology, Psychiatry, Evolution, and Epistemology*. Northvale: Jason Aronson, 1987. Print.
Bateson, Gregory, and Mary Catherine Bateson. *Angels Fear: Towards an Epistemology of the Sacred*. New York: Macmillan, 1987. Print.
Braidotti, Rosi. "Posthuman, All Too Human: Towards a New Process Ontology." *Theory, Culture & Society* 23 (2006): 197–208. Print.
Burke, Kenneth. *A Grammar of Motives*. Berkeley: University of California Press, 1969. Print.
———. "Interactive Bind." Wilder-Mott and Weakland, 331–40.
———. *Language as Symbolic Action: Essays on Life, Literature, and Method*. Berkeley: University of California Press, 1973. Print.
———. "(Non)Symbolic Motion/(Symbolic) Action." *Critical Inquiry* 4, no. 4 (1978): 809–38. Print.
———. *On Human Nature: A Gathering While Everything Flows, 1967–1984*. Edited by William H. Rueckert and Angelo Bonadonna. Berkeley: University of California Press, 2003. eBook.

Clarke, Bruce. *Neocybernetics and Narrative.* Minneapolis: University of Minnesota Press, 2014. Print.

Coupe, Laurence. "Kenneth Burke: Pioneer of Ecocriticism." *Journal of American Studies* 35, no. 3 (2001): 413–31. Print.

Crusius, Timothy W. "A Case for Kenneth Burke's Dialectic and Rhetoric." *Philosophy & Rhetoric* 19, no. 1 (1986): 23–37. Print.

Foerster, Heinz von. "Ethics and Second-Order Cybernetics." *Understanding Understanding: Essays on Cybernetics and Cognition.* New York: Springer, 2003, 287–304. eBook.

Haraway, Donna J. "A Cyborg Manifesto: Science, Technology, and Socialist-Feminism in the Late Twentieth Century." *Simians, Cyborgs, and Women: The Reinvention of Nature.* New York: Routledge, 1991, 149–82. Print.

Hasan, Ihab. "Prometheus as Performer: Toward a Posthumanist Culture?" *Georgia Review* 31, no. 4 (1977): 830–50. Print.

Leeds-Hurwitz, Wendy. *Communication in Everyday Life: A Social Interpretation.* New York: Praeger, 1989. Print.

MacAgy, Douglas, editor. "The Western Round Table on Modern Art." *Modern Artists in America: First Series,* edited by Robert Motherwell and Ad Reinhardt. New York: Wittenborn Schultz, 1951, 24–39. Print.

Pruchnic, Jeff. *Rhetoric and Ethics in a Cybernetic Age: The Transhuman Condition.* New York: Routledge, 2014. Routledge Studies in Rhetoric and Communication. Print.

Rueckert, William H. "Introduction." Burke, *On Human* 1–7.

———, editor. *Letters from Kenneth Burke to William H. Rueckert, 1959–1987.* West Lafayette: Parlor Press, 2003. Print.

Weiner, Norbert. *The Human Use of Human Beings: Cybernetics and Society.* New York: Da Capo, 1954. Print.

Wilder, Carol. "Remembering Gregory Bateson." *Kybernetes* 42, nos. 9–10 (2013): 1–20. Web. 3 Oct. 2013.

Wilder-Mott, C., and John H. Weakland, editors. *Rigor and Imagination: Essays from the Legacy of Gregory Bateson.* New York: Praeger, 1981. Print.

Wolfe, Cary. *What Is Posthumanism?* Minneapolis: University of Minnesota Press, 2009. Posthumanities 8. Print.

2

The Cyburke Manifesto, or, Two Lessons from Burke on the Rhetoric and Ethics of Posthumanism

Jeff Pruchnic

The prefix "post" signifies a formation that is *temporally after but not over* that to which it is affixed. "Post" indicates a very particular condition of afterness in which what is past is not left behind, but, on the contrary, relentlessly conditions, even dominates a present that nevertheless also breaks in some way with this past. In other words, we use the term "post" only for a present whose past continues to capture and structure it.

—Wendy Brown, *Walled States, Waning Sovereignty*

Posthumanism, it has always seemed to me, has a more complex relationship to its referent than the various other "post-" schools of theory and thought that preceded or followed it. For one, the target of posthumanism—the discourse or line of thinking it is attempting to move beyond or leave behind—would seem to be not so much humanism as it is postmodernism. This of course makes sense as, after all, it is the postmodern, much more than the humanist, that was the dominant philosophical and ethical stance of cultural theory preceding the arrival of posthumanism as a recognizable discourse. However, here we might add an even more complex layer to the temporality or positioning of posthumanism within contemporary critical thought, insofar as humanism was itself the vector that postmodern theory, at least in its early days, was meant to rescue us from. Indeed, while it may be largely forgotten decades later, what we would come to call postmodernism and poststructuralism circulated for a time under the rubric of "anti-humanism" in response to its central figures' disaffection with humanist touchstones and methods of analysis.[1] The more specific critique of anthropocentric modes of cultural analysis that has become a hallmark of posthuman thought was also clearly present in the early work of figures like Roland Barthes, Jacques Derrida, and Michel Foucault, works that would lay the "foundation" for the "anti-foundational" discourse we would later call postmodernism.

Indeed, despite the apparent anachronism, a work like Foucault's *The Order of Things* can look much more like a manifesto for contemporary posthumanist work than of postmodernism. Consider, for instance, Foucault's famous depiction in that text of "man" as an "invention of recent date" that is "perhaps nearing its end," and of anthropocentricism as "a stubborn obstacle standing obstinately in the way of an imminent new form of thought" (342).

However, while the critique of the anthropocentric and the humanist that forms the core of posthumanism might be considered a return of the repressed insofar as it mirrors this stance of early postmodern theory, it is equally clear that posthumanism has positioned itself as being a corrective to such work, an attempt to do things differently in regard to everything that came after this critique of humanism within early postmodern thought. Perhaps most notably, if the heyday of postmodern theory was (rightly or wrongly) accused of focusing overwhelmingly on language and other varieties of "discursivity" at the expense of considerations of embodiment and materiality, posthuman theory has reversed this focus in bringing to the foreground the importance of physiology, affect, and various other materialisms in addressing contemporary culture and systems of social power. If the key terms and battlegrounds of early postmodern theory were epistemology and meaning, the key terms of early posthumanism have been ontology and ethics.

This primacy of ethics in posthumanism in particular brings us to a second important difference between the enterprise and its relationship to both traditional humanism and postmodern theory. While anticipating, as noted above, posthumanism's critique of humanism's unexamined premises regarding individual agency, work in postmodern and poststructuralist philosophy and theory, particularly in its heyday, was quite explicitly positioned as a recounting of the unavoidable and obvious changes occurring in recent culture as opposed to functioning as an affirmative or prescriptive program for responding to them. Derrida, for instance, often specifically described deconstruction as not only a particular method of analysis but a faithful description of "what is happening" in contemporary culture, and the same could be said of Jean-François Lyotard's canonical "report" on contemporary knowledge (*The Postmodern Condition*), Foucault's careful recovery of the lost moments in the history of institutional practices, or Fredric Jameson's mapping of the "cultural logic of late capitalism."[2] In other words, while one might be able to detect the strategic and political intent of such works, its purpose was, at least, on the surface, to represent the present accurately; the particular ideals or actions that might be promoted or encouraged by that analysis manifest only at a subsidiary moment, as a corollary to the analysis presented. Indeed, it was this register of at least early postmodern theory that led to accusations of its political quietism, at least in comparison to critical theory of the Frankfurt School variety or other earlier modes of humanistic and cultural analysis indebted to historical materialism.

Here, too, I think we can detect a clear departure in posthumanist theory. Perhaps because of its embrace of materialist methods, the most prominent work in posthumanism has been much more comfortable in embracing a role of advocacy or in offering more explicit prescriptions in alignment with the diagnoses of contemporary cultural life being offered within. Thus, for instance, in a work that was more influential than perhaps any other in popularizing the term in contemporary critical discourse, N. Katherine Hayles's *How We Became Posthuman* offers two possibilities for what may emerge from the titular cultural condition. One is a "nightmare" in which human consciousness and sense of self can be perceived as disembodied, and the worst aspects of triumphant humanism go into overdrive; another, the one forwarded by Hayles, is a future in which human finitude and embodiment are embraced and we can create ethical strategies "conducive to the long-range survival of humans and of the other life-forms, biological and artificial, with whom we share the planet and ourselves" (291). Similarly, in *What Is Posthumanism?*, the work that perhaps comes the closest to providing the thorough mapping of posthuman thought that Jameson accomplished in his magisterial work on postmodernism, Cary Wolfe advocates for a version of posthumanism as ethically attuned as Hayles's, particularly one that is cleanly separated from the excesses and egoism he sees in much "transhumanist" discourse on artificial intelligence and body modification. Without taking away from the rigor of these other analyses of posthuman culture, I think it is safe to say that in addition to functioning as analytical texts, posthuman theory has also been largely *aspirational*. In addition to, and perhaps more importantly than, documenting "what is happening," posthuman theories have offered their own explicit visions of *what should happen*: how to craft more ethical and sustainable futures for life "after" or beyond "the human" as we used to recognize it.

It is in response to these two vectors in particular—the implicit forwarding of posthumanism as an alternative or successor to postmodernism and the prescriptive register of work on posthumanism—that I think Kenneth Burke's work is particularly salient. While Burke has quite frequently been forwarded as anticipating many of the mainstays of postmodern thought, his uniqueness within that context is apparent around many of the same concerns—particularly the importance of human embodiment on cultural experience—that have distinguished the posthuman from the postmodern.[3] Additionally, it is my wager here that Burke's consistent focus on "motivation" rather than meaning, particularly when applied to methods of cultural analysis and the intersection of criticism and politics, has much to teach us about posthuman theorists' focus on advocacy and ethics and these theorists' own rhetorical or "motivational" strategies for convincing readers to accept their particular visions for the posthuman.

Briefly stated, my thesis is that Burke's work on human motivational schemas, particularly those of humanism, can give us particular purchase on what I will argue is the uniquely paradoxical rhetorical strategy of posthuman theory: to convince humans to move beyond humanism by appealing to some of the very aspects of human exceptionalism and agency being simultaneously critiqued as problematically anthropocentric. Furthermore, I'll suggest that, particularly in its focus on the intersections of ethics and politics, posthumanism should be considered alongside other recent work on rethinking human ontology, a context in which, again, I think Burke's work can be particularly useful for clarifying posthumanism's ethical potentials. In short, this essay includes two lessons from Burke on the rhetoric and ethics of posthumanism. Covering this territory will also, I think, allow us to shed light on some of the more cryptic themes of Burke's work relevant to both humanism and rhetoric, ones that might become clearer, as well as more urgent, when they are considered against the backdrop of posthumanism.

Posthuman Rhetoric, or, the Ethical Confusion

At first blush, at least, there is of course one aspect of Burke's work that might make it a particularly odd fit for thinking through the possibilities of posthumanism: his consistent and explicit insistence on the importance, one might say even necessity, of humanism as framework for cultural analysis. Indeed, Burke insistently returns to humanism as a foundational premise for social and political orientations and consistently argues for the value of humanism as a "corrective" or supplement to other modes of analysis, even those that, like posthumanism, take their point of departure via a critique of humanist touchstones (and thus, at different times, various philosophies or systems—such as communism as well as particular concepts or methods unique to Burke, such as "the comic corrective"—come to be described as "synonyms" for humanism). Burke's preoccupation with humanism would seem to emerge from two interrelated presumptions about what constitutes humanism or humanistic methods. For one, Burke tends to take up humanism broadly, as encompassing any approach that forgoes transcendental or theological explanations of human culture and behavior. He writes, for instance, in *Permanence and Change*:

> Metaphysicians at one time began their works with a *philosophia prima*, which had to do with the structure of the universe in general. From this they proceeded to deduce their laws of history and psychology, of the good and the beautiful, their anthropology. Subsequent thinkers, noting the influence of the anthropological in shaping our ideas as to the nature of the universe, reversed this way of proceeding from the cosmos to man. They began with the study of purely human processes, and interpreted our views of the universe as an outcome of our psychological, physiological, ethnological, or historical responses. (25)

While we may now tend to see at least some of the domains that Burke identifies as steps toward the decline of humanism as a far-reaching philosophy, and/or dismiss Burke's abstract association of humanistic inquiry as a whole with humanism as a philosophy, Burke seems to insist stubbornly on attaching humanism to any critical perspective on (human) culture.

Burke makes perhaps a stronger case for the centrality of humanism in the analysis of culture, or even the necessity of an "anthropomorphic" perspective, in addressing the necessarily complex rhetorical work of cultural criticism. Insofar as Burke situates belief and behavioral systems as premised on particular, simplified, and ideologically weighted views of the world, any human understandings of the role of the human provide what Burke calls "the basis of simplification" for such systems. Thus, he writes, any effective "corrective rationalization" to the ideational commonplaces provided by other domains such as science and technology "must certainly move in the direction of the anthropomorphic or humanistic or poetic, since this is the aspect of culture which the scientific criteria, with their emphasis upon dominance rather than upon inducement, have tended to eliminate or minimize" (*Permanence* 65). The more explicit or avowed persuasive appeal of such work, alongside its appeal to a shared definition of what is constitutive of the human, are, for Burke, essential to the work of cultural analysis; these two principles, when coupled, would seem to constitute "criticism" as an endeavor.

Both of these perspectives on the centrality of humanism are, I take it, bound up in another career-long focus of Burke's work: the study of motives.[4] If Burke's work, as has been so often the case these past few decades, can be positioned as both anticipating the central conceits of subsequent schools of thought and theory while also remaining wholly unique, this is likely because of his insistence on positioning "motives" rather than meaning, ideology, or even communication, despite his immense interest in it, as the central defining term for analyzing human thought and behavior. Indeed, while Burke's openness to questioning traditional notions of both human agency and exceptionalism was quite progressive for his time, it was consistently "motive"—and the closely related fields of affect and emotions—that he continually drew from to distinguish the "actions" or humans from the "motions" of nonhumans.

However, while motive becomes important in Burke's work for marking what is unique about the human, Burke simultaneously uses the concept to question many of the same boundaries that would be contested by posthumanism: those between the biological and the cultural, the natural and the artificial, and the individual and the assemblage. As Burke argues in a 1952 essay, there are "three orders of motives"—namely, "bodily (sensory); familial (personal); political, social, civic"—but these categories are not intended to suggest that these motives function independently or that you can consider them as shaping behavior in a sequential process; rather, they exist in what Burke terms a "state of simultaneous mutuality" when influencing human interpretation and behavior ("*Ethan*" 100). As Timothy W. Crusius notes, Burke's insistence on the cultural dimension of motives that seemed to originate entirely in physiological processes (and vice-versa) allowed him to reference and make use of the dominant theories of human agency and subjectivity of his time—namely behaviorism, Marxism, and "Freudianism"—without endorsing any one of them as adequately explaining the complex interactions of motive, interpretation, and behavior (69–72). This ambiguous quality of motives as taking in both internal and external properties of the human is prominently featured near the beginning of Burke's *A Grammar of Motives* around the topic of the "paradox of substance":

> The word "substance," used to designate what a thing *is*, derives from a word designating something that a thing *is not*. That is, though used to designate something *within* the thing, *intrinsic* to it, the word etymologically refers to something *outside* the thing, *extrinsic* to it. Or otherwise put: the word in its etymological origins would refer to an attribute of the

thing's *context*, since that which supports or underlies a thing would be a part of the thing's context. And a thing's context, being outside or beyond the thing, would be something that the thing is *not*. (23)

This Möbius-strip quality of substance is paralleled in Burke's conception of motive and in his approach to reading "motive" as his core hermeneutic concept in *A Grammar of Motives* and *A Rhetoric of Motives*.

Thus, despite the consistent and vocal affirmation of humanism in Burke's work, I think that Burke's unique and oddly prescient take on (human) motives may be immensely valuable in unpacking what I take to be the paradoxical, perhaps even contradictory, goal of much work in posthumanism: convincing humans to reconsider the exceptionalism of the species and thus act in a less anthropocentric, and more broadly ethical, manner in relation to not only other humans but nonhumans as well. It is this endeavor that most distinguishes posthumanism from earlier intellectual movements, and also perhaps the greatest challenge facing the enterprise. When every other aspect of the human previously taken to be eternal or constitutive has been deconstructed or dismissed as an accident of history (or as the result of humanism's supposed and self-congratulatory consideration of human supremacy), the one defining and unavoidable vector of "the human condition" may be what Giorgio Agamben, following the work of Martin Heidegger, calls "the open": the context in which humans cannot help but divide the natural world into categories and decide whether, for instance, animals should be situated as sharing significant ontological attributes with humans. As Agamben suggests, regardless of the decision humans make about "sharing" such ontological attributes, that decision is unavoidably "an undue projection of the human world onto the animal," a boundary-crossing that the human, and only the human, can seem to accomplish (60). Insofar as posthumanisms of pretty much every stripe are premised on such a renunciation of human supremacy, this dilemma is a particularly problematic one for the endeavor; as Agamben suggests, even denying that one has the right to make such decisions constitutes an anthropocentric action.

More specifically, we might say that posthumanism's defining critique of anthropocentrism and human exceptionality burdens it with an additional difficulty in comparison to other, one might say "more humanist," attempts to convince humans to live in more just and sustainable ways with nonhumans. For instance, in one of the classic justifications for the ethical obligation to be kind toward (nonhuman) animals, found in Immanuel Kant's *Metaphysics of*

Morals, sparing animals from unnecessary pain and torment is not premised on some recognition of any sentience of the animal. Rather, kindness to animals is coded as an obligation of the ethical individual only insofar as to do otherwise would degrade the human involved in the action or risk spilling over into the nonhuman realm and thus make her more likely to be "inhumane" to human animals; the ethical duty to avoid causing animal suffering, Kant tells us, can only "belong *indirectly* to a human being's duty with regard to these animals; considered as a *direct* duty, however, it is only of the human being *to* himself" (193). In other words, kindness toward animals is, ethically, only positively val-ued insofar as it carries backward to the humans performing the duty and to their interactions with other humans; in the words of a student of Kant's lec-tures on ethics, "tender feelings toward dumb animals develop humane feelings towards mankind" (Kant, *Lectures* 240). In both cases, the animal is not given any particular pride of place beyond its ability to be a conduit for these other outcomes.

Such appeals, premised as they are on the "proper" goodness of humans and how to achieve it, would seem unavailable to posthumanist discourse because to use them would be to simultaneously undermine the critique of anthropo-centrism being forwarded in the same discourse. Neither, for that matter, does posthumanism have easy recourse to a principle that even Kant rejects: that of arguing that the shared capacities of humans and animals require one to evince toward animals at least some portion of the ethical behavior required of ethical interaction with nonhuman animals. Rather, to do so would be to credit the appeal to the "shared humanity" that posthuman discourses have been careful to avoid, given the long and tragic history of defining humanity in ways that exclude not only "actual" nonhumans but marginalized groups of humans as well; indeed, one might say that the consistent critique of the failure of such humanist appeals to the commonality of humans is the vector that, more than anything else, puts the "post" in posthuman ethics.

Wolfe gives us a particularly striking example of this problematic in a cri-tique of the "Great Ape Project," an altruistic endeavor to raise funds for the protection of (nonhuman) great apes that emphasized their similarity with humans. Such a tactic is ethically compromised, Wolfe argues, because attempt-ing to motivate human ethical concern for "those who are (symptomatically) 'most like us' only ends up reinforcing the very humanisms that seem to be the problem in the first place" (*Animal* 192). In other words, while the campaign may be an attempt to extend the boundaries of the human by emphasizing our shared capacities with some animals, it uses the same logic deployed to exclude our "others" based on a lack of such capacities, and thus is also an extension of the boundaries of the problematical humanism that posthuman ethics would seek to supplant. Rather, Wolfe goes on to argue, insofar as humanist ethics are undermined by a presumption of some form of reciprocity (either an expectation of ethical treatment in return or of a more abstract reciprocity of shared characteristics between the subject and object of such action), ethical behavior that might transcend this problem would have to be outside of such reciprocity and thus toward the truly "other" (such as nonhuman animals that lack the similarities evinced by great apes) (199).

However, such restrictions pose a particular thorny dilemma for posthuman ethics, even beyond the difficulty of escaping ethics' longstanding roots in a shared *ethos*, or some communal connection between individuals interacting with another (an "escape" that theorists of posthuman ethics have been eager to make in their attempts to emphasize the relationalities between humans, nonhuman animals, and machines without privileging the reciprocity of thought or conduct usually restricted to humans). However ironic it may seem, the challenge of engaging in ethics without any presumed form of reciprocation (either directly in some kind of immediate reward, or indirectly through the edict that one should act ethically in hopes that they will receive the same ethical treatment from others) might highlight the impossibility of performing any ethical action that does not have some element of self-interest in it, even if it does not take the traditional form of reciprocity ("one good turn leads to another"). More specifically, the absence of a transcendental schema for ethics (such as religion) or some hope of reciprocation only highlights the ways in which humans are often motivated to "do good" in order to consider themselves "good"; in other words, while one might escape the direct connection Kant makes between acting ethically toward nonhumans in order to develop more humane actions toward humans, the elimination of any connection to this function foregrounds the pursuit of attaining "humaneness" *in itself.*

All of which is to say that ethics, even of the posthuman variety, cannot escape a certain self-interestedness; even if one is not pursuing some immediate tangible reward or reciprocal action, the performance of ethical behavior must be motivated by an interest *in oneself,* in being a "better person" for escaping the "trap of humanism" or becoming a more enlightened "posthuman," and all the corollaries of that action—respect for one's self and one's ethical accomplishments, pride in one's self, pleasure in moving beyond humanism through the exercise of nonreciprocal ethics, etc.—and these vectors are only amplified when performed toward and around other actors, such as nonhumans, who are incapable of such behavior. In this sense, the ethical objectives of posthumanism, however strangely, may be those that most emphasize the anthropocentric, self-congratulatory vectors of humanism that the field has attempted explicitly to move beyond.

Rosi Braidotti's work, perhaps more so than that of any other, has directly confronted the complexities of this dilemma around the question of posthuman ethics. Braidotti warns us against the danger of rejecting what she deems "the most valuable aspects of the humanistic and its most enduring legacy," notably the desire for human "emancipation" and "progressive politics in general," in our rush to critique humanism or embrace antihumanist philosophies (29). At the same time, however, she is as attuned as Hayles or Wolfe to the ways in which events justified by the exceptionalism and anthropocentrism inherent in traditional humanism have contributed to some of the worst tragedies of human history. Thus the challenge, for Braidotti, is to configure an "affirmative" posthumanism that would reject both individualism and "nihilistic defeatism"; such a posthuman ethics, in Braidotti's conception, would promote "an ethical bond of an altogether different sort from the self-interests of an individual subject, as defined along the canonical lines of classical Humanism" and instead be premised on "an enlarged sense of inter-connection between self and others, including the non-human or 'earth' other, by removing the obstacle of self-centered individualism" (49–50). However, it remains difficult to imagine how an ethical bond based on such an expanded interconnection does not lead to the same problems identified by Wolfe in his critique of the Great Ape Project, or whether it is truly possible to mobilize an ethical appeal based on the renunciation of self-interest that does not return to the same problematic of being in some way motivated by one's own satisfaction in "self-overcoming" ("Look at how I've overcome individualism! I'm so free of self-interest!").

It is at this point—this particular paradox of ethics and the specific rhetorical challenges of posthuman discourse—that I think Burke's work on motives can be of particular value. In a section of *Permanence and Change* with the appropriate title "The Ethical Confusion," Burke investigates just such a strange admixture of the self-interested and the selfless under the rubric of "the egoistic-altruistic merger." In conjoining these two terms typically put into opposition with another, Burke attempts to thematize not just the ways in which altruistic action often depends on a certain self-satisfied or even self-aggrandizing egoism—as seen in the example of posthuman ethical appeals, above—but also whether the two might be, however implicitly, always connected to one another. Of particular interest here is the way Burke describes the process through which self-denial or restraint from pursuing self-interests becomes a goal in itself, bringing to its performer its own pleasure and value; interestingly enough, Burke unpacks it in reference to a humanist organization and that organization's "ethicizing" process:

> Perhaps the most complicated case of such "ethicizing" was the American Humanists' concern with the "inner check." Classical philosophers, discovering that a very serviceable principle for promoting human welfare was moderation, advocated moderation so strenuously and so long that it became *not a means of procuring advantages* but an *end to be sought even at the risk of disadvantage.* But once it had become an end rather than a means, a new means was required to promote its attainment. This was supplied by the invention of the "inner check," which prompts us to feel the sanction of moderation. (210)

As Burke goes on to detail, the "inner check" then itself "quickly moves from an instrument into an end, a good-in-itself," following the same process that transformed the role of moderation.

Burke further clarifies that in revealing this process through which means are transformed into ends and self-interest is transformed into self-sacrifice (and vice-versa), he is not merely interested in conveying the "cynical notion that altruism is 'mere egoism'" (211). Rather, he is interested, on one hand, in the ways in which either end of this spectrum can be emphasized by opposing parties: "the Church might interpret the desire to make money as merely a low form of desire to improve oneself; and the Anti-Church would counter by interpreting morals as a mere epiphenomenon of the desire to prosper in the materialistic sense" (211). On the other hand, and perhaps more importantly, he also pursues the ways in which such an emphasis can be used not only in critical interpretations but also in motivational strategies for convincing individuals to act ethically through appeals to motives we would not intuitively code as positively ethical.

Indeed, such an "ethical confusion," for Burke, is intrinsic to the process of human motivation toward ethical action, even if we may tend to emphasize one or the other part of the egoistic-altruistic merger; as Burke writes, while we may tend to weight the selfless or self-interested ends of the spectrum, "in the series itself there is no such weighting, either one way or the other" (211). He goes on to suggest that we should not only draw the dreary conclusion that altruism cannot exist without egoism (in other words, that no "pure" altruism exists), but also the inversion of that process: "The concept of an egoistic-altruistic merger" would also indicate "that egoism cannot exist without altruism. Or, otherwise stated: egoism cannot operate unless it so transcends itself that it becomes *qualitatively* different" (211). It is here, I think, that we are provided with perhaps our best frame of reference for understanding the peculiar mix of egoism and altruism in posthuman ethics: if posthumanist appeals for nonreciprocal ethical action toward nonhumans end up relying on the very humanist anthropocentrism they critique—anthropocentrism being in an important sense the egoism *of the species*—they do so in an attempt to transform it into something *qualitatively different*, to use it against itself, to motivate humans to deploy the same ethical considerations they would give those they traditionally see as equals toward those traditionally excluded from that category.

In another work, I have suggested that various attempts to revise humanism radically or think "beyond" its central tenets might cause us to reject Foucault's famous consideration of humanism in "What Is Enlightenment?" as a kind of floating signifier attached to various (often contradictory) movements, and instead recognize it as a longstanding rhetorical strategy based on a certain unavoidable self-identification by its audience (Pruchnic, *Rhetoric* 54–57). However, thinking through the challenges of posthumanist ethical objectives alongside Burke's work on motives might suggest a much more specific conclusion about the peculiar rhetorical context of posthumanism—namely, that it is by necessity reliant on appealing to many of the same humanist qualities being simultaneously disavowed. Furthermore, the potential for achieving this complex rhetorical strategy may be the most important challenge for posthumanism as an activist or interventionist undertaking. To put it another way, if early work in postmodernism, as predicted in Jameson's famous definition, may have amounted to "not much more than theorizing its own conditions of possibility," then early posthumanism may turn out to be primarily about theorizing its own conditions of *persuadability* (i).

Posthuman Ethics, or, Making a Virtue of Vice

Thus far, I've argued that work on posthuman ethics is dependent on, perhaps even defined by, a complex rhetorical strategy by which a particular vintage of anthropocentric humanism is appealed to while being simultaneously denounced. Even if one wholeheartedly accepts Burke's "egoistic-altruistic merger" as a way of understanding that dynamic and its centrality to appeals to ethical action, I take it there is another concomitant question left unanswered: if posthuman ethical objectives are dependent on a particular rhetorical strategy, then what is the ethics *of that* rhetoric? In other words, it would seem that in addition to the egoistic-altruistic merger, we have another important combination at play, what we might call, after Burke, the "ethical-rhetorical merger" that distinguishes post-humanist thought from both humanism and postmodernism (and indeed, it seems to me that this "other" merger is also an unnamed but recurrent concept in Burke's work). More simply stated, if investigating the ethics of posthuman-ism revealed something important about its rhetoric, can looking at this rhetoric also tell us something significant about posthuman ethics? This is the question I want to turn to now by way of concluding this essay.

I take it that the ethical import of posthumanism, particularly when consid-ered as a corrective or replacement for postmodern ethical thought, is best considered alongside other recent attempts that share such a "post-postmodern" approach and that also, like posthumanism, have attempted to make clearer the connections of critical work done in contemporary theory and its potential to contribute to thinking on ethics and politics (as opposed to "just" epistemology). I am thinking here of the variety of endeavors that foreground ontology (rather than subjectivity) as a crucial concept that have emerged over the last two decades in the works of such thinkers as Giorgio Agamben, Slavoj Žižek, Michael Hardt, and Antonio Negri. Carsten Strathausen has given the name "neo-left ontology" to describe the shared aim of such a diverse group of think-ers, all of whom proceed in some way from Jean-Luc Nancy's call for theory to invent "an ontology of being-with-one-another" in order to develop more prag-matic and ethical strategies for contemporary culture (Nancy 53). The variety of posthumanisms that have emerged in contemporary theory during the same time share this objective, one which might be considered an attempt to move "beyond" progressive or "left" postmodernist approaches that worked through the destruction or deconstruction of problematic cultural binaries or exclu-sions; rather than (just) breaking apart conceptual categories, thinkers in this camp work more to construct or promote particular linkages, ways of "being-with-one-another," that emphasize the responsibilities and shared interests we have to and with each other.

However, here again I take it that this objective is particularly challenging for posthumanism as opposed to other attempts to rethink ontology for ethical purposes. Whereas the latter have tended to emphasize the commonality between humans despite all of their other differences, posthumanism, as we have seen, also highlights the dangers of depending on such a logic insofar as it has tended historically to lead to other exclusions; the "linkages" being sought in posthumanism are most frequently not between humans but *outside of them* and with various nonhuman entities. As a "leveling" of retrogressive or exploitive categorizations of humans, nonhuman animals, and machines, posthumanism does not have the easy recourse of insisting that all humans can, in the famous Kantian formulation, be "ends" in themselves, whereas other entities (such as animals) can be comfortably left in the abject category of "means." Either such other entities must be "elevated" to the same level as the human or, it would seem, the human must be "lowered" to these other levels to create some kind of ethical parity.

I want to suggest that something of the latter is present in posthumanism, but also that it may not have to be ethically problematic. As shown above, the posthuman call for humans to extend certain rights or respect to nonhumans must be considered along two levels: on one, a critique of anthropocentrism is leveled in order to convince humans to accept this proposition and act accordingly, while on the other, by nature of its appeal, this call tends to shore up some of the self-congratulatory or supremacist aspects of humanism that are being critiqued. Insofar as this kind of appeal is at least partially deceptive—by its nature not able to operate alongside the disclosure of its full premises—it may be that it has to treat people as "means" of a sort in order to ensure that both humans and nonhumans might be afforded at least some of the privileges of being "ends"; moving between those two categories is not only necessary to the current rhetorical strategies of posthumanism, but would also seem to be the best way to achieve its ethical imperatives.

As argued above, such a strategy relies on a particularly problematic audience accommodation strategy, one in which humans must be simultaneously elevated and critiqued. Indeed, one might add that one would also have to account for multiple divergences between the types of audiences for such an argument. Indeed, Wolfe, despite his somewhat rigid critique of common animal rights strategies referenced earlier in this chapter, addresses this particular challenge in *What Is Posthumanism?* Assaying the variety of contemporary theories and theorists that might be considered under a broad spectrum of more or less humanist and posthumanist thought, Wolfe also draws our attention to the ways that the common appeals or premises of these different schools may be strategically invoked for particular purposes, even if they appear to conflict with the principles being held to by the rhetor. As Wolfe writes, for instance, "if you are interviewing with the local newspaper about animal overpopulation in your community and you want to win over readers to your point of view, you would do well to gravitate toward the internal disciplinary discourse that characterizes the humanist end of the spectrum" (124). In this sense, then, one can make a distinction between the various "approaches" one might take as well as the degree of (post)humanism held, philosophically, by the rhetor using such an approach, and the two will not necessarily overlap on every occasion; more precisely, canny rhetors would do well to use an approach that does not entirely reveal their ideational stance when it is necessary to win over their audience.

Wolfe's advice here is, I take it, a synecdoche of sorts for the larger rhetorical strategy of posthumanist ethics identified above, and we might question the ethics of that particular strategy insofar as it leads one to "hide" some part of one's stance in order to win over an audience effectively, an uncomfortable situation when ethics is itself the topic and "goal" of the endeavor; in this scenario, the audience is treated as the means to create an ethical action rather than an "end" that might share the rhetor's principles.

Here, too, I think Burke's work on motives can be salutary for untangling the ethical complexities of such a process. Indeed, the phenomenon through which rhetors seem to compromise their own ethics for the "greater good" of motivating the ethical actions that are their goal is a recurrent interest in Burke's work. Among many other examples, for instance, in *Permanence and Change* Burke glosses Sidney Hook's analysis of Karl Marx, in which, Burke explains, Hook identifies what appear to be "inconsistencies" in Marx's thought by identifying how Marx "rephrased his arguments to profit by the particular conviction of the particular group he happened to be addressing" (183). It is no coincidence that Burke would be interested in such strategies, as his own work would seem to show similar patterns, particularly in, apposite to the example of Marx, his shifting depictions of communism in the multiple versions of the works we have come to know as "My Approach to Communism" and *Permanence and Change*.[5]

For Burke, the playing of a role that shields a rhetor's true values was a particularly interesting case for the ethics of rhetoric, one that "often brings rhetoric to the edge of cunning" (*Rhetoric of Motives* 36). He goes on to write in *A Rhetoric of Motives*,

> A misanthropic politician who dealt in mankind-loving imagery could still think of himself as rhetorically honest, if he meant to do well by his constituents yet thought that he could get their vote only by such a display. Whatever the falsity in overplaying the role, there may be honesty in the assuming of the role itself; and the overplaying may be but a translation into a different medium of communication, a way of amplifying a statement so that it carries better to a large or distant audience. Hence, the persuasive identifications of Rhetoric, in being so directly designed for *use*, involve us in a special problem of *consciousness*, as exemplified in the Rhetorician's particular *purpose* for a given statement. (36)

For Burke, it was possible—even necessary—to make a distinction between the rhetors' purpose, their understanding of their own motives, and the tactics they would use to motivate others; if the original motive follows the correct ethical imperative, then one can be forgiven if the motives they produce in others might not have been accomplished in the purest fashion.

Indeed, for Burke it would seem that such an approach is not so much an unfortunate necessity for individuals who hope to be successful in persuading others but perhaps entirely appropriate for the conception of any sustainable cultural or democratic system. As Burke writes in one of his more colorful passages, "once you postulate human virtue as a foundation of a system, you are a dullard indeed if you can't make up a thousand schemes for a good society. A society is sound only if it can prosper on its vices, since virtues are by very definition rare and exceptional" (*Counter-Statement* 114). In this sense, a posthuman rhetorical strategy that focuses on the "vice" in the human tendency toward perceived exceptionality or supremacy, in order to motivate more ethical action toward other humans and nonhumans, might be a far from unethical process for creating more responsible behavior in the world.

In the earlier part of this essay, I argued that the primary rhetorical strategy of posthumanism involved maintaining, perhaps even amplifying, an aspect of anthropocentric humanism that it would otherwise appear to disavow. In detailing the ethics behind that strategy above, we seem to be left with a contrasting conclusion: in at least one important sense, posthumanism subverts an aspect of humanism that it would otherwise seem to be maintaining or amplifying—the treatment of (non)humans as "ends" and not "means"—by motivating humans to act more ethically for the "wrong" reasons. Neither of these cases, I take it, detracts from the value of posthumanist theory and its ethical and political imperatives (as I try to suggest, above, they may even strengthen these vectors).

Indeed, it is this perspective on posthumanism, or on posthumanist *rhetoric* more specifically, that might help us map the next step in adapting the best of (post)humanism for the demands of the present and for thinking through the advantages of posthumanist thought beyond its value as a mere corrective or extension of postmodern or humanist thought. In one of the first essays to thematize posthumanism in relation to rhetoric, John Muckelbauer and Debra Hawhee warned readers over fifteen years ago to be careful of too-easy conclusions that we can easily surpass humanism: "humanism is not an ideological chimera that we have somehow intellectually surpassed; to tell such a story would be a key strategy of humanism" (769). While this sentiment is still worth repeating today, we might have to add that any posthuman future worth supporting will have to figure not only how to critique the excesses of anthropocentrism, but also leverage them for more effective purposes; we will have to, following Burke, think of ways to carve better futures from the manipulation of our "ethical confusion," our less obviously altruistic motives, and our strategies for transforming virtue into vice and back again. After all, as Burke tells us near the conclusion of *The Rhetoric of Religion*, "the future will inevitably be what that particular combination of all men's efforts and counter-efforts and virtues and vices, along with the nature of things in general, inevitably adds up to" (272), and we could do far worse than the future advocated by posthumanism's particular combination of virtue and vice, humanism and antihumanism.

Notes

1. See Martin Halliwell and Andy Mousley's *Critical Humanisms* for an overview of the "anti-humanist" rubric as applied to early postmodern theory as well as a thorough analysis of the relationship between humanism and postmodern and poststructuralist thought.

2. Derrida used this phrase often to describe deconstruction; a reflection on the statement and his use of it can be found in the first volume of *The Beast and The Sovereign* (76).

3. For Burke's focus on embodiment and its relevance to (post-)postmodern theory, see Debra Hawhee's book-length study of the topic and Pruchnic's "Rhetoric, Cybernetics, and the Work of the Body in Burke's Body of Work."

4. Burke's analysis of motives as a conceptual category takes center stage at least as early as his second book ("Motives" being the focus of the second chapter of Burke's *Permanence*

and Change) and finds its fullest analyses in Burke's *A Rhetoric of Motives* and *A Grammar of Motives*. It remains an important part of Burke's final completed book-length work, *The Rhetoric of Religion*, via that text's focus on how cultural values and symbolic systems take over from religious ones in determining the ways humans are "motivated" and attribute motives to others.

5. See Stacey Sheriff for an excellent examination of Burke's drafts of the "My Approach to Communism" essay and Pruchnic, "Burke in/on Public and Private," for a reading of the manuscript versions of *Permanence and Change*.

Works Cited

Agamben, Giorgio. *The Open: Man and Animal*. Translated by Devin Attell. Stanford: Stanford University Press, 2004. Meridian: Crossing Aesthetics. Print.

Braidotti, Rosi. *The Posthuman*. Cambridge, Mass.: Polity Press, 2013. Print.

Brown, Wendy. *Walled States, Waning Sovereignty*. Brooklyn: Zone, 2010. Print.

Burke, Kenneth. *Counter-Statement*. Berkeley: University of California Press, 1968. Print.

———. "*Ethan Brand*: A Preparatory Investigation." *Essays Toward a Symbolic of Motives, 1950–1955*, edited by William H. Rueckert. West Lafayette: Parlor, 2006, 77–102. Print.

———. *A Grammar of Motives*. Berkeley: University of California Press, 1969. Print.

———. *Permanence and Change: An Anatomy of Purpose*. 3rd ed. Berkeley: University of California Press, 1984. Print.

———. *A Rhetoric of Motives*. Berkeley: University of California Press, 1969. Print.

———. *The Rhetoric of Religion: Studies in Logology*. Berkeley: University of California Press, 1970. Print.

Crusius, Timothy W. *Kenneth Burke and the Conversation After Philosophy*. Carbondale: Southern Illinois University Press, 1999. Rhetorical Philos. and Theory. Print.

Derrida, Jacques. *The Beast and the Sovereign*. Translated by Geoffrey Bennington. Chicago: University of Chicago Press, 2009. Seminars of Jacques Derrida 1. Print.

Foucault, Michel. *The Order of Things: An Archaeology of the Human Sciences*. New York: Vintage, 1994. Print.

———. "What Is Enlightenment?" *The Foucault Reader*, edited by Paul Rabinow. New York: Pantheon, 1984, 32–50. Print.

Halliwell, Martin, and Andy Mousley. *Critical Humanisms: Humanist/Anti-Humanist Dialogues*. Edinburgh: Edinburgh University Press, 2003. Print.

Hawhee, Debra. *Moving Bodies: Kenneth Burke at the Edges of Language*. Columbia: University of South Carolina Press, 2012. Print. Studies in Rhetoric/Communication.

Hayles, N. Katherine. *How We Became Posthuman: Virtual Bodies in Cybernetics, Literature, and Informatics*. Chicago: University of Chicago Press, 1999. Print.

Jameson, Fredric. *Postmodernism, or, The Cultural Logic of Late Capitalism*. Durham: Duke University Press, 1991. Print.

Kant, Immanuel. *Lectures on Ethics*. Translated by Louis Infield. New York: Harper & Row, 1963. Print.

———. *The Metaphysics of Morals*. Edited and translated by Mary Gregor. Cambridge: Cambridge University Press, 1996. Cambridge Texts in the Hist. of Philos. Print.

Lyotard, Jean-François. *The Postmodern Condition: A Report on Knowledge*. Translated by Geoff Bennington and Brian Massumi. Minneapolis: University of Minnesota Press, 1984. Print.

Muckelbauer, John, and Debra Hawhee. "Posthuman Rhetorics: 'It's the Future, Pikul.'" *JAC* 20, no. 4 (2000): 767–74. Print.

Nancy, Jean-Luc. *Being Singular Plural*. Translated by Robert D. Richardson and Anne E. O'Byrne. Stanford: Stanford University Press, 2000. Meridian: Crossing Aesthetics. Print.

Pruchnic, Jeff. "Burke in/on Public and Private: Rhetoric, Propaganda, and the 'Ends(s)' of Humanism." *Burke in the Archives: Using the Past to Transform the Future of Burkean Studies*, edited by Dana Anderson and Jessica Enoch. Columbia: University of South Carolina Press, 2013, 120–42. Studies in Rhetoric/Communication. Print.

————. "Rhetoric, Cybernetics, and the Work of the Body in Burke's Body of Work." *Rhetoric Review* 25, no. 3 (2006): 275–96. Print.

————. *Rhetoric and Ethics in the Cybernetic Age: The Transhuman Condition*. New York: Routledge, 2014. Routledge Studies in Rhetoric and Communication. Print.

Sheriff, Stacey. "Resituating Kenneth Burke's 'My Approach to Communism.'" *Rhetorica* 23, no. 3 (2005): 281–95. Print.

Strathausen, Carsten. "A Critique of Neo-Left Ontology." *Postmodern Culture* 16, no. 3 (2006). Web.

Wolfe, Cary. *Animal Rites: American Culture, the Discourse of Species, and Posthumanist Theory*. Chicago: University of Chicago Press, 2003. Print.

————. *What Is Posthumanism?* Minneapolis: University of Minnesota Press, 2010. Posthumanities 8. Print.

3

Revision as Heresy | Posthuman Writing Systems and Kenneth Burke's "Piety"

Chris Mays

In a 1998 article about writing, pedagogy, storytelling, and revision, and in the middle of an in-depth discussion of Mikhail Bakhtin's concept of the polyphonic novel, Nancy Welch comments that texts, as Bakhtin conceives of them, can "[become] . . . willful, active speaking [subjects] in [their] own right" ("Sideshadowing" 381). A few years later, writing about the lives and "wants" of pictures, W. J. T. Mitchell remarks that while "art historians may 'know' that the pictures they study are only material objects that have been marked with colors and shapes . . . they frequently talk and act as if pictures had feeling, will, consciousness, agency, and desire" (31).

What is interesting about these discussions is that each advances, in an almost casual way, the quite significant premise that texts, visual or written, can exert something resembling a will of their own. While the idea may appear a bit tongue-in-cheek, there is a history of arguments in composition and writing studies scholarship that features this same point: that texts, on their own, exert agency. One quintessential example could be found three decades ago in Peter Elbow's argument that a text in the process of revision may settle on "a pattern or configuration" that, he writes, "*it* was trying to get to" (25; emphasis added). The implication of Elbow's premise, that a text in itself "tries to get" somewhere, is worth taking seriously. This chapter aims to do just that, to consider the possibility that texts having agency is not only reasonable, but also that it can yield useful insights about the behavior of those texts and of texts in general. Moreover, this chapter asserts that exploring this premise can tell us a great deal about our relations with complex systems—texts included—that we have a hand in creating.

By taking seriously the notion that texts themselves can have agency, this chapter complicates commonplace notions of writing and, in particular, of *revision*.

While commonplaces of revision link it to writing, and to rewriting, explicating the concept in terms of complex systems theory reveals that there is more to revision than the dutiful and linear reworkings of a creator on her creation, ever striving toward a singular perfection devoid of "mistakes." Complex systems theory posits revision as transdisciplinary, challenging our understanding of creation more broadly and highlighting the relevance of revision and complexity in a posthuman context that transgresses pedagogical, disciplinary, and epistemic boundaries. Specifically, this chapter proceeds from a posthumanist premise that texts (along with writing in general) are complex systems, which attributes agency to texts and reveals the significant yet invisible dynamics of what could be called their "systemic" behavior. One revelation of posthuman/systems thinking is the expansion of how we think about agentic relations in the world—a move that has cut across various disciplines. Here, this chapter argues that revision is another concept ripe for expansion. By arguing that the creation and revision of complex texts are governed by the nonlinear workings of complex systems, this chapter upends traditional notions of these concepts and instead highlights the multiplicitous and dynamic nature of creation as well as the nature of complexity as never still and never completely under one's control. Insights gained from thinking of revision in terms of multiplicity and instability are relevant not only to writing studies but also to broader transdisciplinary posthumanist discourses, which are similarly beset by multiplicity and instability.

Complication as a Posthuman Methodology

An important point of departure in this chapter is the use of Kenneth Burke's work to add another dimension to posthumanist inquiry. While Burke is often considered a humanist, this chapter argues that his work is not only compatible with posthumanist inquiry, but is itself marked by posthumanist valences. Moreover, Burke's work usefully (and uniquely) complicates posthumanism. In this case, thinking through Burke's concept of "piety" yields an understanding of revision that reveals its expansiveness, versatility, and complexity.

In considering Burkean and posthumanist epistemological traditions in tandem, this chapter's approach takes inspiration from a concept Gregory Bateson calls a "difference that makes a difference" (212). This notion gets at the heart of how combining two somewhat divergent perspectives can actually enhance our understanding of a concept or situation. Bateson—cyberneticist, complex systems theorist, and nascent posthumanist—considers in his work a remarkably similar question to one dealt with here: "What bonus or increment of knowing follows from *combining* information from two or more sources?" (63). Bateson's focus to some extent concerns how we might more productively view inductive evidence as contributing beyond its apparent scope, as with the way in which observations from two local sources can combine to shed light on larger complex questions that probe "how the universe is integrated" (64). The general premise of Bateson's method, though, has significant implications beyond straightforward local data-gathering—namely, the method can apply when combining two epistemological perspectives (e.g., Burkean thought and complex systems theory).

The central point of Bateson's method is that the *difference* between any two perspectives should itself be considered information, and that this information is a degree—as he puts it, a "dimension"—more useful (65). This is because, as Bateson describes, this dual-perspective and higher-order information (which he calls "news of difference") provides a unique depth that a single perspective may lack (64). Thinking in terms of the "difference that makes a difference" that is achieved by contrasting two perspectives enhances our understanding; without this "news," our knowledge is flat.

A methodological approach that embraces Bateson's "difference that makes a difference" sits at the intersection of both Burkean and posthuman emphases on *complication*. Within posthumanist discourses—especially complexity theory and complex systems theory—complication emphasizes multiplicity and articulates center-less networks as the paradigm for human and nonhuman activities and structures.[1] But complication as a key term in posthumanist methodology is also usefully understood in the sense of a verb: posthumanism complicates our understandings of processes heretofore thought to be straightforward. Julie Jung sums this up: "complexity science responds to the questions, 'How do things happen?' and 'How do my students learn?' with, 'It's complicated'" ("Systems"). Posthumanism, and the exploration of complexity that is a crucial part of it, forces a reconsideration of what we often take for granted, and the new answers are never simple.

Observing the difference that makes a difference by thinking through two epistemological positions gives us, Bateson argues, a more "complex synthesis" (65). Describing this approach in terms of vision, Bateson writes that the additional dimension of perception "improve[s] resolution at edges and contrasts," gives us a "better ab[ility] to read when the print is small or the illumination poor," and "create[s] . . . information about depth" (65). "From this new sort of information," he writes, "the seer adds an extra *dimension* to seeing" (65).

Important to this work with revision, Burke's work read in tandem with posthumanism gives us this extra dimension, and moreover, many of Burke's concepts contain a depth and multiplicity of their own that are revealed when they are read across other perspectives. His notion of "piety," for example, will be shown to *complicate* a complex systems assessment of revision. On the surface, piety appears to have religious or (at least) spiritual overtones, a reading that might seem incompatible with complex systems theory, which tends not to be discussed in these terms.[2] To read piety without its religious overtones in order to make it more amenable to systems theory, though, can elide key ramifications of Burke's use of it. As will be elaborated later in this chapter, Burke's piety cannot be captured by a simple religious/nonreligious reduction. However, if we do not try to reconcile piety strictly with secular systems theory terms—if we read these discourses instead in terms of their "difference[s]" that make "difference[s]"—we can more fully account for the nuances of piety and at the same time provoke new understandings of systems theory and, significantly, of revision. Specifically, such a multiplicitious reading opens up a *both-and* understanding of piety that allows its more religious or "devotional" aspects to coexist with the secular. In this way, piety becomes an indispensable complement to our understanding of revision by casting revision simultaneously as a deeply personal process that inspires intense feelings of ownership as well as an impersonal function of a complex system neither owned nor created by any one person or agency.

Complicating Revision

To return to an earlier premise here: the complicating force of posthumanism can shed new light on a concept familiar to most rhetoric and composition scholars: revision. A heavily theorized area of study in these fields, revision is considered a crucial component of a wide range of writing pedagogies (McComiskey 49–53), and many writing scholars have extolled the transformative complexity of revision in its potential for creating alternative ways of knowing and acting in the world (Jung, *Revisionary* 38; Welch *Getting*). As William Germano et al. write, revision "isn't merely a process applied to writing, it's writing itself."

Whether an integral part of writing or "writing itself," revision *seems* a simple concept—changing writing that already exists in order to improve it. Of course, it's more complicated than that. Revision is part of the complex process of creation, one that extends beyond writing and thus beyond traditional disciplinary borders. In a broad sense, revision is a key part of our interactions with the complex systems that inhabit and define our world.

However, to better understand this complexity of revision, we can *start* by rethinking its function in writing. Such a rethinking begins by understanding writing itself as a complex system. This is not a new premise: the specifics of writing as a system have been explored thoroughly in disciplinary scholarship (see Dobrin; Mays; Yood). Here, though, by considering the implications of a systems view of revision, we will take this exploration a step further, complicating extant understandings of writing, revision, creation, and even systems themselves.

Put in systems terms, revision means a change in the (writing) system. As complexity theory tells us, in any complex system there is a nuanced relationship between stability and change—namely, systems tend toward stability. In this sense, systems "want" to stay stable. Systems theorists repeatedly assert this premise: Stuart Kauffman writes extensively of the fundamental drive of systems toward order (he calls this principle "order for free" [71]); Humberto R. Maturana and Francisco J. Varela describe a system's crucial feature as a maintenance of order via "continuously generat[ing] and specif[ying] its own organization" (79); and Jung explains that "[system] boundaries assert agency by maintaining system stability in contexts of ongoing change" ("Systems"). In each of these explanations of systems, it is clear that the drive toward order is a nontrivial component of the systems' existence. A system *depends* on its stability. This is perhaps easiest to comprehend by thinking of biological systems, in which a breakdown of order and the corresponding loss of stability means, simply, death. Such a death may not be as literal (in a traditional sense) for other types of complex systems; however, as a natural consequence of systems' function, they nevertheless tend to avoid such destabilization.

Once we consider writing as a complex system, we can presume a similar tendency toward stability in texts. Like other systems, texts "want" to stay stable. Importantly, this premise exceeds the aforementioned scholarly assertion that the agency of texts is distinct from the agency of a writer. When writing theory intersects with systems theory, we can see that not only do texts exert their own agency but this agency also manifests in part as a drive toward stability.

Such a drive can become apparent in the writing classroom, a frequent site for observing the difficulties of revision. Welch discusses these difficulties of revision in terms of a resistance to the "possible futures" of a text ("Sideshadowing" 383). Welch's discussion of "sideshadowing" foregrounds the difficulty entailed by this "surplus [of] possibilities" for a given text (378). As teachers, our comments on student writing often suggest one possible future for a text. As Welch argues, and as systems theory further explains, such a narrowing is often strongly resisted—often to a point that seems unreasonable.

Revision may seem to broaden the possibilities of a text, and in a sense, the idea of revision *is* an opening up of possibilities: it embodies the potential to take up one of the many possible directions created by the text. But this notion obscures the point that writing is *already* revision; any act of writing narrows an excess of possibilities, as the very act of creating a text is itself a reduction of a text's surplus of possible futures. The text-as-system has in its prior development already been reduced countless times with every decision made at an infinite number of steps along the way in writing it. Thus, a teacher's suggestion to revise—which, as Welch notes, suggests only one possible future—is in fact a suggestion of a trajectory and development that destabilizes the current configuration of the system.

Revision is not resisted because a text *cannot* change. Systems theory tells us that a system *is always changing*, constantly reorganizing as a way to maintain stability in the face of a changing environment. But while a text always evolves, it does so within the parameters of its previous system development, and so to attempt to force a change is to attempt to prompt a reconfiguration of the system. Of course, what writing teachers may call "cosmetic" changes—fixing comma splices and subject-verb agreement, condensing wordy constructions— often maintain the integrity of the old system and so do not constitute the type of revision typically resisted (in fact, these cosmetic changes may evolve as defense mechanisms that keep the basic integrity of the text intact while staving off attempts to force more major changes).

This articulation of texts as systems complicates to some extent the agency of texts: is it the text-as-system that has the agency? Or is it the author? As systems theory tells us, a text has a cohesion and vitality of its own and can certainly evolve on its own, changing signification for different audiences or mutating as it interacts with other authors, other texts, and other material environments. Indeed, this is what many theorists of textual and rhetorical circulation argue.

Rebecca Dingo, for example, discusses "malleable" texts that change as they move (146), and Laurie Gries describes rhetoric "unleashed," moving and evolving "across genres, media, and forms" in "nonlinear, inconsistent, and often unpredictable ways" (7). Systems theory also tells us, though—along with writing studies, rhetoric theory, new materialist theory, and posthumanist theory—that some form of relational or shared agency is a more appropriate model.

Changes in a text, in a sense, occur naturally once that text is "in the wild" in rhetorical circulation. However, prior to this circulation a text often exists bound up in an agentic relation with the author. This system configuration is "created" by both the author and the text itself, and is itself stable: in fact, what makes a text meaningful *is* the stable constitutive relation of text and (human) agent. Notably, this stable relation also shares agency with elements in the environment that are neither author nor text. This is a key move when thinking of complex systems: the collective functioning of what Jane Bennett calls an "agency of assemblages" or "confederate agency" reveals that neither texts nor authors are ever sole agents of creation. Rather, agency is constituted in concert with the other agents with which (and with whom) the text is in relation.

For this discussion, more important than identifying who or what has how much agency is identifying how a shared agency in a system functions as a binding force, one that has the potential to lock in a particular system configuration and constitutes the force of a resistance to revision. As mentioned, constituting a system in a particular way is done via the agency of several participants; crucially, for these participants, in that moment, the system is stable. And it wants to stay that way.

So, for those who are participating in the system of shared created meaning of a text, any significant change is a destabilization of the system. Such change actually forces the creation of a *new* system configuration, and *this* is what is resisted. Systems theorist Niklas Luhmann explains this in his assertion that our experience of stable knowledge is produced by closing off divergent definitions. The creation of "meaning," he writes, reduces the "endless horizon of possibilities" to specific "points of consensus" (64–66). Luhmann does argue that this "closure" creates the possibility of new meaning in the future or, in other words, the possibility of system evolution. But, in that moment of closure, meaning is stabilized by closing off alternative possibilities. Asking for revision reopens those possibilities, and thus asking for revision is asking for a stable meaning—a stable system—to become destabilized.

Burkean Complications

This is a point of intervention where Burkean ideas can intertwine and productively complicate systems theory, adding a new "dimension" to our perspective on these issues. Burke discusses in *Permanence and Change* what he calls an "orientation," a concept that (in a striking parallel to systems theory) he describes as "largely a self-perpetuating system, in which each part tends to corroborate the other parts" (169). This type of orientation defines how a person sees the world and bears a distinct resemblance to what Luhmann calls an "ordering perspective": a perspective from which stable "meaning" is formed (136).

Burke's idea of orientation is complicated (of course); he doesn't always use the term "orientation," and throughout his corpus he refers to similar ideas using different labels. In his retrospective afterword for *Permanence and Change*, written four decades after the first edition of the text, he mentions that his choice of "orientation" shifted as his work evolved, and that over the years he was continually "shopping around for terms connoting the suggestiveness of 'models' or 'perspectives'" (313). He explains that in *Attitudes Toward History*, for example, he "use[d] the term 'frames' a lot, often 'frames' of acceptance" (304). Other choices included Thomas H. Kuhn's "paradigm" (which "wasn't on the market" when *Permanence and Change* was written) (313), *Weltanschauung* ("attitudes toward life"), and *Zeitgeist* ("as per 'climate of opinion'"), and he even mentions the term "design" as containing elements of this idea (304).

Despite the shifting of the term, the ideas about orientation that Burke develops in *Permanence and Change* are particularly useful when looking for those previously mentioned posthuman valences of Burke's notions. "Valences" imply capacities for reactivity among elements. Here, it is ideas that are reactive: Burke's ideas about orientation can be made to react with complexity theory and with revision, and these reactions give us that very posthuman "difference that makes a difference" as well as a newly complicated way of looking at writing.

One of the notable features of orientations is "piety." Orientations *produce* piety. As Burke explains it, piety is "a desire to round things out, to fit experiences together into a unified whole" (74). Piety is also, he writes, a "confiden[ce]" in "knowledge" (78) as well as a "system-builder" (74). All this adds up to the notion that the "piety" produced by orientations causes these perspectives—these "ordering perspectives," in Luhmann's terms—to crystallize once they become established. Furthermore, orientations tend to "corroborate" their component "parts," and this corroboration is realized as a *relational strengthening*—

the strength of one part contributes to the strength of the others in its relation with them. Thinking along the lines of relations, we can see that *interaction* is key to such crystallization. What serves to strengthen a particular orientation is the interrelated aggregate of decisions made within our orientations or, put another way, the interaction of our "bundle of judgments as to how things were, how they are, and how they may be" (Luhmann 14).

In a vivid illustration of this idea of interrelation and interaction as key to the crystallization of an orientation, Burke writes, "Certain of one's choices become creative in themselves; they drive one into ruts, and these ruts in turn reënforce one's piety. Once one has jumped over a cliff, for instance, he can let events take care of themselves, confident in the knowledge that he will continue to maintain and intensify his character as one-who-has-jumped-over-a-cliff" (78). Each choice one makes leads to an orientation—or a "character"—and each subsequent choice made is influenced by that established orientation, by that initial choice. Subsequent choices are influenced by (and interactive with) those previous choices as well as that previous orientation. This continued interaction further strengthens the orientation and further influences future choices, and so on. The interactions here lead to "ruts," and these ruts give rise to piety.

This articulation of orientation illuminates our understanding of the way that *writing* creates a crystallized perspective. In writing, one may not have gone so far as to have "jumped over a cliff." However, the choices made in writing do commit one to an orientation, and this orientation to a significant extent ends up "tak[ing] care of [itself]." The choices made in order to write, that is, are commitments to a particular "meaning" or "orientation," and these commitments tend to "drive one into ruts" and so tend to "reënforce one's piety."

As Debra Hawhee writes, Burke makes a concerted effort to "crack open piety and disentangle the word from its strictly religious associations whereby piety often comes with prepackaged notions of 'good' and 'evil'" (69). She argues that Burke's usage can be read, in fact, as a "direct counterresponse" to the type of "moralizing" wherein people are judged via simplistic categories of good and evil (69). Burke may well have intended to dereligify the basic sense of morality implied by the term. However, in the context of the argument here, while the notions of "good" and "evil" may be less immediately useful, what *can* be productively used are the ideas of devotion and attachment that may indeed be associated with more religious connotations of piety. Specifically, piety in a devotional sense suggests that the attachments one has to a perspective, orientation, or system defy what outside observers may consider "rational." This is key: systems attachments in this sense can be thought of as almost doctrinal or *faith*-based—even, perhaps, dogmatic. And thus, scholars including Ann George and Jack Selzer support a "quasi-religious" reading of Burke's use of piety, arguing that it is meant to suggest people's "deep psychological or emotional investments" (103). The point here is not to ascertain what Burke's religious intentions were with respect to piety. Rather, the point is to show how retaining the religious aspects of piety when applying it to revision highlights the dogmatic and, from a certain point of view, nonrational resistance to changes in a text. Put simply, thinking of piety in this way when theorizing revision radically recontextualizes resistance—even when the need for revision seems clear.

System Revisions

A revision suggestion may seem obvious to a teacher of writing. Suggestions for the student, such as "this is unclear," or perhaps "your points here are completely indecipherable: please rewrite this section," might in some cases entail revisions that will require a good deal of effort from that student. But for the person giving the suggestion, that request seems straightforward enough. Within the logic of the writing system, however (and thus for the writer her- or himself), the text may already be perfectly clear, and, moreover, the revision suggestion may seem a threat to the coherence that already exists, from the writer's point of view, in the text. When the changes requested are bigger, more substantive, the threat—and thus the resistance—is that much greater.

As mentioned, thinking in terms of piety can suggest irrationality, such as with an author's unreasonable devotion to a version of a text that clearly can be improved. How is it that they don't see the "problems" with the text? Even in the case of revisions undertaken by authors themselves, key aspects of the text are often sacrosanct, with any suggested changes to these sections necessarily coming from outside readers. From a systems point of view, however, this resistance is a completely rational impulse—a rationality, that is, that operates within the boundaries delineated by the system itself. The system's own internal "logic" dictates that the system structure remain the same. To someone outside the system—to the writing teacher, perhaps—the revision is easy, and it is obvious. But to one caught up in the system, revision threatens destabilization, the potential "death" of the text.

Welch writes that as writing teachers, "we assume that our responses . . . should foreshadow a particular revision, one toward which a draft currently points or needs to be redirected" ("Sideshadowing" 378–79). We see the text as we feel it *should* be: "we respond with the aim of increasing the coincidence between the draft-as-it-is and the essay-it-could-be," and these responses "[seek] to direct the writer toward a particular future for a text" (379). Welch points out that this teacherly move is problematic, though, because it shuts down the vibrancy of the text. Regardless, a systems point of view reminds us of another problem with teacher suggestions: that taking these suggestions will unavoidably destabilize the current textual configuration in which the student is invested and entangled. In both cases, engaging with revision practices, as teachers, as students, or as writers is more complicated than it might seem.

Against all these roadblocks, Luhmann explains that systems always *do* change, and combined with Welch's insights this reminds us that texts as systems are vibrant and multiple. Luhmann (paralleling Welch from a different perspective) also explains that it is this very "excess" that creates this vibrancy and that drives stable meanings to change and so allows revisions to occur. Luhmann's description of meaning, however, is that which "drift[s]" into new forms as a system reorganizes in response to its changing surroundings (514n17). This description tells us two things: One, that a writing teacher or any other external agent may create the change in the surroundings—the exigency—that gets a text/system to reorganize. This is a more hopeful point, and will be discussed below. Two, in a less hopeful vein, this point about system reorganization tells us that systems tend to persist, and that they do not change (significantly) from the inside. The movement of "drift" does not entail easy pivots and quick changes in direction: not only will any threat to the system be resisted by anyone substantively entangled within the system (including the "author"), but the inertia of the text as a stable system will also provide its own substantial resistance. Instead of substantive change, there will be small compensatory changes in the system in response to suggestions for revision, and these changes will primarily serve to keep intact the system's original formulation.

Writing, Systems, and Change

To recap: Texts as systems tend to persist. Writers are bound up with texts in such a way that limits their ability to perceive other ways of knowing and other ways of writing the text (i.e., revisions). If, following Burke, stable systems exist in/as ruts, then we can say that the participant in a system is in a rut so deep that she cannot see over the tops of its walls. Luhmann describes this phenomenon as "binding," which he writes "fixes, through the structure of an emergent system," the meaning created by that system (221). Such bindings come about by "selections that eliminate . . . other possibilities" (223). In other words, systems "acquire a tendency to reinforce themselves" by seeming natural (223). Systems bound to a particular meaning make it seem like there is no other way for them to be.

N. Katherine Hayles writes that "among systems theorists, Luhmann is remarkable in seeing that every system has an outside that cannot be grasped from inside the system" (160). Luhmann's insights thus intertwine well with Burke's "piety," and both combine to illustrate that for those caught up in a system, directives to revise it seem impossible, irrational (even, perhaps, heretical). Just as for those outside that system, the choice by those in the system *not* to revise may seem similarly irrational.

The dilemma here would paint revision as a nearly hopeless possibility, as an act against the natural tendency of systems and thus against the natural tendency of writing itself to bind to a particular meaning and configuration. To be sure, such an acknowledgment is found in a great deal of scholarship on revision. The "reality" is, as Jung writes, "that people do not always want to hear what we have to say" (*Revisionary* 11). A simple observation of an online argument would seem to confirm this point beyond a doubt. In an even more ostensibly dire sentiment, Welch describes that students view revision not as a "liberating opportunity" but rather as something to be "resisted as *death-work*" (*Getting* 36). Of course, from a systems point of view, revision *is* a type of "death-work"—substantive structural change is the death of the system.

There is, though, a consistently documented record of students' actually *engaging* in revision, and any writer can tell you that revision is not only possible but necessary (dissenters on this point may exist but may also be conveniently forgetting their own revision practices). So, in this sense, it must be the case that revision—and so the destabilization and even the "death" of a system—*is* possible.

Here again, Burke provides the basis for a potential route to this type of hopeful possibility. In *Permanence and Change*, Burke's intent is to ask questions such as why people resist change, whether perspectival or social. And he spends a great deal of the book focusing on the question of how, given piety, we might alter another's orientation.

Burke writes that while an "orientation is largely a self-perpetuating system
... for all [its] self-perpetuating qualities ... it contains the germs of its dissolution" (169). Blending complexity theory and Burke's overarching points here, we
could say that any system configuration leaves elements out that eventually need
to be dealt with via a system "reorientation" and thus via a "[shift] of perspective"
(169). The general idea here—that any system leaves elements out that eventually need to be reckoned with—is remarkably consistent with the aforementioned principle that *excess* is a crucial factor in system evolution. While
Luhmann argues that excess drives the "drift" of a system into new forms, we
might think of Burke's description of "secular conversions" as adding another
layer to this type of "drift."

Burke writes that psychoanalysis, for instance, can be thought of as one of
these "technique[s] of non-religious conversion" (125). He writes, "It effects its
cures by providing a new perspective that dissolves the system of pieties lying at
the roots of the patient's sorrows or bewilderments. It is an *impious* rationalization, offering a fresh terminology of motives to replace the patient's painful terminology of motives.... By selecting a vocabulary which specifically violates the
dictates of style and taboo, it changes the entire nature of his problem, rephrasing it in a form for which there is a solution" (125). What changes the "entire
nature of [the] problem" in terms of a system is precisely the introduction of
elements previously left out. Burke calls this "Perspective by Incongruity." And
he also calls it "Exorcism by Misnomer": we "[cast] out demons by a vocabulary
of conversion, by an incongruous naming, by calling them the very thing in all
the world they are not" (133). In other words, we could say that this casting out
entails an introduction of what is *wrong*, ostensibly, to a perspective, and so by
introducing this incongruity we destabilize it. From yet another point of view,
we could say this whole process is akin to Welch's argument that texts—we
could call them, even, perspectives—contain a surplus of possibilities that must
be acknowledged, and that this acknowledgment of other possibilities can spur
our revisions. All of this—the mixing of Burke and posthumanism, of the secular and the religious, of talk of the revision of texts and of the exorcism of
pieties—points to the generative difference between the terminologies used and
to the intertwined mechanics of the function of systems and of texts.

What is common to all of these insights about system reorganization (and
thus revision) is the notion that change—or conversion—does not occur via
any direct mechanism. Causality does not proceed in any smooth or straight
line, as we cannot simply will our perspectives to change, nor can we demand a

revision and expect to receive exactly what we asked for. The agency, as has been repeatedly asserted here and in various ways throughout (and beyond) the post-human theoretical edifice, does not inhere in any one element. In fact, it may not even be discursive elements that bring about such change: Burke writes, at one point in *Permanence and Change*, that "any important change in the *material* conditions" may result in "old systems of piety" being "throw[n] into disorder" (270n2; emphasis added). Rather, the system responds to myriad changes and elements on its outside that all arise in various direct *and* deferred ways as a consequence of the system's own existence. This is to say, again: Systems aren't "willed" into new configurations. They "drift" into them.

As Burke reminds us, though, there are ways to create destabilization, to initiate the drifting that leads into new orientations. And Hayles writes that while change in a system configuration is not an "inevitability," it is a possibility, as any system is itself an "exhilarating and chaotic space of constructions that are contingent on time and place, dependent on specific women and men making situated decisions, partly building on what has gone before and partly reaching out toward the new" (160–61). Change, reorientation, and revision, then, are always possible but are fundamentally unpredictable, dependent on a vertiginous host of individual decisions and actions at moments ostensibly far removed from the immediate and observable situatedness of the system.

Such changes do happen, though. And they *can* be markedly affected by our actions. The key to better understanding how this happens is to recognize what are often invisible effects of our actions and to negotiate and plan our intentional efforts to change a system and initiate revision by observing the ways a change *in the conditions* in which the system exists can spark a corresponding change *in the system*. There is no direct line from intention to effect (or from intervention to conversion), but it is possible to effect a significant change within a system that is a result of an aggregate of smaller actions outside of it. Such a process illustrates a principle of systems and complexity called emergence. While the emergence of change is ultimately unpredictable, it is inevitable that changes on the outside of a system create the conditions for internal change. We may never be able to pin down the one action that "caused" a specific change (and, in fact, there is never a single cause), but we can certainly recognize the conditions out of which change emerges and act in ways that may move the situation toward those conditions.

In short, writers can revise and be prompted to revise, but neither they nor we are in full control of those revisions. As Welch argues, we should not view writers as "needing just a strategy or two for making [their] intentions apparent on the page" ("Sideshadowing" 375). Instead, texts—as systems—drift into revision in concert with the writer and in concert with the other elements interacting with and in the system. Correspondingly, this means that those who advocate specific revisions are neither in full control nor are fully aware of the total effects of their efforts. We can strive to advocate revision, but we can never guarantee precisely what that revision will be. This point should force us to recognize the ways our intentions may result in revisions that would be unthought and even impossible prior to our own efforts to initiate revision—that is, prior to our interactions with the system. In this sense, *all interactions* with a system *are interventions* in that system. This means that change can happen, and we can cause it. But we can never fully intend or predict it.

Revision and Complexity Beyond Writing

There is a myth in quiltmaking that, traditionally, the very best practitioners would leave an error in each of their quilts that was almost undetectable. If you've ever seen an intricate quilt, this is not difficult to believe. The patterns are dizzyingly complex, and so one misplaced block, a slightly turned shape, or a subtle color shift goes easily unnoticed. The practice is often referred to as the inclusion of a "humility block." As the reasoning goes, to demonstrate imperfection in quiltmaking is to demonstrate one's remove from God and, thus, humility. Versions of the humility myth can be found in a variety of cultures from a variety of historical periods. In Ovid's *Metamorphosis*, for example, there is the story of Arachne, whose weaving was so perfect, and she so proud of that fact, that Athena was provoked into challenging her to a weave-off. Athena lost and then (resenting Arachne's lack of humility, it would seem) proceeded to turn Arachne into a spider, a form in which Arachne could continue her "perfect" weaving for the rest of eternity.

The commonality of this myth suggests, for one thing, the commonality of imperfection, and the value of accepting this. Deeming a desire for perfection to be the result of hubris makes our own inevitable errors a bit more tolerable. In other words, errors are ubiquitous, and we should be okay with that—we shouldn't think so highly of our own work as to imagine it above that fact.

But this interpretation of the myth leaves out an important point: that expert quilters scoff at the idea that they can be perfect in the first place and would therefore need something like a "humility block" to offset supposed perfection. Quilt historian Bobbie Aug writes that Amish quilters she asked about that humility block story "were aghast" ("Humility"). To them "an intentional error is saying just the opposite—that their work is perfect and that they would have to be purposeful in order to make mistakes" ("Humility"). This point highlights the notion that the very *idea* of perfection is a folly. Even for these experts, perfection was never a possibility.

If perfection itself is the real myth, then the very notion of "mistakes" is a red herring—the real lesson in humility is in learning that imperfection is the default state. This lesson also foregrounds an important point about complexity, one that transcends the narrower discussion of writing that has dominated this chapter: in any complex system, there are no true "mistakes." Rather, the system simply evolves. Our deeming things "mistakes" *to be revised* is in fact a product of our seeing complexity from another perspective. Complex systems theory reveals that complexity is never still and never "perfect." In fact, to assume there is such a thing as a perfect complex system is to miss the entire point of complexity. If a text is a system, then there can never be a way to pin down or initiate the changes needed to "perfect" it.

These points about quiltmaking, perfection, and complexity also illustrate that revision is not only about writing; rather, revision is about creation. As Manuel DeLanda writes, complexity theory is remarkable in its revelation of "behavioral isomorphism" across diverse complex systems. While no two complex systems are exactly alike, systems' general organizational characteristics are found across diverse physical systems, as well as less strictly "physical" systems, in "rhythmic patterns that have nothing to do with the movement of matter in space" (12–15). Ilya Prigogine and Isabelle Stengers go even further, arguing that "human creativity and innovation can be understood as the amplification of laws of nature already present in physics or chemistry" (Prigogine 71). Notwithstanding one's belief in the "laws of nature," in short, it is likely that our creation (and revision) of anything complex is subject to the mechanisms that govern complexity.

~~Perfect~~ Imperfect Complexity

Revision isn't about mistakes; it is about remaking. There is always another, (potentially) better configuration, always another perspective to be adopted. It is this remaking that can seem so frustrating, and can be so resisted. As Richard

McKeon writes, our "new insight[s]" continually require us "to modify the inter-pretation of facts previously known and to necessitate the adjustment or aban-donment of theories previously held" (203–4). This is, as one would expect, not easy. Revision involves adopting a perspective that many times seems wrong—that is, one's view of a system is one's own, and it is difficult to accept on faith that the way you see something is not the only way to see it.

This idea of revision comes largely from a complexity perspective, and a post-human perspective. But the notion that we need to accept on faith the validity of other views of a system is also directly—and uniquely—relevant to a Burkean perspective. Burke's piety may not be a thoroughly religious piety, but it neverthe-less suggests that our attachment to the "ruts" in which we dwell is a form of devotion, and our potential transcendence of these ruts, a conversion. Consider-ing this devotion in tandem with the points made by Luhmann and Hayles—that we cannot directly "see" what is outside the system in which we are entangled—creates a triangulated view of what is our involuntary participation in systems. Considered together, Burke's piety and the logic of complex systems create Bateson's "difference that makes a difference." Together, they allow us to see the situation in greater depth and with an added dimension of clarity. This dimension helps us productively complicate commonly held assumptions about the process and the difficulty of revision. And this complication recasts, within the act of revision, the role of stability, change, agency, and intention—notions that go beyond writing and exist in a distinctly transdisciplinary space.

As an answer, "it's complicated" has a distinct Burkean resonance; Burke's famous refrain, "It's more complicated than that," is the obvious echo. More important to this chapter, though, is that in asserting complication as a key term, Burke opens up his own ideas to alternative perspectives. If we consider Burke's work as its own ordering perspective—as itself a complex system—then we can consider the way that this system may evolve in response to changes in its environment, or become something different when taken up and provoked by a reengagement with a more current—and incongruous—perspective. Post-humanism, which may have been left out of Burke's original formulation, now becomes the excess that provides the impetus for a change, a revision.

Notes

1. Complexity and complex systems theory are a key focus in much posthumanist work, and complexity theory—a theory of complication itself—is a fast-rising mode of inquiry in many fields. According to Nobel laureates Ilya Prigogine and Isabelle Stengers, complexity

and systems theory have initiated the "beginning of a new scientific era" (Prigogine 7), in which the "so-called hard sciences" are intertwined with the "softer sciences of life" (Toffler xvii), or as Rosi Braidotti renames them, the "hard" and "subtle" sciences (154). Across disciplines, complexity and the posthuman discourses that engage it have given us new ways of understanding a wide variety of physical, social, and discursive phenomena.

2. This tendency is not an absolute, of course. Some complex systems theorists do draw at times on religiously inflected discourse. Ervin Laszlo, for instance, writes that systems theory fills a "need for a creative extension of the traditional fundaments of the great religions, to complete and complement the rational worldview that is already emerging within the new sciences" (91). Laszlo's primary emphasis, however, is on the "rational" components of the theory, and his terministic choices tend to reflect secular language. This secular emphasis is the norm for many of the discourses on systems and complexity. The larger point here, though, is that the methodology employed in this chapter helps us talk about systems theory *and* Burkean theory using a *new constellation* of terms, out of which can emerge a differential understanding of both bodies of knowledge.

Works Cited

Bateson, Gregory. *Mind and Nature: A Necessary Unity.* 1979. Cresskill: Hampton Press, 2002. Print.

Bennett, Jane. *Vibrant Matter: A Political Ecology of Things.* Durham: Duke University Press, 2010. Print.

Braidotti, Rosi. *The Posthuman.* Cambridge: Polity Press, 2013. Print.

Burke, Kenneth. *Permanence and Change: An Anatomy of Purpose.* 3rd ed. Berkeley: University of California Press, 1984. Print.

DeLanda, Manuel. *Philosophy and Simulation: The Emergence of Synthetic Reason.* New York: Continuum, 2011. Print.

Dingo, Rebecca. *Networking Arguments: Rhetoric, Transnational Feminism, and Public Policy Writing.* Pittsburgh: University of Pittsburgh Press, 2012. Print.

Dobrin, Sidney I. *Postcomposition.* Carbondale: Southern Illinois University Press, 2011. Print.

Elbow, Peter. *Writing Without Teachers.* New York: Oxford University Press, 1973. Print.

George, Ann, and Jack Selzer. *Kenneth Burke in the 1930s.* Columbia: University of South Carolina Press, 2007. Print.

Germano, William, David J. Bartholomae, Cathy L. Birkenstein-Graff, Willis Regier, Susan Gubar, and Jeffrey J. Williams. "Revision as Writing, Writing as Revision." *Modern Language Association* (2016). Web. 15 Jan. 2016.

Gries, Laurie. *Still Life with Rhetoric: A New Materialist Approach for Visual Rhetorics.* Logan: Utah State University Press, 2015. Print.

Hawhee, Debra. *Moving Bodies: Kenneth Burke at the Edges of Language.* Columbia: University of South Carolina Press, 2012. Print. Studies in Rhetoric/Communication.

Hayles, N. Katherine. "Making the Cut: The Interplay of Narrative and System, or What Systems Theory Can't See." *Observing Complexity: Systems Theory and Postmodernity,* edited by William Rasch and Cary Wolfe. Minneapolis: University of Minnesota Press, 2000, 137–62. Print.

"'Humility' Blocks." *Hart Cottage Quilts* (2010). Web. 14 Feb. 2016.

Jung, Julie. *Revisionary Rhetoric, Feminist Pedagogy, and Multigenre Texts.* Carbondale: Southern Illinois University Press, 2005. Print.

————. "Systems Rhetoric: A Dynamic Coupling of Explanation and Description." *enculturation* 17 (2014). Web. 15 Jan. 2016.

Kauffman, Stuart. *At Home in the Universe: The Search for the Laws of Self-Organization and Complexity*. New York: Oxford University Press, 1995. Print.

Laszlo, Ervin. *The Systems View of the World: A Holistic Vision for Our Time*. Cresskill: Hampton Press, 1996. Print.

Luhmann, Niklas. *Social Systems*. Translated by John Bednarz Jr. with Dirk Baecker. Stanford: Stanford University Press, 1995. Print.

Maturana, Humberto R., and Francisco J. Varela. *Autopoiesis and Cognition: The Realization of the Living*. Dordrecht: Reidel, 1980. Print.

Mays, Chris. "Writing Complexity, One Stability at a Time: Teaching Writing as a Complex System." *College Composition and Communication* 68, no. 3 (2017): 559–85. Print.

McComiskey, Bruce. *Teaching Composition as a Social Process*. Logan: Utah State University Press, 2000. Print.

McKeon, Richard. "A Philosopher Meditates on Discovery." *Rhetoric: Essays in Invention and Discovery*, edited by Mark Backman. Woodbridge: Ox Bow Press, 1987, 194–220. Print.

Mitchell, W. J. T. *What Do Pictures Want? The Lives and Loves of Images*. Chicago: University of Chicago Press, 2005. Print.

Ovid. *Metamorphoses*. Translated by Anthony S. Kline. *University of Virginia Library* (2000). Web. 14 Feb. 2016.

Prigogine, Ilya. *The End of Certainty: Time, Chaos, and the New Laws of Nature*. New York: Simon and Schuster, 1996. Print.

Toffler, Alvin. "Foreword: Science and Change." *Order Out of Chaos: Man's New Dialogue with Nature*, edited by Ilya Prigogine and Isabelle Stengers. London: Heinemann, 1984, xi–xxvi. Print.

Welch, Nancy. *Getting Restless: Rethinking Revision in Writing Instruction*. Portsmouth: Reed Elsevier, 1997. Print.

————. "Sideshadowing Teacher Response." *College English* 60, no. 4 (1998): 374–95. Print.

Yood, Jessica. "A History of Pedagogy in Complexity: Reality Checks for Writing Studies." *enculturation* 16 (2013). Web. 20 Jan. 2014.

4

Burke's Counter-Nature | Posthumanism in the Anthropocene

Robert Wess

While posthumanism is widely discussed today, so is the Anthropocene. What tends to pass without commentary is the irony of the coexistence of the two. As posthumanism continues decentering the human being, it appears increasingly likely that the geological epoch in which we live will be officially named after humankind.[1] Indeed, talk of the Anthropocene is becoming the elephant in the room, but it needs to build on posthumanism, not abandon it, just as posthumanism needs to join the Anthropocene conceptually or risk marginalizing itself in the years ahead. The time is ripe for posthumanism to evolve into Anthropocenic posthumanism.

My argument for this new posthumanism consists of four parts. Posthumanism (the first part of this chapter) is reoriented toward Anthropocenic posthumanism (the fourth part) through the intervention of Burke's concept of counter-nature. Counter-nature theorized the Anthropocene *avant la lettre* (the second part). It also prompted Burke's self-revision in the afterwords for the third editions of *Permanence and Change* (1935) and *Attitudes Toward History* (1937), which were completed in 1983 (*Permanence* 336; *Attitudes* 430); in turn, this self-revision enriched the theorizing of the Anthropocene (the third part), providing a framework for reorienting posthumanism.

By theorizing Anthropocenic posthumanism, counter-nature demonstrates that it merits more attention than it has received, even in Burke studies. Counter-nature may well be more important today than when Burke conceived it. Furthermore, it could become much more important in the decades ahead if posthumanists and Burkeans join together to use it to turn theorists toward Anthropocenic posthumanism.

Posthumanism

This first part blends an introduction to posthumanism with an account of its neglect of the Anthropocene, then argues that posthumanism should both engage the Anthropocene and turn to Burke to do so.

One reason for this neglect can be found in history. The prominence of the term "Anthropocene" is relatively recent, proposed as a name for our epoch in 2000 (Crutzen and Stoermer), whereas critiques of humanism have been piling up for half a century or more. Cary Wolfe dates the emergence of the term "posthumanism" in the mid-1990s, but stresses that anticipations of it include the memorable conclusion to *The Order of Things*, first published in 1966, that envisions the erasure of "man," as Michel Foucault phrases it, "like a face drawn in sand at the edge of the sea" (Wolfe, *What* xii; Foucault 387). N. Katherine Hayles alludes to the same passage from Foucault in her history of the emergence of posthumanism (2n5). In *The Posthuman*, Rosi Braidotti offers a more complex history, which is perhaps a more informative history precisely because of its complexity. In her historical narrative, there are not two stages—first humanism, then posthumanism—but three: humanism, antihumanism, posthumanism. In the 1960s and 1970s, an antihumanism emerged (16). Posthumanism, by contrast, is not just an "anti"—a "no" to humanism's "yes"—but is itself a new "yes" to embrace. Antihumanism anticipates, in some ways, the posthumanism that follows, but posthumanism is distinctive. Furthermore, it was not "historically inevitable" (25). A "no" to a "yes" does not guarantee affirmation of a new "yes." From a Burkean standpoint, these two stages—yes versus no, yes versus yes—are distinguishable in historical transformations, with the completion of a transformation marked by a turn to a new "yes."[2] "No" is transitional. The discourse of posthumanism thus emerged and matured before the term "Anthropocene" acquired its current status. Hayles's landmark *How We Became Posthuman* even appeared in 1999, a year before the seminal proposal to use this term to designate our geological epoch.

A deeper reason for this neglect is theoretical. The Anthropocene makes humans central, whereas posthumanists go in the opposite direction, rejecting humanist assumptions that distinguish humans from and elevate them above all other inhabitants of planet Earth. Wolfe illustrates these assumptions with a quotation from Wikipedia too long to reproduce in full here. Suffice it to say that the quotation centers on "rationality": by virtue of their reason, humans can anticipate consequences so that they are responsible for their actions. That makes them autonomous beings, determining rather than determined: "In focusing on the capacity for self-determination, humanism rejects the validity of transcendental justifications, such as a dependence on belief without reason, the supernatural, or texts of allegedly divine origin" (*What* xi). Hayles similarly underlines the humanist assumption that "mind thinking" distinguishes humans, citing the iconic example of Descartes (2–3). Braidotti also identifies humanism with the assumption of a subjectivity consisting of "consciousness, universal rationality, and self-regulating ethical behavior" (15). Additionally, she adds a humanist body in the form of Leonardo da Vinci's Vitruvian Man: an image of two men superimposed on one another, with arms and legs outstretched in different directions, one fitting perfectly within a circle, the other just as perfectly within a square (14). Here, even the human body is informed by rationality in the form of geometric figures. This "iconic image," she suggests, "is the emblem of Humanism as a doctrine that combines the biological, discursive and moral expansion of human capabilities into an idea of teleologically ordained, rational progress" (13).

While Wolfe, Hayles, and Braidotti agree in targeting humanist assumptions, there are nonetheless explicit disagreements among them that reflect fundamental divisions among posthumanists. Together, they constitute a representative sample of posthumanism. On one side of the main divide are posthumanists who focus on relations between humans and new technologies. Hayles's "posthuman view configures human being so that it can be seamlessly articulated with intelligent machines" (3). For Hayles, "mind thinking" is not prior, as in Descartes, but secondary to informational patterns programmable in machines. Demoted, "mind thinking" is "an epiphenomenon . . . an evolutionary upstart trying to claim that it is the whole show when in actuality it is only a minor sideshow" (3).

On the other side of the main divide, Wolfe characterizes his posthumanism explicitly as the "opposite" of Hayles's, contrasting his emphasis on "embodiment" with a "triumphant disembodiment" that he sees in her technological emphasis, even if she resists the "transhumanism" that, by envisioning technology turning humans into superhumans, is really "an *intensification* of humanism" (*What* xv). Wolfe emphasizes "embodiment" to critique the speciesism in the view that "the full transcendence of the 'human' requires the sacrifice of the 'animal' and the animalistic" (*Animal* 6). Wolfe relies heavily on the decentering of the human subject in Derrida's deconstruction. He quotes a long passage from a Derrida interview—promising to return to it "more than once" (*What* 25)—in which Derrida concedes that language can be defined in a way that makes it unique to humans but contends that what makes language possible (i.e., mark, trace, iterability, *différance*) also makes possible "the complexity of 'animal languages,' genetic coding, all forms of marking" (Derrida 116). Derrida thus provides Wolfe a basis for overturning speciesism.

Among posthumanists on the side of "embodiment," there is a notable division. Braidotti explicitly respects Wolfe and deconstruction, but she also has "some impatience with the limitations of its linguistic frame of reference" (30). Her overturning of speciesism is based instead on the vital force of life flowing through human and nonhuman forms, "coded as *zoe*" (60). She rejects extending to animals the "principle of moral and legal equality" because that implicitly privileges "the hegemonic category, the human, toward the others" (79). She affirms, instead, "*zoe*-centered egalitarianism," in which life is no longer "codified as the exclusive property or the unalienable right of one species, the human, over all others" (60).

Braidotti is the exception that proves the rule insofar as she theorizes posthumanism but also introduces the Anthropocene into her book by name: "The fact that our geological era is known as the 'anthropocene' stresses both the technologically mediated power acquired by *anthropos* and its potentially lethal consequences for everyone else" (66). More precisely, she adds later, just a segment of *anthropos* exercises this power when "you consider the difference in carbon print between richer and poorer nations" (88). True enough, but the problem remains of theoretically squaring her posthuman "*zoe*-centered egalitarianism" with her recognition of Anthropocenic inequality by which human power dominates.

While the concept of the Anthropocene breaks with posthumanism insofar as it is a centering rather than a decentering of humans, it does not revitalize humanist assumptions of rational self-determination and progress. The Anthropocene exhibits not humanist progress toward an ideal end but a colossal unintended consequence, as Dipesh Chakrabarty insists (221), not a reason to celebrate rationality but a catastrophic exhibit of the limits of reason. Human actions, Chakrabarty stresses, have irrationally put at risk "conditions (such as the temperature zone in which the planet exists) that work like boundary parameters of human existence" (218). It is arguable that nothing undermines humanist assumptions more than the Anthropocene itself. For this reason, posthumanists should welcome a turn to Anthropocenic posthumanism. But such a turn would require theoretical reorientations in posthumanist projects.

A proposal to posthumanists, especially those unfamiliar with Burke, that they turn to Burke is likely to meet resistance because of Burke's consistent theorizing of language to distinguish humans from the rest of Earth's inhabitants. But Burke's interest in human difference is actually suited to the Anthropocenic difference that undermines the humanist difference. For Burke consistently sees that what makes us different is no reason to make us proud. For example, "We can distinguish man from other animals without necessarily being overhaughty. For what other animals have yellow journalism, corrupt politics, pornography, stock market manipulators, plans for waging thermonuclear, chemical, and bacteriological war? I think we can consider ourselves different in kind from the other animals, without necessarily being overproud of our distinction" ("Terministic" 50). It is plausible that it was precisely because of this view of humans that Burke was particularly ready to see the Anthropocene emerging *avant la lettre*.

Furthermore, while Burke theorizes language to distinguish humans from nonhumans, his theorizing also encompasses levels, *à la* posthumanist "embodiment," in which human and nonhuman are indistinguishable. His theoretical tracing of the origin of language to the negative, for example, includes the "postulat[ion] [of] a prehistorical beginning of language in which a word such as *no* meant something positive like 'Look at his,' or 'Look at that'" ("Dramatistic" 424). This is a beginning that one can envision occurring not only in humans but also among nonhumans capable, for example, of warning one another of danger. Similarly, in *Permanence and Change*, Burke begins famously with his argument that "all living things are critics" because living entails discriminating, such that, for example, fish who learn to discriminate between "bait" and "food" outlast fish who do not (5). Human discriminations, Burke goes on, include linguistic abstractions that capacitate humans to make discriminations on levels nonhumans never attain. But this distinctive human capacity sometimes lowers rather than elevates humankind. "No slight critical ability is required," Burke satirizes, "for one to hate as his deepest enemy a people thousands of miles away" (6). One can find in Burke, then, affinities with some posthumanist themes, but what makes him most valuable to posthumanism is counter-nature, which is a theoretical pathway to Anthropocenic posthumanism.

Counter-Nature

Counter-nature is one sign of Burke's ecological concerns, which first appeared early in his career. His 1937 prediction that we would one day need to pay more attention to ecology than was common at that time was even cited in 1970 as one prediction from the 1930s that "has since come to seem exceedingly perspicacious" (Bowen 198). But this praise made no mention of the book in which the prediction appears (Burke, *Attitudes* 150), so, Burke lamented, the congratulatory "pebble caused nary a ripple" in sales (412).

Counter-nature appears in the first editions of neither *Permanence and Change* nor *Attitudes Toward History*, but it appears at the beginning of Burke's 1983 afterword to *Permanence and Change*, where it is introduced from the standpoint of Burke's late definition of humans: "bodies that learn language" ("Poem" 263). Both afterwords are subtitled "In Retrospective Prospect." Together, they amount to a small book, totaling one hundred pages, far from the perfunctory texts that might have served for new editions. Burke devoted considerable effort to looking back at these books from the standpoint of counter-nature to forge a prospect for looking forward.

This late definition is much shorter than Burke's earlier five-part definition in his essay "Definition of Man."[3] But Burke thought that the two definitions were not "fundamentally different," indicating a preference for the later one mainly because it "led [him] to further observations, and made [his] position easier to present" ("In Haste" 340–41), as illustrated at the beginning of his *Permanence and Change* afterword, in which he derives four categories from "bodies that learn language," with the fourth introducing counter-nature. Two categories present themselves immediately: "bodies" and "language." For Burke, language coexists with the "thinking of the body."[4] Language distinguishes humans from nonhumans, but as we have seen, some dimensions of language are shared by humans and nonhumans. Unlike Derrida, Burke distinguishes humans on the basis of their linguistic prowess, but he does not celebrate human superiority on the basis of this prowess, unlike humanism. Burke's third category consists of magical and mythic dimensions of language, derived from the learning in infancy that connects body and language.[5] The fourth encompasses the "kind of *attention* and *communication* that make possible the gradual accumulation and distribution of instrumental devices (inventions by humans in the role of *homo faber*)" (*Permanence* 295–96). Counter-nature derives directly from the proliferation of technologies and indirectly from language, which makes proliferation possible.

The term "counter-nature" solved for Burke a terminological problem arising from his recognition that the effects of technology were becoming so massive that they were producing conditions of living, in his words, "quite alien to the state of nature to which our prehistoric ancestors successfully adapted," even introducing threats to survival (296). Burke saw the need for a new term to designate these "alien" conditions of living. The "counter" in "counter-nature" seems to name these new conditions in a purely negative way, as "against" nature, echoing "alien." Yet in an essay published a few years before the 1983 afterwords, Burke drew on etymology to find a second meaning, a meaning surprisingly positive. "The term 'Counter-Nature,'" Burke explains, "has the etymological ambivalence of the Latin preposition *contra*, from which the prefix 'counter' is derived. It can mean 'against' both in the sense of 'opposed to' and in the sense of 'in close contact with,' as in the sentence 'To brace himself he leaned against a tree'; and the same root, *contra*, gives the patriot his proud expression, 'my country'" ("Variations" 167). The "close contact with" ingredient in "counter-nature" is suggested later in the same essay when Burke observes, "'Fore-ordination' of some sort is implicit in the fact that the foetus of one animal does not develop into the offspring of another. And if the presently emergent skills of biogenetic engineering develop to the point where transformations of exactly that sort can be proposed . . . the same underlying laws of motion that made such a development impossible without the intervention of human bioengineering would still circumambiently prevail" (170–71). Bioengineering counts on these "laws" continuing to prevail in the very act of intentionally intervening so that their operation produces an outcome different from what would occur without the intervention. As an analogy, imagine that a driverless car is going to New York by following a computer program when someone intervenes to change one command in the program to make the car end up in Chicago. The programmed driving is the law that remains in effect throughout, while the intervention is the small change in the program that comes from outside the process to change the result of the process. The intervention is "counter" but it works by "close contact with."

In the context of counter-nature, Burke adds, our bodies remain conservative insofar as they are "still much like those of our ancestors in the remote past," unlike the environment in which they now live. This can change: Burke theorizes the possibility that "microscopic creatures" could enter the body and in time become "naturalized as an integral part of its economy" (*Permanence* 297). But that takes a long time, so that the body in its conservatism is likely to remain out of step with the counter-nature in which it lives for the foreseeable future.

Burke's conceptualization of counter-nature to theorize massive human-caused change in conditions of living thus anticipates the proposal made by

Paul J. Crutzen and Eugene F. Stoermer in 2000: "Considering these and many other major and still growing impacts of human activities on earth and atmosphere, and at all, including global, scales, it seems to us more than appropriate to emphasize the central role of mankind in geology and ecology by proposing to use the term 'anthropocene' for the current geological epoch" (17). This role prompts Chakrabarty to invent terms to distinguish "biological agents" from "geological agents": all bodies have biological agency, but human bodies acquired additional geological agency when human activities collectively attained "a scale large enough to have an impact on the planet itself" (206–7).

This impact's philosophical significance appears in Bruno Latour's recent "Agency at the Time of the Anthropocene." Latour remarks that his early work tried to explain how scientists construct facts about phenomena, but that now, in the context of the Anthropocene, "a new problem arises: how to understand the active role of human agency not only in the construction of facts, but also in the very existence of the phenomena those facts are trying to document?" (2). Discussing this problem, Latour draws heavily on Michel Serres, who proclaims in *The Nature Contract* that "global history enters nature; global nature enters history: this is something utterly new in philosophy" (4). In philosophy before the Anthropocene, humans were on one side and an objective world without humans was on the other. Now, this division dissolves because, as Latour puts it, "human action is visible everywhere" (5). Looking back at Burke with the benefit of later writers such as Serres and Latour, one can see him using counter-nature to theorize emergent realities of the Anthropocene that would later assume a clearer form.

Burke's Self-Revision

The 1983 afterwords contain materials relevant in varying ways to *Permanence and Change* and *Attitudes Toward History*. Materials relevant to Burke's revision of himself appear in both, beginning in the afterword to *Permanence and Change*, then carrying over to the afterword to *Attitudes Toward History*, which begins with analogues to the newly discovered open-endedness in the revision of *Permanence and Change*. Burke's self-revision authorizes in effect a freedom of interpretation, but a freedom within limits insofar as it is based on something in Burke's concept of perspective by incongruity that was always there, just not seen clearly.[6] This something became more visible in the context of counter-nature. Counter-nature motivated the self-revision, and in turn, the self-revision enriched the theorizing of counter-nature.

The revision stresses the coupling of perspective by incongruity and transvaluation. Among Burke's most often cited concepts, perspective by incongruity can be introduced to anyone new to Burke with his simple example of "decadent athleticism" (*Permanence* 90–91). In a context in which athletics is considered wholesome, "decadent" advances a perspective that is incongruous. This incongruity, in turn, effects a transvaluative movement of athleticism from the category of wholesomeness to that of decadence. In Burke's self-revision, the scope of perspective by incongruity is enlarged and its significance is altered.

The link between counter-nature and this enlarged scope derives from Burke's view that a technology is a perspective and thus may be a perspective by incongruity. The obvious objection to this view is that technology is not a perspective because it applies science, which is objective. Burke counters this objection in the afterword to *Permanence and Change*, where he rejects the "'heavenly' derivation of 'applied' science [i.e., technology] from 'pure' science" (319). Burke's meaning centers in his equation of "heavenly" to "pure"—that is, to the notion that science is "pure" because it is not a perspective but is instead objective, a "view from nowhere," as phrased in Thomas Nagel's famous title. "Heavenly" adds to this meaning the notion that such objectivity is godlike, so that the trustworthiness of what comes from science is indisputable. When technology is viewed as applying "heavenly" science, it partakes of the same supposed objectivity and trustworthiness. Burke's alternative view is that technologies evolve out of ideological perspectives. Astrology is an example. Astrology's origin, Burke observes, is ideological: "the first of humankind's eschatologies" (*Permanence* 319). But in this ideological project, humans produced technologies of observation that played a role later in astronomy: "the astronomy that grew out of it relied greatly on the instrumentation of accumulated recordings" (319). This "instrumentation" originated in an ideological perspective, not a "heavenly" science. But it cannot be reduced to this ideological origin, for insofar as it survives Burke's test of "recalcitrance" (255–61) it acquires a degree of objectivity, not the pure objectivity of the "view from nowhere," but the objectivity of dependability. A technology that works dependably passes the recalcitrance test to achieve the purpose for which it was designed, but this purpose derives from a perspective, not from a godlike transcendence of perspective. By passing the recalcitrance test, technologies of observation developed for astrological purposes could be used later, even if one rejected astrology. Later ideological projects can take up earlier technologies and modify them to make new technologies: "Technology can be neither criticized nor controlled nor corrected without recourse to still more Technology" (*Attitudes* 396).

This last point merits underlining. Despite all his misgivings about technology, Burke sees that only technology can correct technology: "Counter-Nature is here to stay" ("Variations" 182), Burke stresses this elsewhere, adding, "Environmentalism is but an intelligent species of technology's self-criticism" (182).

Burke's perspectival view of technology means that from one perspective a technology may work, dependably passing the recalcitrance test (e.g., automobiles work), even while from another perspective the same technology is a disaster (automobiles pollute). Many technologies that dependably achieve their purposes also produce the unintended consequence of the Anthropocene that, as Chakrabarty suggests, it endangers human beings, the producers of technologies—a variant of the Frankenstein narrative. Burke's perspectival view of the technologies producing counter-nature thus offers a theoretical understanding of how the Anthropocene is occurring.

An illustration of a technology producing a transvaluative perspective by incongruity appears in Burke's example of an audience at a drama. Analogous to the incongruous juxtaposition of athleticism with decadence, Burke incongruously juxtaposes an "audience's sympathetic personal response to the unfolding of a drama" with "the use of mechanical 'sensors' to detect concomitant bodily responses (such as changes in blood pressure, temperature, respiration, heartbeat)" (*Attitudes* 380). This technological perspective, Burke suggests, is a "transcendence sideways . . . represent[ing] various kinds of outcries, but with no more personal feeling than the vibrations in the air that make them audible" (381). Such transcendence sideways is a transvaluative perspective by incongruity that shifts human response to a drama from the category of the "*personalistic*" to that of the technologically "*instrumental*" (379).

The proliferation of technologies giving rise to counter-nature is thus for Burke a proliferation of perspectives by incongruity producing a multitude of transvaluations. As a result, the significance of perspective by incongruity undergoes an alteration. Originally, its significance derived from its role in effecting transitional "de-formation[s]," as suggested by Burke's use of the title "Perspective by Incongruity" for the second of *Permanence and Change*'s three parts, a structure that Burke summarizes as "formation, de-formation, re-formation—a design which, in opting for the theme of group *cooperation*, could end on a metaphorical reference to an ideal state of favorable mutual adjustments among the various sectors of the community as a '*poetry* of action'" (*Permanence* 305). That communism might facilitate such an "ideal state" by establishing stability was part of its appeal to Burke at that time. "Under a stable environment," he explains, "a corresponding stability of moral and esthetic values can arise and permeate the group—and it is this 'superstructure' of values which the artist draws upon in constructing an effective work of art" ("My Approach" 20). In his 1953 "Prologue" to *Permanence and Change*, Burke characterizes it as the type of book that authors in the 1930s "sometimes put together, to keep themselves from falling apart" (*Permanence* xlvii). The book did this for Burke in its three-stage narrative, ending in stabilities that would promote great art.

But by the 1980s, the stabilities that Burke envisioned in the 1930s had yet to appear. Instead, instability reigned in proliferating technologies, resulting in counter-nature. The significance of perspective by incongruity underwent alteration, as it proved to be not transitional but the new normal of counter-nature.

At this point, the philosophical implications of Nietzschean perspectivism, which had inspired the idea of perspective by incongruity in the first place, impressed themselves on Burke more clearly. For the ultimate implication of perspectivism is that there is nothing prior to the principle of perspective itself, so that any particular perspective is at most provisional, here today but possibly displaced by another tomorrow. Transformation from perspective to perspective is universal. Stressing the universalizing of perspective that follows from this priority, Burke saw *Permanence and Change* in a "notably different" way (301).

> But when the second part was given as title a key concept adapted from Nietzsche, more was thereby let free to range than I suspected at the time. For when a mode of "perspectivism" is aimed, as Nietzsche's is, at "the transvaluation of all values," in effect we have introduced a method which *universalizes* the principle of "transformation"—and in that sense my third stage could be but a modified continuation of what got let loose in the second. For "transformation," as a synonym for "transvaluation," is so intrinsically expansive a term that even "formation" is rather like a "being-formed." (308)

Perspective by incongruity thus ceases to be transitional, becoming instead a perspectival open-endedness that cannot be closed off.[7] The section of *Permanence and Change* titled "An Incongruous Assortment of Incongruities" (111–24) was conceived originally as a compilation of strategies of instability preparatory to a new stability, but viewing this section retrospectively, Burke proposes that it is "better characterized as a disjunct clatter of random *beginnings* than as the makings of a simplification that would provide the organizing principle of a 'new order'" (306). Burke goes on, as noted earlier, to identify analogues in *Attitudes Toward History* to this newly discovered open-endedness in *Permanence and Change*. Of these, the concept of bureaucratization of the imaginative is where he comes closest in the 1930s to the revision he presents in the 1980s (*Attitudes* 378).

Theorized by this revised perspective by incongruity, counter-nature is open-ended, consisting of new beginning displacing new beginning without any beginning leading to an ending. Theorized by this enriched model of counter-nature, the Anthropocene cannot be corrected by a "heavenly" science that straightens everything out once and for all in godlike fashion. Instead, open-ended experimentation displaces any "grand narrative" toward an ideal humanist end. Counter-nature, in short, theorizes an Anthropocene that posthumanism can join conceptually.

Looking back and unpacking the philosophical implications of his perspective by congruity, Burke thus revises himself to see "verbalizing bodies whose ancestors imagined the realm of the *Supernatural* now so variously transform its vestiges in response to the ever-expanding realm of technological *Counter-Nature*" (*Permanence* 297). This contrast registers the sense in which Burke sees counter-nature as a new epoch breaking with the epoch of the supernatural. This is not a distinction at the level of geological time-scale; insofar as Burke is not thinking on that level, counter-nature is not equivalent to the Anthropocene. Nonetheless, counter-nature does effectively theorize the Anthropocene, and Burke does see it breaking with millennia of the supernatural, whose "vestiges" he sees surviving even after centuries of humanist secularization, vestiges he has been particularly expert at tracing.[8] Burke seems to see this transformation from super-nature to counter-nature as fundamental in the sense that the more firmly counter-nature entrenches itself, the more difficult it is to go back, so that counter-nature appears unstoppable going forward.

Because of counter-nature, Burke suggests, "manmade Technology begins to look like a kind of 'fulfillment' (call it, as you prefer, 'voluntary' or 'compulsive')," adding that it is "a kind of 'destiny,' a fulfillment of peculiarly human aptitudes. Viewed thus, Technology is an ultimate direction indigenous to Bodies That Learn Language.... The result is a somewhat aimless 'pluralism' of speculations that now proliferate in response to the many diversified methods and perspectives suggested by the advances of Technology itself" (*Permanence* 296–97). Here, Burke implicitly invokes the language of nature, where "compulsive" and "voluntary" are synonymous: humans do what their nature compels them to do, but they do it voluntarily because it is their nature to want to do it. The paradox of this "destiny" is that it presupposes that nature produces in humans something that turns nature on its head, although not completely, as suggested by the earlier discussion of the "close contact with" meaning among the multiple meanings of "counter." Whether counter-nature is viable over the long run is, in effect, an experiment that is underway not in a laboratory but in reality on planet Earth. This "destiny" is open-ended transvaluative perspectives by incongruity rather than humanist rational progress toward an ideal end.

Anthropocenic Posthumanism

In his 1983 afterwords, Burke offers, in place of the ideal end that he envisioned in the 1930s, examples of the two main directions that perspectival transvaluations may take, one tending toward a Nietzschean will to power, the other going in the opposite direction. That more technological transvaluations will occur is predictable; where they will ultimately go is open-ended. The perspectivist reason for Anthropocenic posthumanism thus displaces humanist transcendent reason.

Ironically, because only technology can correct technology, that which brought about the Anthropocene is nonetheless that to which we must turn going forward, albeit with a difference. The Anthropocene is posthuman in the sense that its existence is a critique of the human-centered assumptions that helped to cause it. For the foreseeable future, however, the Anthropocene "is what it is," rather than something that can be simply erased. Other variants of posthumanism, by contrast, can be transvaluations that aim to transform the planetary force that humankind exercises. In other words, they can aim not to erase the Anthropocene but to change its characteristics. These posthumanist transvaluations can be affirmed, as in the example of Braidotti's distinction between antihumanism's "no" and posthumanism's "yes." To reorient these posthumanisms toward Anthropocenic posthumanism, the one thing needed is to direct the transvaluations they affirm toward a positive change in the planetary force that humankind exerts. Such change would be Anthropocenic insofar as humans would cause it, but it would produce an Anthropocene that differs from the present one.

Hayles exemplifies one of Burke's two contrasting directions, while Braidotti and Wolfe exemplify the other, Braidotti doing so better than Wolfe. Consideration of ways to reorient Hayles and Braidotti, however sketchy, can at least suggest the possibility of conceptually reorienting posthumanism toward Anthropocenic posthumanism across the board.

Because Hayles focuses on linkages between humans and computer technology, she belongs to the general line of transvaluations that Burke traces to the linkage between Nietzsche's "will to power" and "the exponential curve of technological 'progress' during the past two centuries" (*Attitudes* 385). As noted earlier, what is sometimes called "transhumanism" to distinguish it from posthumanism takes this linkage to "superman" extremes, but Hayles explicitly rejects that. Near the end of *How We Became Posthuman*, she considers the speculation that linkage of humans with intelligent machines may someday offer the chance "to download yourself into a computer, thereby obtaining through technological mastery the ultimate privilege of immortality" (287). Hayles disowns this aspiration, arguing that such a technological linkage "is not abandoning the autonomous liberal subject but is expanding its prerogatives into the realm of the posthuman. Yet the posthuman need not be recuperated back into liberal humanism," Hayles explains, because technologically "distributed cognition replaces autonomous will; embodiment replaces a body seen as a support system for the mind; and a dynamic partnership between humans and intelligent machines replaces the liberal humanist subject's manifest destiny to dominate and control nature" (287–88). Note, by the way, how the commonplace "dominate and control nature" is shattered by the Anthropocene, which evidences dominance but not control because it is an unintended consequence rather than the realization of a goal. Leaving that aside, the main revision needed to reorient Hayles's posthumanism centers in the value of her trio of "distributed cognition," "embodiment," and "dynamic partnership," which Hayles affirms in the name of decentering the "liberal subject."

At this point, she stops. For her posthumanism, this decentering is enough. But it is not enough in the context of the Anthropocene. Recognizing that technologies typically can be used for diverse purposes, Anthropocenic posthumanism insists that Hayles's technological trio be designed carefully to ensure that it changes the planetary force that humankind exercises in a direction that is ecologically friendly. It is not enough simply to assume that transvaluative movement of the subject from the category of autonomy to that of technological dependency has automatic ecological value. Reorientation is needed to define a dependency whose ecological value is more clearly demonstrable.

Burke illustrates the other general transvaluational direction with lines of verse titled "The Body Beautiful," a title that he characterizes as "in the dimension of the *humanistic*" (*Attitudes* 387). In this verse, perspectives by incongruity translate the idealized "body beautiful" first into its organs, metaphorized as plumbing, then ultimately into the "primeval slime" from which we all descend (386). "'Bacteriological' connotations," Burke elaborates, "are one with the very essence of *Nature*: the human body inherits a cellular way of life from times before there were such things as human bodies for cells to inhabit or to compose by collectively inhabiting, thereby to become the physiological dwelling-places for human tenants that are identified as individual citizens" (388). This transvaluation is akin to Braidotti's posthumanism, which of the three in my sample is the one that overlaps most with the new materialist recognition that human existence depends on multiple material processes (Coole and Frost 1). Wolfe is on the slope toward Braidotti. Whether he gets as close to Burke's transvaluation depends on whether the linguistic intersects with the genetic as deeply as Derrida proposes.

While technology is central to counter-nature and to Burke's self-revision, this "Body Beautiful" example reminds us that transvaluative perspectives by incongruity are obviously not always technologies. But even without fostering the invention of new technologies, perspectives that are not technologies can still have Anthropocenic effects. Speciesism informs human actions that impact nonhumans, so that overturning it can lead to different actions with different effects. The terms of the overturning mark where posthumanist critique of speciesism can be reoriented toward Anthropocenic posthumanism.

Braidotti's "*zoe*-centered egalitarianism" achieves its transvaluative force by broadening calls for greater equality in human relations to include human and nonhuman relations. Whether this is what Anthropocenic posthumanism needs, however, may be questioned. When Braidotti says, as quoted earlier, that her "egalitarianism" requires that life no longer be "the unalienable right" of only one species, one needs to ponder exactly what this means.

Note first that the transvaluative perspective by incongruity here works by extending "unalienable right" far beyond the human realm. One question to ask is whether this extension, by centering on the liberal idea of "unalienable right," still privileges the "hegemonic category, the human," something Braidotti explicitly resists, as we saw earlier. A deeper question focuses on the extension itself. Does extending this "inalienable right" to all species of life mean that even viruses deadly to humans, such as Ebola, have this same "right"? That transvaluation in the name of posthuman "zoe-centered egalitarianism" prompts such questions indicates that this egalitarianism is so abstract that it becomes empty, impossible to apply consistently.

Anthropocenic posthumanism suggests instead a transvaluation that substitutes "interdependence" among species for "egalitarianism." Interdependence stresses mutual dependency among different species, making extinction a problem not only for a species in danger of extinction but also for other species, including potentially the human species. Transvaluative stress on interdependence would modify the planetary force that humankind exercises in the direction of ecological interdependence, so long as it did not degenerate into concern only for species humans need for their own survival.

Theorizing Anthropocenic posthumanism from the standpoint of Burke's counter-nature inscribes it in an open-ended world. This open-endedness cautions against idealized humanist ends. Instead, one must always be tentative, ready to reevaluate what happened yesterday in preparation for tomorrow, rather than to be married to one transvaluation forever. Additionally, one must expect the unexpected, such as that coming from a surprising new technology. Counter-nature replaces rational progress toward an ideal end with open-ended movement without a certain outcome. Counter-nature is humankind's experiment with itself. Humankind may survive; then again, it may not.

Notes

1. Elizabeth Kolbert, author of *The Sixth Extinction: An Unnatural History*, reports in a recent article that the issue of whether to adopt "Anthropocene" as the official name for our epoch may be brought to a vote in 2016 at a meeting of the International Commission on Stratigraphy (49), which maintains the official geological time scale. But regardless of how the professionals voted, the term is so embedded in culture already that its use is likely to continue. See also Chakrabarty (210).

2. For a discussion of this distinction in Burke, see Wess (222–23).

3. Burke also revises his title—"Definition of Man"—rewriting it as "Definition of [Hu]-Man[s]" (*Attitudes* 424).

4. "The Thinking of the Body (Comments on the Imagery of Catharsis in Literature)," among Burke's most well-known essays, appeared in 1963 and is reprinted in *Language as Symbolic Action*. For a valuable study of Burke's interest in the body, see Debra Hawhee's *Moving Bodies*. Perhaps Burke's best example of the "thinking of body" appears in an essay,

also reprinted in *Language as Symbolic Action*, titled "*Somnia ad Urinandum*: More Thoughts on Motion and Action," which Hawhee neglects. In this essay, Burke analyzes urination dreams that wake the dreamer to the reality of needing to urinate as quickly as possible.

5. For a fleshing-out of this derivation, see Burke's "Post-Poesque Derivation of a Terministic Cluster."

6. In Burke's 1983 revision of *Permanence and Change*, his view of the book differs from his view of it in a chapter titled "Prologue" that he added for its 1953 edition. In 1953, Burke depicts this book as a "monologue" that became from the standpoint of "his later books more like one voice in a dialogue," centering particularly on the issue of proportions of bodily and linguistic motivations, with the 1953 voice putting less weight on the body than the 1935 voice (l–li). By contrast, in 1983 Burke sees *Permanence and Change* in a way that differs from the view he had of it when he wrote it (301). His revision, in effect, displaces the 1935 monologue with a 1983 monologue.

7. Kant also figures in this revision (*Permanence* 301), albeit in a role secondary to Nietzsche. Burke refers to Nietzsche as "Kantian" (311), the point being that Nietzschean perspectivism is implicit in Kant's three critiques (326–27). Burke stresses that Nietzsche's extreme perspectivism would horrify Kant, just as Marx would not have pleased Hegel (311; see also 333), but suggests that one cannot put the perspectivist genie back into the bottle that Kant let it out of. By making noumena inaccessible, Kant left one with indirect phenomenal perspectives that never reach that which is beyond phenomena.

8. William H. Rueckert argues persuasively that Burke's "dramatistic theory . . . systematize[s] a naturalistic, linguistically oriented, secular variant of Christianity. Burke has retained the principal ideas of Christianity and worked out dramatistic equivalents for them with astonishing thoroughness" (133).

Works Cited

Bowen, William. "Our New Awareness of the Great Web." *Fortune* (1970): 198–99. Print.
Braidotti, Rosi. *The Posthuman*. Cambridge, Mass.: Polity Press, 2013. Print.
Burke, Kenneth. *Attitudes Toward History*. 3rd ed. Berkeley: University of California Press, 1984. Print.
———. "Definition of Man." *Language*, 3–24.
———. "A Dramatistic View of the Origins of Language." *Language*, 419–79.
———. "In Haste." *Pre/Text* 6, nos. 3–4 (1985):329–77. Print.
———. *Language as Symbolic Action: Essays on Life, Literature, and Method*. Berkeley: University of California Press, 1966. Print.
———. "My Approach to Communism." *New Masses* 10, no. 16, (1934): 18–20. Print.
———. *Permanence and Change: An Anatomy of Purpose*. 3rd ed. Berkeley: University of California Press, 1984. Print.
———. "Poem." *The Legacy of Kenneth Burke*, edited by Herbert W. Simons and Trevor Melia. Madison: University of Wisconsin Press, 1989. Print.
———. "Post-Poesque Derivation of a Terministic Cluster." *Critical Inquiry* 4, no. 2 (1977): 215–20. Print.
———. "Terministic Screens." *Language*, 44–62.
———. "Variations on 'Providence.'" *Notre Dame English Journal* 13, no. 3 (1981): 155–83. Print.

Chakrabarty, Dipesh. "The Climate of History: Four Theses." *Critical Inquiry* 35, no. 2 (2009): 197–222. Print.

Coole, Diana, and Samantha Frost, editors. *New Materialisms: Ontology, Agency, and Politics.* Durham: Duke University Press, 2010. Print.

Crutzen, Paul J., and Eugene F. Stoermer. "The 'Anthropocene.'" *Global Change Newsletter* 41 (2000): 17–18. Web. 12 May 2015.

Derrida, Jacques. "'Eating Well,' or the Calculation of the Subject: An Interview with Jacques Derrida." *Who Comes After the Subject?*, edited by Eduardo Cadava, Peter Connor, and Jean-Luc Nancy. New York: Routledge, 1991, 96–119. Print.

Foucault, Michel. *The Order of Things: An Archaeology of the Human Sciences.* New York: Random, 1973. Print.

Hawhee, Debra. *Moving Bodies: Kenneth Burke at the Edges of Language.* Columbia: University of South Carolina Press, 2009. Print. Studies in Rhetoric/Communication.

Hayles, N. Katherine. *How We Became Posthuman: Virtual Bodies in Cybernetics, Literature, and Informatics.* Chicago: University of Chicago Press, 1999. Print.

Kolbert, Elizabeth. "Annals of Extinction Part Two: The Lost World: Fossils of the Future." *New Yorker* (23 Dec. 2013), 48–56. Print.

Latour, Bruno. "Agency at the Time of the Anthropocene." *New Literary History* 45, no. 1 (2014), 1–18. Print.

Nagel, Thomas. *The View from Nowhere.* Oxford: Oxford University Press, 1986. Print.

Rueckert, William H. *Kenneth Burke and the Drama of Human Relations.* 2nd ed. Berkeley: University of California Press, 1982. Print.

Serres, Michel. *The Natural Contract.* Translated by Elizabeth MacArthur and William Paulson. Ann Arbor: University of Michigan Press, 1995. Print.

Wess, Robert. *Kenneth Burke: Rhetoric, Subjectivity, Postmodernism.* Cambridge: Cambridge University Press, 1996. Literature, Culture, Theory 18. Print.

Wolfe, Cary. *Animal Rites: American Culture, the Discourse of Species, and Posthumanist Theory.* Chicago: University of Chicago Press, 2003. Print.

———. *What Is Posthumanism?* Minneapolis: University of Minnesota Press, 2010. Posthumanities 8. Print.

5

Technique–Technology–Transcendence | Machination and *Amēchania* in Burke, Nietzsche, and Parmenides

Thomas Rickert

Hippoi tai me pherousin, hoson t' epi thumos ikanoi . . .
(The mares that carry me as far as longing can reach . . .)
—Parmenides, *Peri Phuseos* (On Being)

The German band Kraftwerk's 1978 album *Die Mensch-Maschine* (*The Man-Machine*) explores the merger of natural and artificial, human and nonhuman, living being and machine. The members of Kraftwerk pose as robots on the album cover, evoking futurist and constructivist art of the past; but as robots, they gaze blankly into an unknown future. The music itself is highly techno-logical, created with synthesizers, machine-treated vocals, and drum machines; and the lyrics—quite spare—deal with robots, cities, spacelabs, and, of course, the titular subject itself, the man-machine (although "human-machine" might be more accurate, as *mensch* was not originally a word only for the male; the use of *wesen*, "living being," reinforces the broader interpretation). The lyrics to the title track read,

Mensch-Maschine	Man-Machine
Halb Wesen und halb Ding	Half [living] being and half thing
Mensch-Maschine, Maschine . . .	Man-Machine, Machine . . .
Mensch-Maschine	Man-Machine
Halb Wesen und halb Überding	Half being and half over-thing
Mensch-Maschine, Maschine . . .	Man-Machine, Machine . . .

Kraftwerk's man-machine traffics favorably with later, posthuman theorizations of human-machine symbiosis such as, for instance, Donna Haraway's ground-breaking theory of the cyborg. Both are clearly mythic, of course, but Kraftwerk emphasizes a twist in ontological meaning different from Haraway's emphases on partiality, irony, responsibility, and an attendant politics (151, 181). Kraftwerk's *Überding* reverses the Nietzschean *Übermensch*, and the move from *mensch* to *ding* is striking. This is the ontological twist, for the meshing of human and machine isn't a simple unity that emerges from "half being" and "half thing," but rather a transcendence to a new order on the part of the machine—something over, super, above. From this perspective, there can be no demonization of technology to preserve a human essence, as the human is only half anyway, but neither is there any harmonic whole. The *über* unbalances the symbiosis. There is both similarity and dissimilarity with Haraway on this point. Similarity in that the machine is given the nod in the same way that Haraway picks the cyborg over the goddess, and dissimilarity in that there's an ontological asymmetry between beings and machines, or, at least, a greater emphasis on it (181). This point is brought home by Kraftwerk's iconic imagery and musical performance, in which human vocals are streamlined and machined, and the band present themselves to be as robotic as possible. "Becoming robot" isn't a direct human choice but a merger that is already technological. Still, the accomplishment is unequal: ÜBERding. Or, as band member Ralf Hütter explains, "We are playing the machines, the machines play us, it is really the exchange and the friendship we have with the musical machines which make us build a new music" (qtd. in Price). Looking at the photos that adorn the album cover and booklet, one sees the band made up as robots attending to the machinery. This reinforces the *Überding*, in that the technology is not bent toward the human, but vice versa: the human is already technologized and, in that technologized form, further attuned to the machinic. To make music, that most *human* of arts, presupposes techniques themselves already technological for further working with technology. The point that Kraftwerk crafts for us is that the human is doubly technological, a becoming technological of the human that in turn fosters further technological relations. The *Überding*, then, marks not simply the priority of the machinic but the idea that transcendence is itself on the side of the machine, whether for beings or technology. Technics reside primordially.[1]

The gesture beyond the human spurred by the question of the technic will be my focus here. Posthumanism, a contemporary theoretical movement pushing toward a new understanding of human beings' relation to the (nonhuman) world and technology, is thus also at issue. Certainly, posthumanism and technics provide a near-irresistible combination beckoning toward some new way of being in the world. I will resist the temptation to think posthumanism as a temporal shift responding to recent technical advancements such as digital media, biotechnics, ambient computing, and so on. Instead, I see the posthuman as a capacity or trajectory already implicit in the question of the human (and what lies beyond it), going back to our earliest intellectual works and practices. Such a premise has many advantages, but perhaps foremost among them is to highlight how the technics of technique and technology continually intermerge and inflect each other.[2] This, indeed, was the point of my using the opening Kraftwerk example, and it differs from the idea of the cyborg in subtle ways. It declines to see posthumanism in terms of a technical augmentation but sees it rather as something equally implicit in *technologies* of the self, so long as we understand the "self" as fundamentally indistinct from the technical. Technologies are not augmentative because they presuppose ways of being technical including forms of technique; and technique, whether in terms of psychic or somatic training, also presupposes a technical attitude in advance. That is, technique requires a perspective whereby the body or mind is seen as something that can be transformed, augmented, machined, perfected, or transcended.[3] This technical *attitude* necessarily suffuses every technique in advance.

In what follows, I put a trio of thinkers—Parmenides, Nietzsche, and Burke—into conversation about the posthuman issue of human and nonhuman relations, specifically their relations to technology. Does technology overcome the human and so generate a transcending separation between the human and the machinic? Such a transcendence is variously understood, of course, but most positions come down to one of two poles: either technology moves us into a future rendered precarious by the loss of a nontechnical human essence, or it moves us beyond human limitations in order to reach a promising future. Posthumanism jettisons this binary, seeing the human and the technological (or the nonhuman in general) as mutually enmeshed. But how are we to conceive of this human/nonhuman meshwork? Parmenides, Nietzsche, and Burke each offer insight into how technique, which is typically associated with the human body and psyche, gets caught up in the technological, and one of the major pathways is through forms of transcendence. This issue has long been with us, I note—it shows up in Plato, as we shall see—even if it remains murky. One reason for its occlusion is that many definitions of technology come down to "the making or using of artifacts," "the extension of humanity," and similar concepts (Mitcham 1; Rothenberg xvii). In other words, harbored in the technique/technology distinction are body/world, human/nonhuman, or (why not?) *ding*/non-*ding* binaries. While such commonsense distinctions have their value, they are not secure, and it is attending to their erosions and modulations that will help us foster different relations to technology. As for transcendence, not only is it visible in technology's gesture to a beyond, but it is seen in technique as well, in particular in the forms of *askesis*, or spiritual training, that appear (perhaps surprisingly) in Parmenides, Nietzsche, and Burke. But I will also argue that Kraftwerk's *Überding* helps illuminate how transcendence is also a manifestation of technic's disequilibrium—that is, a transcendent beyond is already immanent to technicity's unfolding. If technics are always part of how being in the world gets transformed, what marks them as *über* is this sense of never catching up to where they gesture next. If this is so, then posthumanism, rather than gathering disparate solutions to human/nonhuman and human/technology dichotomies, might be better conceived as the name of a problem: an instability at the heart of the human, one name for which is technicity.

It Wasn't Me. It Was My Attitude

What we have ascertained so far is that technology has an attitude problem.[4] It is always out of—over or perhaps above—step with itself. Alongside its compatriot science, technology promises transcendence. Whoever and whatever the human is, technology can augment, improve, perfect, swerve away from, or dominate it. Even technology's failures primarily work to galvanize greater efforts, as if there is something in the technology itself, something that ushers us ever forward on the seduction of its promise to transcend where we are now and grant us something better. Many thinkers have noted such, of course, and Burke was among them. One of his pithiest encapsulations of this notion occurs at the end of his "Towards Helhaven" essay, in which he describes technology in a mock tricolon, complete with all caps: "ONWARD, OUTWARD, and UP!" ("Towards" 25). Furthermore, he was keenly observant of the isomorphism between technology's trouble-producing material instantiations and the social attitude driving technological production. Looking back on his early career from 1972, Burke says that he viewed the cult of technologic progress as a cultural absurdity rather than as "the grave economic problem it now shows signs of 'progressively' becoming" (*Dramatism* 17). The punning shift in progress's meaning here is telling: progress's promise of something more and better shifts progressively into the worse and worsening.

In this way, we see how well Burke's thoughts on technology mirror other aspects of his thought, particularly his emphasis on entelechy, the idea that one always "goes to the end of the line," brings something to its uttermost completion ("Why" 314). For Burke, technology's attitude is transcendent in precisely this sense: a going to the end of the line on the back of the faith in progress that drives it along. When technology's advocates are confronted with technological problems, the solution is inevitably better technology. Car pollution a problem? Electric cars are the answer. Climate change an issue? The answer is conservation via improved technologies, or even outright denial, motored by the idea that more technological progress is of far greater benefit. And so on. From Burke's perspective, this fulfills well the principle of entelechy. And indeed, Burke saw technology as increasingly interconnected, constituting something like a world order (*Attitudes* 357). In some essential way, technology accomplishes a separation between human beings and the world, from which catastrophic consequences ensue.

This, then, sketches the problematic that I want to address in terms of Burke, Nietzsche, and the Presocratic philosopher Parmenides. What does it mean that technology has an attitude problem—that it motivates a transcendence that captures and endangers human beings even as it holds the greatest of promises? Faith and hope are explicitly manifest in both these perspectives, too, and because of this, I want to attend to the mystical and religious dimensions here, which perhaps offer insight into how new perspectives can be achieved.[5] I argue that all three tackle this issue head on, offering what might be called forms of practical spiritual instruction—or *askesis*—that work on emotional, intellectual, and spiritual aspects of human beings in order to transform them.[6] This transformation would, in turn, affect our relation to the world, including technology, suggesting other ways of inhabiting the world. *Askesis* as I explore it here will rework a theme found in Parmenides—namely, that most people lack world-wise, cunning techniques, or *mêtis*, that allow them to thrive where uncertainty and illusion hold sway. If we are, then, *amēchania*—that is, lacking *mêtis*—then *askesis* can be considered one possible way to cultivate it. Furthermore, given that *askesis* is a *technē*, we can gain a more precise understanding of the relation between the human and the technological, finding that the ground of technique is itself the technological (not vice versa), making the transcendent paradoxically immanent to worldly being. Finally, I will briefly turn to Plato's *Euthyphro* to offer some conditional remarks about *technē* itself, suggesting that it cannot be equated with rationality and efficiency only, and that alternative modalities such as caring and attending are readily available within the technic. But this possibility is already given a provocative direction in Parmenides, Nietzsche, and Burke.

Parmenides: The System of a Thousand Lies

I begin with Parmenides, who may seem an unusual figure to explore in this context. Technology, in the common understanding as externalized artifact, is not an issue for Parmenides. However, if we engage with his use of spiritual and intellectual techniques, we will see that Parmenides has much to offer us about technology. Parmenides is one of the first to ask why things are the way they are in a way that sets us on the road to theoretical knowledge. Parmenides marks where technique steps into rational account and thereby gets its -logy (although this is simply a disclosure of a primordial technological attitude).[7] However, there have been recent challenges, most notably by Peter Kingsley, to the philosophical picture of Parmenides as a protophilosopher who offered one of the first rational accounts of the cosmos. These challenges open up other aspects of his surviving poem, *Peri Phuseos* (On Being), demonstrating that Parmenides was interested in truth as persuasion; that metaphysical, revelatory elements are integral to his thinking; and that he was interested in teaching *mêtis*, which is understood as a form of cunning, worldly wisdom, a polymorphous intelligence open to fluid, evolving situations (Detienne and Vernant 2–5). Rather than simply setting us on the road to science via the rational acquisition of knowledge, Parmenides suggests that truth may be unattainable in its purest forms for human beings, and even deeper truths may require other, even divine, sources. Wisdom begins there, with the necessity of learning *mêtis* to cope with the snares and traps of the world that trick us into thinking that we have knowledge that we do not. Let me highlight here the isomorphism between theorizing technologies of knowledge production as insufficient in themselves to offer ethical or practical guidance and our current situation, in which, increasingly, technologies of machine and digitality are also insufficient. We will return to this below; for now, let us look at how Parmenides makes his case.

Parmenides's poem begins with his description of being carried off to Hades, led by mares and lesser goddesses, where he is greeted by an unnamed goddess, who is most likely Persephone, Queen of the Underworld. Complexly interwoven into his *katabasis* are themes of capture, spellbinding, initiation, and the power of persuasion. The proem describes a powerfully rendered mystical experience in which Parmenides is greeted and spellbound by Persephone, becoming the vehicle for her words of power. "I will do the talking," she tells him, "and it's up to you to carry away my words" (F2). Parmenides's description of a journey to the underworld, where he is transfixed by a goddess, is not simply allegory or fictional framing but rather a metaphysical performance (Burkert). While what Parmenides relates as the "still heart of persuasive truth" (*alētheiēs eupietheos atremes ētor*) cannot be separated from his innovative logical techniques (F2), neither can it be separated from metaphysical techniques. Logic and rationality are to be lauded and pursued, but they are not to be understood as a pure solution unto themselves.

Grounds for a new understanding of Parmenides were spurred by the discovery of a medical compound unearthed in the late 1950s in Velia—formerly Elea—on the southern coast of Italy. The Apollo-associated compound ran for nearly five hundred years. Archaeologists have found much of interest there, including medical paraphernalia, an underground chamber, and a few busts of the compound's leaders. The name given for these figures is *iatromantis*, meaning healer-prophet. What was surprising to many is that a bust of Parmenides was also found there, with no year given, suggesting that he was a founding figure (Kingsley, *Dark* 106–8). Another term used to describe these healer-prophets is *phôlarchos*, which means something like "lords of the lair." It is related to the word *phôleos*, meaning "to lie down in a cave or den like an animal" (Ustinova 191–92, 197–99; Kingsley, *Dark* 77–79). A *phôlarchos* is a healer-prophet trained in the proper techniques, such as fasting, breathing exercises, the use of intoxicants, and so on, who would lie down in a cave, den, or underground sanctuary in order to achieve altered states of consciousness proper for receiving divine revelation. This practice was called "incubation." It was often referred to by another word, *hēsychia*, meaning stillness.[8] As we know from the Greeks and from comparative study with other cultures, stillness refers to the sensation of utter quiet and connection to the world that accompanies trance states such as incubation.

What surprises here is not that the Greeks are known to have practiced incubation but that we find Parmenides, the supposed "Father of Western Rationality," associated with a society of medically oriented incubants and evoking incubatory states in his philosophical poem (see Kingsley, *Dark*; Gemelli Marciano). It places a religious element, or more precisely a technics of psychic alteration, at the heart of rationality and truth. Rather than a philosopher using the techniques of rational thought—logic, the principle of noncontradiction, and dialectic—we have the techniques of rational thought accompanied and inspired by a communion with reality and the divine. This metaphysical experience results from the meeting of specific techniques, human neurological affordances, and environmental potentials. The body's biological affordances—meaning its susceptibility to fasting, chant, intoxicants, and so on—induce transformations in brain states. Numerous psychological and neurological studies have demonstrated the physical and mental changes that we undergo during such experiences.[9] We have the forging of techniques stemming from the body's unique affordances, and the performance of those techniques in suitable environments, whether adapted—such as caves—or built—such as underground chambers— for the biotechnical production of metaphysical experience. Here, we see a concrete instance of one of my themes—namely, that technology has a religious dimension. For Parmenides, that religious dimension appears as bringing divine truth to the mortal realm for purposes of instruction, healing, and knowledge. As we have known since at least Walter Ong, writing is a technology that restructures thought; we can now say the same thing about meditative and other altered states such as incubation. *Incubation is a technology that restructures thought.*[10] It increases neuronal connections, stimulating happiness, well-being, concentration, empathy, and the ability to pursue less ego-centered forms of thought, including the exploration of a "spiritual world," among other effects (Winkelman 1–26).

Why does Parmenides temper his rational pursuit of understanding being with metaphysical considerations? We might take cues from Nietzsche's famous claim that dialectic convinces no one; it is as if we see this insight given incipient form at the very dawn of what we call scientific rationality.[11] Parmenides hedges on reason alone because he understands it to be insufficient on its own. Large portions of the poem are devoted to the idea that there are two paths one can go by—the route of being and the route of nonbeing. But it turns out that the way of nonbeing is impossible (F2). Yet at the same time, there is an isomorphism between thinking and being, as if to say that anything we can think in some fashion exists (and therefore, no "actual" nonbeing exists) (F3). There is no separation from being—from all of being. Thought is manifold, and as such, has its reality; measuring thought against the world cannot finally qualify or negate thinking's reach. There is no "reality" that will finally bring the manifoldness of thought to rest—there is no separation (Kingsley, *Reality* 71–75). Yet this insight sounds improbable, to say the least, when so articulated. This helps us understand why what Persephone relates to Parmenides is simultaneously performed and specified. The poem creates effects that mimic incubation to accompany the more rigorously logical content—and in places, the logical content moves so quickly as to generate transporting effects as well. More simply: the poem seeks to achieve what it says—that is, to describe, perform, and recreate (in others) a metaphysical experience that includes yet also exceeds the rational. Again, technics reappear: the efficient production of transformative experience described in the poem and the psychosomatic effects of the entire poem as delivered to an audience.

What the poem strives to achieve is a receptive state of mind for the dizzying claims and logic games delivered by Persephone; as they spellbind Parmenides in the context of the poem, they also spellbind the listener. The poem uses misdirection, illogic, sound effects, ambiguity, density of meaning, and rapid word flow to mesmerize, dazzle, and confound (Gemelli Marciano 32–33). These performative effects are mirrored in Persephone's description of the plight of everyday people. In F6, for instance, Persephone tells us that they know nothing, calling them "two-headed," "undiscerning," and "helpless." "Two-headed" (*dikranoi*) indicates that people are at loggerheads, of two minds. They cannot adjudicate. To describe them as "undiscerning" (*akrita phula*) exploits ambiguity by suggesting both the masses that one cannot distinguish individuals among and the inability to decide. The masses are all the same, presumably, in their inability to find the proper knowledge to steer their way forward. We saw why above: thought is manifold. While I cannot make the argument here for lack of space, I will suggest that this is already a step toward sophistic thought, in which a logos and an antilogos are understood to be replete in the world—a version, I suggest, of Parmenides's sense of never finding something to bring thought to rest. There is no guide in thought we might find, and in this way we find ourselves two-headed, undiscerning, helpless.

Helpless, or *amēchania*, refers to being without a ruse; in the context of the poem, it means that people lack *mētis* (Kingsley, *Reality* 91; see also, Detienne and Vernant 23n3, 40–41, 78, 144). *Mētis* is cunning wisdom, often tethered to hunting, contest, and other forms of practical or performative success.[12] *Amēchania* is the privative of *mēchanē*, a term linked to a series of other words, including *technē*, all associated with *mētis*. What the goddess means is that people have no remedy for their plight, no cunning wisdom for deciding wisely and successfully, but rather they are bound to the world's deceptions and traps. *Mēchanē*, meaning an instrument for doing, making, or constructing something, is a resonant word here, as it is the root for our word "machine"; and thus it is perhaps no surprise to see how it is associated strongly with *technē*, and thus technology. A machine is an instrument or tool of human artifice, a device. As such, even here the association with *mêtis* bears out, as device can also mean a clever ploy, trick, or maneuver. The word *mēchanē* is rooted in Proto-Indo-European *mogh-* and *megh-*, which mean "to have power" (and are thus related to German *macht* and *machen*, which also mean "power"), and even to the English word "may" (Mitcham 167). A machine as a constructed artifact, then, never sheds its associations with machinations such as scheming or crafty action. Furthermore, the possibility of a machining of the human remains ever-present, and this includes rhetoric, which might be well described as the machining of language (Brown 496, 498; Rice 367).

Parmenides's embrace of logical techniques—also a machining of language—is but one trick in his overall project. And the reason why is already performed for us: metaphysical experience, divine guidance, and a distrust of human-centered devices suggest that reason alone cannot transcend or abolish human helplessness. Reason and knowledge are not the only forms of intelligence necessary to achieve *mêtis*, exactly, because they offer hope that truth has been achieved while actually binding and blinding us to its own illusions—although they don't appear as illusions, of course. They appear as new thoughts—that is, new techniques, technologies, machines, and machinations, with all their attendant promises of transcendence and improvement. It is worth noting that philosophers have long claimed that Parmenides's logic is faulty and that the cosmology of one being that he offers is incoherent. What is missing in this read is the deeper thread of *mêtis* that amounts to existential insight into finding life's course in a world of deception, trickery, traps, and illusion. Logic, reason, and knowledge can produce great benefit, as Parmenides himself demonstrates; but in the end they do not suffice on their own to render the truth of being because they, too, are prey to surfeit, leaving us to what Persephone calls our "sightless eyes" and "echoing ears" (F7). Before one quickly dismisses Parmenides's point, it should be recalled that contemporary science is continually finding that our sense of reality is not reason-based, but modulated strongly by emotion, morals, perspective, and the neurological contributions our brains make to establishing what we see as reality, contributions that are frequently characterized as hallucinatory (see, for instance, Haidt and Greene on emotion and morality and Thomson for a summative view of hallucination). Even if one disregards such research as "wrong" science, Parmenides is borne out, since we still see the restlessness of thought, its continual and irrepressible generation.

The theme of traps—of being bound within limits and false knowledge—runs like a golden thread throughout Parmenides's poem. Contra Plato's cave myth, there's no escape from illusion, and truth is always accompanied by persuasion. Our best hope—and this amounts to Parmenides's *askesis*—remains the wisdom of *mêtis*, which begins with two tightly interrelated points. The first of these is somewhat speculative, but given the evidence, we might surmise that Parmenides places importance on incubation, whereby one is persuaded to the illusiveness of our conceptual, rational understanding of reality through the experience of a profound interconnectedness of everything, a oneness that exists beyond all mutability. This oneness is itself persuasive; it is an integral part of the "still heart of persuasive truth" Persephone promises to deliver. Even Aristotle recognizes the power of such experience, as when he comments that the mysteries do not teach one anything but create life-transforming encounters, as happened for thousands who came every year to experience the Eleusinian Mysteries. With this ecstatic experience came the traditional religious benefits of happiness, tranquility, and fortitude in the face of death. As Cicero describes, it is via the mysteries that initiates "get the idea not only of how to live in joy, but also how to die with hope for the best" (*De Legibus* 2.36). In an odd twist, then, technology along with reason and logic are put in service of dissolving our faith in their promises. Parmenides's poem is akin to a deprogramming session (Gemelli Marciano 41). So, the second part to his *askesis* is to accept that these illusions of the world cannot be overcome via logic, knowledge, or reason. Whatever remedy they offer is compromised, because faith in reason alone is the path to further illusion and the propagation of still more *amēchania*. As Persephone says, the path of all—all people, all things—is backward-turning (F6). *Mêtis* begins with this acceptance. But it does not end there, for the poem suggests that, in accepting illusion as our lot, we are still bound within the necessity of persuasion, and here we see why the poem combines metaphysical performative elements with logical argumentation. Experience alone, even of this profound cosmological stillness, is also helpless—as the goddess Persephone says, truth is always attended by persuasion (F2). We are not abandoned to reason but neither can we abandon reason.

In sum, then, Parmenides illuminates technology in numerous ways for us. First, he provides an early test case for how technique and technology are conjoined to produce truth, knowledge, and life-changing experiences. That is, Parmenides showcases an ancient version of a bioenvironed technics. But, second, his work reflects back on such techniques, suggesting that human beings are *amēchania* without other forms of help. This is not necessarily an ontological claim about divinities or metaphysics; rather, it is a claim that the experience showcases how technics of biopsychic alteration have material effects on brain neurofunctioning that, in turn, manifest as changes in thought patterns and insights. They are technics. These experiences, that is, are looped into the biomaterial ecology productive of ideas and persuasiveness. And furthermore, this suggests a profound ambiguity about technology. It offers much—indeed the means for the very transcendence someone like Parmenides seeks—and yet it also produces a surfeit that nets us in its promises without delivering on them. From this perspective, technology's attitude, its entelechial push to reach the great good place, becomes a key means for grounding a new attitude toward technology, one that sees it as another snare that binds us to illusion if we accept it without deeper insight.

Nietzsche: The Rhythm of Earth

Nietzsche provides a fitting comparison to Parmenides, because he reworks several Parmenidean themes yet also provides new points of departure. And, like Parmenides, the connection to technology can be indirect. Yet if we recall the Burkean mantra "Onward, outward, and up," we can already bring the theme of transcendence into view and see how technological transcendence and Nietzsche's recurring thematic of self-overcoming the human (the *Übermensch*) overlap. Indeed, in many respects, Nietzsche is the first thinker of the modern era to pursue *embodied* techniques for posthuman existence. Furthermore, Nietzsche, like Parmenides, pursues new forms of initiation—one might even say that that Nietzsche's Dionysian pursuit is itself a new piety. This piety, not dissimilarly to Burke's conception of "piety," entails not simply new beliefs, but also the reorganization of one's heart, one's motives, one's very sense of world. And again, we see the connection to Parmenides, who through his transformative *askesis* sought to fundamentally rework one's sense of and place within reality. Lastly, both Parmenides and Nietzsche have profound insight into the traps and limits of reason, and thus also reason's extensions through the rationalizations of technique into technology. Nietzsche, we will see, seeks a new piety to counter decadence, and this new piety, as for Parmenides before him, requires an *askesis* (Benson 10–12).

Nietzsche's thought is complex, so I plan to focus on two main motifs: overcoming (hence, transcending) the self and the transvaluation of values. Obviously, the two are conjoined. One can see this in any number of ways, but perhaps of particular clarity is Nietzsche's sparring with Socrates, which happens continuously throughout his writing career. In his first book, *The Birth of Tragedy*, Nietzsche explicitly casts Socrates as the first who could live and, more significantly, *die* within the scientific/rationalist mindset and who thought that the powers of rationality could not only penetrate the deepest abyss of being but *correct* it (*Birth*, Section 15). However, Nietzsche also allows that Socrates demonstrates doubt about his pursuit of the rational at all cost when, during his imprisonment just prior to his death, Socrates admits that many times during the course of his life a dream-voice came to him saying, "Socrates, practice music" (*Birth*, Section 14). This is telling, on Nietzsche's part, for in many respects music plays a key role in self-overcoming, just as music exemplifies the Dionysian values Nietzsche seeks. These values pertain to the irrepressible Becoming of life, which is ever-changing, uncontrollable, uncorrectable, and, in an essential way, beyond our understanding. Rational thought, science, and technology cannot, for Nietzsche, allow us to transcend this Becoming; they will not through their operations deliver on their incipient promises to arrive at a better, truer, safer world than this one. Music, on the contrary, affirms this becoming, attunes us to its rhythms beyond good and evil, seeks neither correction nor understanding but immersion and experience. It is no accident that when Nietzsche claims to philosophize with a hammer, he means it in a musical sense: sounding out idols as with a tuning fork—that is, shattering them by finding the appropriate resonant frequency (*Twilight*, preface).

In terms of *askesis*, music provides Nietzsche something analogous to Parmenides's incubation. Just as incubation fosters a deep, insightful mindset that includes reason and technology as part of its practice, so, too, does music. Just as the profundity of Parmenides's incubation provides an experience of our completeness in being that resists articulation, so, too, does music convey for Nietzsche the abyssal depths of life's becoming and thereby say things that philosophy cannot. Indeed, this helps us understand why, when Nietzsche looks back on *The Birth of Tragedy* several years later in "An Attempt at Self Criticism," he admits that it appears as if he is a "mystical, almost maenadic soul" stammering with difficulty, and that rather than speaking, he should have "*sung*" (*Birth* 4; emphasis in original). Music's "supreme revelations" cause us to feel, claims Nietzsche, the crudeness of imagery and language ("On Music" 112, 117).

When Socrates denies the voice that urges him to learn music, he thereby holds to the claim of language and reason to explain reality and justify existence, which is crucial insofar as Nietzsche reads Socrates's *askesis* of the dialectical exchange as reason leading to self-transformation. Nietzsche thinks that music's powers are greater than reason's, in part because Nietzsche's embrace of a vital, worldly becoming revalues the body. Music provides an experience and, with the best music, that experience is transporting, taking us out of ourselves, providing, he states, "joy. A Trinity of Joy: elevation, illumination, calm, a unity of all three" (qtd. in Benson 173). Music grips and raises the body and, in so doing, raises the mind. We might recall Nietzsche's criticism of dialectic: that it convinces no one, and that the turn to dialectical reason is already an indication of decadence because that turn evidences that the instincts have eroded and become unsure of themselves (*Twilight* 6). Regardless of our views of his high esteem of aristocratic values, we see that, for Nietzsche, belief and value are embodied and performed. Indeed, we must see in this light Nietzsche's odd *ad hominem* argument that Socrates was decadent because he was ugly (7). What is an otherwise objectionable point nevertheless evinces the insight that thinking is always embodied. Nietzsche's riposte to Flaubert sharpens the point. Flaubert states that one can only think and write while sitting; Nietzsche responds, "I've caught you, you old nihilist!" (34). The sedentary life is a sin: "Only thoughts reached by walking have value" (34). In these and other passages, Nietzsche teaches that "one must first persuade the *body*" (47). Insofar as music grips the body, as rhythms get in the muscles and melodies move the heart, music is not only more fulsome than dialectic but has greater power to transform. In this fashion, music not only induces a reevaluation of reason's powers, but it also persuades us bodily of the power of more affective, worldly values. From a Nietzschean perspective, it is thus little wonder that great changes in music always appear as cultural disruptions and that, historically, music has always been regarded as the most dangerous and suspicious of the arts. It bypasses rational gatekeeping, getting into our sinews and synapses through irrepressible sound and rhythm.

This returns us to our technological thread. Music, of course, is technological, whether techniques of voice or bodily rhythm or the technologies of musical instruments. And while Nietzsche may not explicitly address technology often in his writings, it is clearly incipient in that he is ever aware of the dissolving separation of body and environment. He also provides germinal insights about our technological scaffolding. This is especially true since music, insofar as it becomes the dominant paradigm for describing transformation, moves into a technological modality. Music generates a unique sort of transcendence for Nietzsche, then—not an overcoming of this world, but rather an overcoming of what in us deafens us to what this world asks us to embrace. It is a transcendence into worldly immanence achieved via musical *askesis*. Music performs in a technological fashion to transform our worldly existence. Nietzsche and Parmenides, then, share a common concern with the technics of transcendence and transformation, and how concrete practices inhabit a technological orientation in order to be brought to bear on questions of how to achieve a better life. This is how we are to understand Nietzsche's controversial notion of the *Übermensch*. Often considered a type of superbeing, in actuality, the "overman" is a person who has overcome a life organized around the values associated with a transcendent realm or being in favor of an affirmation of worldly immanence. And the key to overcoming this decadence—literally a "de-cadence," as a falling out of rhythm—lies in the worldly technics of *askesis*, especially those in a musical key that reattune us to the Earth's rhythms (Benson 4–5).

It is from this perspective that we should understand Nietzsche's embrace of the typewriter. By the late 1800s, shortly before his slide into insanity, Nietzsche was a physical wreck: near blind, with shaking hands and incapacitating headaches. He sought out the typewriter so that he might continue writing after handwriting had failed him. Indeed, Friedrich Kittler calls Nietzsche the first "mechanized philosopher" (200). In a letter, Nietzsche remarks that "our writing tools are also working on our thoughts" (qtd. in Kittler 200). It is a remarkable statement but, given what we have seen about Nietzsche's views of music and the body, perhaps not surprising. If music works on the body, and so in turn works on our thoughts and attitudes, potentially leading us to a new Dionysian piety, why would technology not also work on our bodies and, hence, also our thoughts and attitudes? Thus, Kittler goes on to argue that the typewriter modified how Nietzsche wrote, inducing him to pursue further the aphoristic style that he had already gravitated toward. Short, clipped, concise—what Kittler calls "telegram style"—the aphorism and the typewriter allowed the physically ailing Nietzsche to continue writing when he might otherwise have lapsed into silence. And it transformed in subtle ways the form and, to some extent, the contents of his thinking.

Finally, then, for Nietzsche, technology is complexly considered. First, Nietzsche denies any common notion of transcendence, seeing that overcoming takes place immanently, in the world of appearance. Music is, thus, a key element of his Dionysian *askesis*, but we must see that technology has a role to play here, too, as evidenced in his thoughts about the typewriter. This contributes to post-humanism not only because it shifts values but also by reworking the material and technological scaffolding integral to formations of body and mind. It is in this context that we should understand an odd little poem that Nietzsche wrote about the typewriter:

> The writing ball is a thing like me: made of
> iron
> yet easily twisted on journeys.
> Patience and tact are required in abundance,
> as well as fine fingers, to use us. (qtd. in Kittler, 200)

Nietzsche's identification with the machinic is profound here, and certainly not utopian.[13] In other passages in his oeuvre, Nietzsche attends to some of the ill effects of technology, particularly how its machinic thrust levels the desire to climb higher; factory work, he points out, dissipates workers' energies and potentials (McGinn 683, 690). Still, in the passage on the typing ball, we see that the separation among the bodily, the technological, and the discursive is subject to dissolution, and the possibility of self-overcoming—with the self understood as a hybrid, technological self—via *askesis* remains as not just a possibility but a call. In this sense, Nietzsche's main concern both takes part in and reworks technology's attitude and, thus, for all its differences, runs a course similar to Parmenides, which is to seek primarily some overcoming of humanity, and, via this *askesis*-driven reawakening to the Dionysian, cultivate fortitude and greatness in life.

Burke: What's the Frequency, Kenneth?

Nietzsche is entirely characteristic in seeking to affirm technology—even when he notes its ill effects—and in pursuing that affirmation through self-transformation and a transvaluation of values. Burke maintains some striking differences from Nietzsche on this score. When Burke discusses the possibility of an affirmation of technology, as in the "Helhaven" essay, it is leavened with a strong dose of satire ("Towards" 56). More characteristic, perhaps, is his actual way of life, which, as Ian Hill notes, entailed living on a farm without running water, electricity, or much other technology until the 1960s. Burke's antitechnological lifestyle coincides with that of another famous of critic of technology, Martin Heidegger, who also—and infamously—kept a hut deep in the Black Forest that lacked running water, electricity, and so on until the 1960s. The parallel is worth noting because, similarly to Heidegger, Burke saw what he called "Big Technology" as a "master psychosis," one with inherent motivations and its own particular "occupational psychosis" that opens up particular ways of seeing and feeling and closes down others (*Permanence* 44–49). Thus, as I mentioned earlier, technology motivates technological solutions, even to technological problems, because technology fulfills itself: if it's the motor for the greatness of modern civilization, then other solutions are closed from view. Put together with Burke's principle of entelechy, then, technology's motivation both blinds us to other possibilities and aims to perfect itself—that is, to maximize its capabilities to the very end.

It is thus the case that Burke understands technology's attitudes as caught up in particular terminologies. While human imperfection ironically preserves us, perhaps, from extinction, there remain better means to challenge, delimit, or otherwise use technology. The main and best one, of course, is to transform the controlling discourse. Given that technology is socially embedded—meaning that its motivational force is activated and pursued through our social vocabularies, beliefs, feelings, sustaining rituals, and the material infrastructure—we see that challenging what Burke characterizes as the "technological psychosis" is no easy matter. For instance, consider how difficult it apparently is to transition from gasoline- to electric-powered vehicles, even in the face of energy and climate-change threats. Technologies are deeply interlocked: we see cars, for example, threaded through innumerable other technologies, industries, infrastructure, and financial networks. So, second, to transform a vocabulary requires that we address many different and variably connected arenas. One quickly sees that while powerful rhetorical possibilities are available, they are difficult to predict, control, and implement. There is occasionally great potential here, of course, as Rachel Carson's *Silent Spring*, the 1970s antipollution movement, or today's Green Movement each demonstrate through their powerful interventions. That they are limited, or that their time of effectiveness eventually wanes, is no objection to them. Yet at the same time, it is important to point out that each of these appeals connected with profound questions about how to dwell and included possibilities such as innovative techniques for living or alternate technologies.

It is these deeper technical connections that must be noted, because tackling the technical psychosis goes beyond a single, limited interruption. For instance, as I write this, I see in my Facebook feed that someone has posted that pesticides are implicated in declining bee populations. And then I recall that someone posted a story that a Harvard robotics lab has developed robot bees to pollinate plants.[14] And so it goes. I write on my laptop—linked to sophisticated Internet-based and news-gathering technologies—about problems caused by technology that in turn shape my attitudes toward technology, and confront how the most improbable technological solutions seem like the Great Leap Forward to many. Indeed, RoboBees do not even sting, but they have surveillance capability. One immediately senses other technological connections in the make; the RoboBees, intended for one technologically produced problem, immediately offer themselves as the solution to another problem not initially conceived.

Burke saw how technology formed impenetrably dense systems, beckoning onward, but he nonetheless remained committed to numerous forms of symbolic transformation. The comic frame, achieved perhaps best through satire, works aesthetically to reorient attitudes. The aforementioned "Helhaven" essay is so rich as to defy summary, dripping with acidic comments about the gospel of "Total Futuristic Promotion" (20), "the cult of industrial power" (24), and "new needs" (16), which amounts to a "Hypertechnologism" ascendant (19) in which we achieve our happy ending: "an apocalyptic development whereby technology could of itself procure, for a fortunate few, an ultimate technological release from the very distresses with which that very technology now burdens us" (20). Burke continually notes the paradox of paradoxes, that technology itself is the condition of possibility for his vision of the technoapocalypse. Burke would have had a deep appreciation for the stinging ironies of RoboBees.

At this point, however, I want to shift gears. Satire and other forms of aesthetic and terminological transformation, that is, perspectives by incongruity, have their value. Pushing hard on a vocabulary, pushing it past its perfectible limit into new attitudinal territory, retains powerful potential. But there may be reservations about satire as well: Burke himself seems to understand that his "Helhaven" essay, and other of his interventions seem more tragic than comic. I confess to having doubts about the powering focus on the symbolic and, hence, to being less than enthusiastic about its overall potential, even if I enjoy Burke's skill and bitter humor. Still, perhaps the larger lesson here is in the vocabulary that Burke continually reaches for when discussing technology, and not only in the "Helhaven" essay. We should note how that terminology is itself religious, even mystical, which brings us back to Parmenides and Nietzsche. Certainly, Burke himself shows various forms of give-and-take affinity with Nietzsche, having learned well the lesson that cultivating a new relation toward technology's attitudes requires a Nietzschean "revaluation of all values."[15] At the same time, I wonder whether Burke was able to perfect—as far as he might—some of the implications of such an insight. Is Burke's *askesis* best understood as operating within the realm of symbolicity, even if he has a sophisticated understanding of language's grip on the body and emotions? Put differently, if achieving a better comportment toward technology requires fundamental changes in valuation and behavior, why would our focus remain solely on symbolicity?

My suggestion, inspired by some of Debra Hawhee's work on Burke and mysticism, is that there are already in Burke untapped potentials at odds with the dominance elsewhere of his symbolically oriented *askesis*. That is, there are connections to some of the insights given in Parmenides and Nietzsche to which bodily and experiential perspectives, enacted through technique and technology, offer alternatives, including perspectives by incongruity that cannot be fully explicated within the symbolic. Indeed, that itself offers a perspective— the opening of a beyond to language and technology. Still, it can seem as if Burke declines these openings. His *Rhetoric of Religion* perhaps best encapsulates this point for me. In the foreword, Burke admits that religion speaks of God and an original Edenic oneness, with endless varieties of action and passion. Thus, religion forges attitudes proper to religious belief, experience, and behavior—piety in its most spiritual key. Yet he then quickly shifts to the idea that religion is primarily words and, hence, open to terminological analysis. We have to wonder at this shift, for, while this strategy certainly works on contemporary religion and what we call Religions of the Book, there is little here that would apply to what is called traditional religion, which can be described as experiential and ecstatic.[16] Here, we see again the importance of Nietzsche and especially Parmenides, for both of them, albeit differently, perform aspects of traditional religion. Their forms of *askesis* seek what is beyond the word. And, as perhaps Neoplatonists such as Olympiodorus exemplify best, even the turn toward the power of the rational word can take mystical, experiential form—a rationality of the ineffable, we might say.[17]

But again, it is not as if Burke lacks insight into these matters, because he acknowledges that mysticism is a powerful attitude. Hawhee notes that mystic imagery and language suffuse Burke's work, and that he took especial interest in mystics such as Gurdjieff.[18] What Hawhee argues is that the mystic experience centered on the body—an immediate apprehension of the ineffable, of the oneness and infinite connectedness of all the cosmos—remains as a possible component of his *askesis*. For instance, Gurdjieff, Hawhee tells us, reworked ancient forms of dance and body awareness, such as the stop exercise, during which dancers freeze in pose upon command; the exercise is designed to break the automatism of everyday life and movement and, thus, gain the experience-based resources to find new movements, new thoughts (39–40). As Burke argues, there remains profound power in the step from principles to the principle of principles and, hence, an "ultimate order" that both fulfills and transcends the previous order (*Rhetoric* 189). The wrenching of experience via mystic techniques may well contribute to such transcendence within the current order.

The connections here to Parmenides and Nietzsche are profuse, in that both of them also sought forms of *askesis* that interrupted our soporific, daily routines—precisely the routines that mark us as the unknowing masses whom Persephone describes for Parmenides, the ones who are *amēchania*, helpless, lacking not just the *mêtis* that might aid them but also the sense that they are even in need. And what, I think, connects all of these figures—Burke included— is the drive to rouse us from the dangers that stem from this "waking sleep" (Hawhee 41). Thus, inspired by Gurdjieff, Hawhee writes, Burke complains that a ballet audience is too sluggish, making the performance an empty spectacle rather than a transforming experience (43). Like Nietzsche, Burke sees in dancing—that combination of rhythm, melody, and movement—a vital art that can project us beyond language and, in that sense, tap into the mystical (44). And in so doing, it provides nonsymbolic resources and, hence, a potential *askesis*, in the face of mass *amēchania*.

The Way of the Non-*Ding*

In what is considered to be one of Plato's earliest dialogues, the *Euthyphro*, Socrates questions Euthyphro about what holiness or piety is. As the dialogue develops, the conversation turns to the idea that holiness has something to do with proper attention to the gods. At this point, a striking set of correspondences is set up. "Attending to" means the art of working on, crafting, or making something in the right or proper manner. Socrates goes through a list of such arts, including horsemanship, hunting, housebuilding, doctoring, and shipbuilding.

All of these are characterized as "arts" in translation, which can lead to resonance with the notion of *technē*.[19] So, for instance, Socrates will ask, "What is it which the art that serves shipbuilders serves to produce?", to which Euthyphro dutifully responds, "Evidently, Socrates, a ship" (13E). While other dialogues would use the term *technē*, here, perhaps because of the religious context, Plato chooses two other terms: *therapeia* (typically translated as "attending to") and *hypēretikē* (typically translated as "service" or "art"). The willingness here to put skill or art across a large swath of activities *including* the spiritual is striking.

But I think there are a number of interrelated points nestled here that bear upon technology and attitude. What is at stake in characterizing shipbuilding in terms of *hypēretikē* or *therapeia* rather than *technē*? While *technē* highlights both technique and technological artifact, *hypēretikē* and *therapeia* assume technics within an orientation that might best be characterized as ethical. There is care, humility, perhaps even a certain acquiescence that characterizes the relationship between who makes and what is made, who does and what is done to. There is devoutness and deference built into what is still technical activity. What is made or attended to speaks to the activity or has some value, some weight in shaping how things proceed. It is here that we might recall where I started—namely, with Kraftwerk's evocation of the *Überding*. The band characterizes their relationship with their musical instruments as a friendship. We obtain a different tonality in the attitude toward technology here. It is neither mastery nor servitude, although there is a sense of service as care-bound attending-to. The *über* is not a devaluation of the non-*ding*, but rather a marker of deference to the *ding* within the technological relationship. While the technical is primarily characterized in terms of rationalizing efficiency, here we see that other styles of being with technology already exist within technics. Efficiency may well be an attractor—that is, a habitual state toward which the technical gravitates—but *it is not the only attractor*. Jenny Edbauer Rice, who also explores this theme, remarks that the machinic offers not reduction or routinization but "another way of caring for the world" (379). Thus, balance, ecological awareness, gratitude, deference, and care are also possible styles of being with technology.

This is finally one of the deeper lessons we can take from the forms of *askesis* offered by Parmenides, Nietzsche, and Burke. *Askesis* works within the technological to forge other ways of being, including ways of being with technology. In each of these three, a technological attitude toward the body and the world emerges. Technique emerges from this technological attitude. There is a gap. The *Überding* is, I suggest, one way to create an image of this gap. There is an over, an above, a transcendence in the technological for which technique fits us. But it can never close that gap. Because technique always contributes to further technologization, it can never catch up. Technology, then, is an always-incipient way of being toward the world, whose aspects manifest as being capable of something. This is why the capacity for a technological attitude already resides within animals. Technique, then, would be equivalent to styles of *being with* the technological. Techniques and technologies share a transcendent push, with technique emerging as the machining of the human that has sprung a technological attitude.

But to return to a key Parmenidean theme, there is still something troublesome here. What incubation revealed to Parmenides is that there is no escape from the (rational, technical, or other) traps of the world. It is sobering to consider Parmenides's thoughts in relation to the many skeptical arguments emerging today about the possibility even of science to self-correct.[20] The irony of scientific work's arguing science's fallibility is simultaneously delicious and troubling. So, we must wonder whether the insights of Parmenides, Nietzsche, and Burke about finding an *askesis*—a new way of being with the rational, scientific, and technological—have bearing for us. The hope they provide is precisely the counter to a false sense of transcendence. They ask us to confront that helplessness and cultivate via a transformative experience—*itself technic*—certain types of fortitude or—pushing through with Plato—perhaps a different relation to the technic that nevertheless resides within it. Perhaps this amounts to a type of sacralization of technology and material ecology, or a granting of the *über*, which should not be confused with the fantasies of our dominant technoromanticisms. These are naïve in that they indicate a belief in the transcendent promise. But this is not all that technical relations offer, and hence this cannot be the goal that shapes our technical relations. Indeed, this is Plato's lesson about service or attendance. Neither can we turn to forms of separation or escape from the technological that privilege some remaining aspect of the human, the non-*ding*, as if this would provide shielding from the narrowing of efficiency and rationality. The technics of *askesis* do not, of course, provide any answers or tell us what to do; rather, they place us before a different future horizon, being a technical source for establishing a fundamental technicity, within which new attitudes are possible and achievable.

Notes

1. In this essay, I use "technics" to conjoin technologies and techniques in a way that emphasizes their common root in *technē*.

2. We might provisionally define technique as experientially acquired procedures for doing or making within an environment, and technology the externalization, via technique, of the doing or making that in turn transforms our environs and hence also our techniques. The modernist understanding of the nature/culture split emphasizes the rationality and efficiency in technology that overcomes the human; the posthuman understanding emphasizes the dissolution of body-world, human-nonhuman dichotomies for a new hybridity, thereby leaving dislocated, or unsettled, how we might reconceive of what efficiency and rationality might be. I will have occasion to return to this later.

3. One could lay out a similar argument on the artifice/artifact split: artifice requires that one take an artifactual perspective toward the application of the art.

4. Burke's use of "attitude" evolves during the course of his work and is not easily defined. Perhaps its fullest expression is given in *Attitudes Toward History*, in which he defines as the mediating point between symbolic action and nonsymbolic motion (394). I take Burke to mean that an attitude indicates a stance incipient in a situation, where stance includes beliefs, feelings, and motivations as expressed in a context, which includes one's body and one's environs. Technology is precisely attitudinal in that, from this robust conceptualization of situation, it produces a motivational impulse—one oriented toward betterment, onwardness, perfection.

5. It is worth recalling that technology's ties to the religious were quite the topic starting in the late 1990s, with books by Erik Davis, Margaret Wertheim, David F. Noble, and John Horgan; this spiritual dimension may even be returning, if John Durham Peters's recent book on new media is any indication. They demonstrate that technology offers transcendence, mystic immersion, the promise of heaven, and a glimpse of the divine, among other religious orientations.

6. See Mailloux, who is exploring this issue extensively in terms of Jesuit spiritual practices.

7. This point underscores why technologies inevitably provide ways of thinking about the world. Heraclitus famously understood the cosmos in the tension of a strung bow; today, computers are a dominant explanatory mode. Every era has its dominant machinic narratives. As Rothenberg remarks, "the explanatory power of what we construct should not be underestimated" (3). It's at this point we see the power of Heidegger's claim that technology is a form of revealing (see Heidegger, "Question").

8. This word was picked up by Christianity and is still used with regard to meditative and mystical Christian practices; see Patton.

9. See Winkelman—in particular "Introduction to Shamanism and Consciousness"—for the biopsychosocial particulars, including the neuroscience of altered states of consciousness.

10. Neuroscience is demonstrating through numerous studies that meditation does alter the brain. See Davidson and Lutz on the topic of Buddhist meditation and its effects on practitioners. A summary in the popular press of various studies can be found at http://www.huffingtonpost.com/2013/08/05/how-you-can-train-your-mi_n_3688660.html.

11. As Nietzsche writes, "One chooses dialectic only when one has no other means. One knows that one arouses mistrust with it, that it is not very persuasive" (*Twilight* 1.6).

12. Detienne and Vernant present a book-length elaboration of *mêtis* in *Cunning Intelligence in Greek Culture and Society*.

13. This point is contrary to the utopian talk about notions of the Singularity, as proposed by Vinge, Kurzweil, and others.

14. The robot bees have been developed by Harvard's Wyss Institute. They have a splash page announcing their progress with the technology: https://wyss.harvard.edu/technology/autonomous-flying-microrobots-robobees/.

15. This phrase refers to the subtitle of Nietzsche's collection *The Will to Power*, "An Attempt at the Revaluation of All Values," referring to the attempt to revalue cultural values on non-Christian grounds.

16. Hayden provides a book-length elaboration of this argument.

17. Uždavinys argues at length in *Philosophy and Theurgy in Late Antiquity* that the Neoplatonists elevated their belief in rationality to a religious doctrine that required meditative and transcendent techniques to be fully accessed.

18. Burke also read William James's work on mysticism. James's mystic experiments led him to discover empirically the sense of immersive oneness common to all mysticism. He also claimed to have understood Hegel better afterward. See Nicotra.

19. See, for instance, Rothenberg, who interprets the passage as being about *technē* (4).

20. For a small selection of such work, see Stroebe, Postmes, and Spears; Haidt; Greene; Ioannidis; and "Unreliable."

Works Cited

Benson, Bruce Ellis. *Pious Nietzsche: Decadence and Dionysian Faith*. Bloomington: Indiana University Press, 2008. Print.

Brown, James J., Jr. "The Machine That Therefore I Am." *Philosophy & Rhetoric* 47, no. 4 (2014): 494–514. Print.

Burke, Kenneth. *Attitudes Toward History*. 3rd ed. Berkeley: University of California Press, 1984. Print.

———. *Dramatism and Development*. Barre: Clark University Press, 1972. Print.

———. *Permanence and Change: An Anatomy of Purpose*. 3rd ed. Berkeley: University of California Press, 1984. Print.

———. *The Rhetoric of Religion: Studies in Logology*. Berkeley: University of California Press, 1970. Print.

———. "Towards Helhaven: Three Stages of a Vision." *Sewanee Review* 79, no. 1 (1971): 11–25. Print.

———. "Why Satire, with a Plan for Writing One." *Michigan Quarterly Review* 13, no. 4 (1974): 307–37. Print.

Burkert, Walter. "Das Proömium des Parmenides und die 'Katabasis' des Pythagoras." *Phronesis* 14, no. 1 (1969): 1–30. Print.

Cicero. *De Legibus*. Translated by Clinton Walker Keyes. Cambridge, Mass.: Harvard University Press, 1928. Print.

Davidson, Richard J., and Antoine Lutz. "Buddha's Brain: Neuroplasticity and Meditation." *IEEE Signal Processing Magazine*, no. 1 (2008): 176–174. Web. 1 Jan. 2008.

Davis, Erik. *Techgnosis: Myth, Magic, Mysticism in the Age of Information*. New York: Harmony, 1998. Print.

Detienne, Marcel, and Jean-Pierre Vernant. *Cunning Intelligence in Greek Culture and Society*. Translated by Janet Lloyd. Chicago: University of Chicago Press, 1974. Print.

Gemelli Marciano, M. Laura. "Images and Experience: At the Roots of Parmenides' *Aletheia*." *Ancient Philosophy* 28, no. 1 (2008): 21–48. Print.

Greene, Joshua. *Moral Tribes: Emotion, Reason, and the Gap Between Us and Them*. New York: Penguin, 2014. Print.

Haidt, Jonathan. *The Righteous Mind: Why Good People Are Divided by Politics and Religion*. New York: Pantheon, 2012. Print.

Haraway, Donna. *Simians, Cyborgs, and Women: The Reinvention of Nature*. New York: Routledge, 1991. Print.

Hawhee, Debra. *Moving Bodies: Kenneth Burke at the Edges of Language*. Columbia: University of South Carolina Press, 2009. Studies in Rhetoric/Communication. Print.

Hayden, Brian. *Shamans, Sorcerers, and Saints: A Prehistory of Religion*. Washington, DC: Smithsonian Books, 2003. Print.

Heidegger, Martin. *The Question Concerning Technology, and Other Essays*. New York: Harper and Row, 1977. Print.

Hill, Ian. "'The Human Barnyard' and Kenneth Burke's Philosophy of Technology." *KB Journal* 5, no. 2 (2009). Web.

Horgan, John. *Rational Mysticism*. New York: Mariner Books, 2004. Print.

Ioannidis, John. "Why Most Published Research Findings Are False." *PLoS Med* 2, no. 8 (2005). Web.

Kingsley, Peter. *In the Dark Places of Wisdom*. Point Reyes: Golden Sufi Center, 1999. Print.

———. *Reality*. Point Reyes: Golden Sufi Center, 2003. Print.

Kittler, Friedrich A. *Gramophone, Film, Typewriter*. Translated by Geoffrey Winthrop-Young and Michael Wutz. Stanford: Stanford University Press, 2000. Print.

Kraftwerk. *The Man-Machine*. Capitol, 1978. LP.

Kurzweil, Ray. *The Singularity Is Near: When Humans Transcend Biology*. New York: Viking, 2005. Print.

Mailloux, Steven. "Jesuit *Eloquentia Perfecta* and Theotropic Logology." *Studies in Philosophy and Education* 34, no. 4 (2015): 403–12. Print.

McGinn, Robert E. "Nietzsche on Technology." *Journal of the History of Ideas* 41, no. 4 (1980): 679–91. Print.

Mitcham, Carl. *Thinking Through Technology: The Path Between Engineering and Philosophy*. Chicago: University of Chicago Press, 1994. Print.

Nicotra, Jodie. "William James in the Borderlands: Psychedelic Science and the 'Accidental Fences' of Self." *Configurations* 16 (2008): 199–213. Print.

Nietzsche, Friedrich. *The Birth of Tragedy and the Case of Wagner*. Translated by Walter Kaufmann. New York: Vintage, 1967. Print.

———. "On Music and Words." Translated by Walter Kaufmann. *Between Romanticism and Modernism: Four Studies in the Music of the Later Nineteenth Century*, edited by Carl Dahlhaus. Berkeley: University of California Press, 1980, 103–20. Print.

———. *Twilight of the Idols*. Translated by Walter Kaufmann. *The Portable Nietzsche*. New York: Viking, 1968. Print.

———. *The Will to Power*. Translated by Walter Kaufmann and R. J. Hollingdale. New York: Vintage, 1968. Print.

Noble, David F. *The Religion of Technology: The Divinity of Man and the Spirit of Invention*. New York: Penguin, 1999. Print.

Parmenides. *The Texts of Early Greek Philosophy: Part 1*. Edited and translated by Daniel W. Graham. New York: Cambridge University Press, 2010, 203–44. Print.

Patton, Kimberley C. "'A Great and Strange Correction': Intentionality, Locality, and Epiphany in the Category of Dream Incubation." *History of Religions* 43, no. 3 (2004): 194–223. Print.

Peters, John Durham. *The Marvelous Clouds: Toward a Philosophy of Elemental Media*. Chicago: University of Chicago Press, 2015. Print.

Plato. *Euthyphro, Apology, Crito, Phaedo, Phaedrus*. Translated by Harold North Fowler. Cambridge, Mass.: Harvard University Press, 1914. Print.

Price, Andy. "Landmark Productions: Kraftwerk—*The Man Machine*." *MusicTech.net*. Web. 10 Dec. 2014.

Rice, Jenny Edbauer. "Rhetoric's Mechanics: Retooling the Equipment of Writing Production." *College Composition and Communication* 60, no. 2 (2008): 366–87. Print.

Rothenberg, David. *Hand's End: Technology and the Limits of Nature*. Berkeley: University of California Press, 1993. Print.

Stroebe, Wolfgang, Tom Postmes, and Russell Spears. "Scientific Misconduct and the Myth of Self-Correction in Science." *Perspectives on Psychological Science* 7, no. 6 (2012): 670–88. Print.

Thomson, Helen. "You Are Hallucinating Right Now to Make Sense of the World." *New Scientist*. Web. 2 Nov. 2016.

"Unreliable Research: Trouble at the Lab." *Economist*. 19 Oct. 2013. Web.

Ustinova, Yulia. *Caves and the Ancient Greek Mind*. New York: Oxford University Press, 2009. Print.

Uždavinys, Algis. *Philosophy and Theurgy in Late Antiquity*. San Rafael: Sophi Perennis, 2008. Print.

Vinge, Vernor. "The Coming Technological Singularity: How to Survive in the Post-Human Era." *Vision 21: Interdisciplinary Science and Engineering in the Era of Cyberspace*. NASA. Lewis Research Center. SEE N94–27358 07–12, 11–22. http://ntrs.nasa.gov/archive/nasa/casi.ntrs.nasa.gov/19940022855.pdf. Web.

Wertheim, Margaret. *The Pearly Gates of Cyberspace: A History of Space from Dante to the Internet*. New York: W. W. Norton, 1999. Print.

Winkelman, Michael. *Shamanism: A Biopsychosocial Paradigm of Consciousness and Healing*. 2nd ed. Santa Barbara: Praeger, 2010. Print.

II Futures

6

The Uses of Compulsion | Recasting Burke's Technological Psychosis in a Comic Frame

Jodie Nicotra

If the thinly veiled autobiographical protagonist of Burke's short story "The Anaesthetic Revelation of Herone Liddell" was "haunted by ecology," then Burke himself was haunted by technology. Or perhaps it would be more accurate to say that he was "goaded" by technology, given his repeated attempts both to theorize it and uncover some sort of symbolic action that might serve as its corrective. Beginning with "Waste, or The Future of Prosperity," a prescient satirical essay from the late 1920s, the problem that Burke later termed the "technological psychosis" turns up again and again over the course of his career. But his later writings especially reveal what Ian Hill characterizes as "full apocalyptic overtones," an intensifying dread of technologically based environmental destruction that Burke, with comic ambivalence, viewed as the perfection, the logical, entelechial outcome of the rational animal's rationality.

This persistent anxiety about humanity's terrible, inevitable, final goal manifests in Burke's later works as what William H. Rueckert and Angelo Bonadonna describe as a "[relentless attack] on hyper-technologism" (1), expressed as an incessant rehashing of ideas about technology, Burke's "late compulsion to refer back to earlier and other works of his, and to quote himself often" (6). Indeed, Burke himself acknowledged that his thinking about technology took a rather obsessive cast. In one late essay, he describes "fixations about the problems of what I would call either 'technologism' or the 'technological psychosis'" ("Realisms" 105). In another, he writes, "for several years I had been compulsively taking notes on the subject of technological pollution—and I still do compulsively take such notes" ("Why" 72). While he loathed this activity and longed to stop thinking about the issue, "even," he wrote, "to the extent of inattention by dissipation," it continued to nag at him (72). If, as we can glean from reading this account, Burke took to drink (not that he likely needed an excuse) in order to shut off his obsessive attention to technology, the anxiety must have been intense, indeed.

We might find Burke's view of technology through the frame of rejection somewhat surprising for one whose central concept is the "comic frame," the "attitude of attitudes" that promotes an attitude of affirmation, one that says yes to the world rather than rejects it. If satire for Burke functions as a frame of rejection, in the comic "the frame of *acceptance* is uppermost" (*Attitudes* 43). As a number of scholars have noted, this attitude of affirmation is central to our understanding of Burke (see, for example, Carlson, "Gandhi" and "Limitations"; Christiansen and Hansen; Demo; Nicotra). The question here becomes whether and how Burke's concept of the comic can serve as a corrective to his own decided rejection of technology. Specifically, I demonstrate that one can productively read Burke against himself: adapting the very mechanism of compulsion that in Burke's satire functions as a frame of rejection also proves useful as a strategy of amplification and, ultimately, a program for a response to technology that *affirms*, rather than critiques or distances.

What is to be gained from this affirmative program? While Burke's professed resistance to the human technological impulse would seem to position him as a straightforward humanist, his own compulsive thinking about technology combined with his critical perspective help to illuminate the relationship to technology not as instrumental (a humanist view) but as co-constitutive (a posthumanist view). In particular, Burke's satires of technology, which necessitate close attention and amplification of the human-technology relationship, position him as a transitional figure between humanism and posthumanism. Though overtly gloomy about the perceived loss of human control of technology, Burke's concepts of entelechy and compulsion belie a nascent understanding that the "human" as such is only a fantasy, a "normative convention," as Rosi Braidotti puts it (26) that, ontologically, what's referred to as "human" is actually much more complex and relational, co-constituted by and with nonhuman forces that include technology. In other words, though it manifests in his satires as a frame of rejection, Burke's strategy of amplification offers an affirmative program that might be reengineered to embrace the posthuman subject.

The Technological Compulsion

I am but asking that we view [technology] as a kind of "destiny," a fulfillment of peculiarly human aptitudes.
—Kenneth Burke, *Permanence and Change*

While Burke cheerfully affirmed throughout his career that "bodies that learn
language" ("Poem" 263) are inevitably used by their symbols, he consistently
characterized technology as a symbol-guided force and, hence, treated it and
what he viewed as its inevitable by-products—waste, pollution, and nuclear
holocaust—elegiacally. "Man" in Burke's definition is "separated from his natural
condition by instruments of his own making" (*Language* 16); technology is an
irresistible impulse that ends inevitably in death and destruction. Burke's char-
acterization reveals a longing for a human free from the grasp of technology,
though Burke is too realistic to see this as a possibility. Instead, his discussions
about technology are colored by persistent gloom.

As the opening epigraph for this section suggests, technology for Burke is
not simply neutral or passive but has an inbuilt "ultimate direction" (*Permanence*
296), an implicit reference to his appropriation of Aristotle's notion of entelechy,
which is "the notion that each being aims at the perfection natural to its kind"
(*Language* 17). Entelechy for Burke is the "perfection" of language, such that the
establishment of a particular terminology or nomenclature carries within itself
its own "terministic compulsion" or inevitable end (19). Because technology is
inextricable from symbol systems, this entelechial drive is also inherent to technologies. As Burke explains in the afterword to *Permanence and Change*, human
history has involved the turn from an early mythic orientation to a "'perfect'
secular fulfillment in the empirical realm of symbol-guided Technology's
Counter-Nature, as the human race 'progressively' (impulsively and/or compulsively) strives toward imposing its self-portraiture (with corresponding vexa-
tions) upon the realm of non-human Nature" (336).

As the language of impulsivity and compulsion suggests, the fulfillment of the
technological imperative isn't just a passive happenstance of directionality, but
an active *drive*. Enmeshed in Burke's notion of entelechy is this idea of an impetus or compelling force—*something* pushing through the perfection of symbol-
guided technology. "Compulsion," a term that crops up frequently in Burke's
discussions of technology, appears most overtly in this passage from his satirical
essay "Towards Helhaven": "Frankly, I enroll myself among those who take it for

granted that the compulsiveness of man's technologic genius, as compulsively implemented by the vast compulsions of our vast technologic grid, makes for a self-perpetuating cycle quite beyond our ability to adopt any major reforms in our ways of doing things. We are happiest when we can plunge on and on" (61). Burke's language here echoes the central Freudian concept of the repetition compulsion. In *Beyond the Pleasure Principle*, Freud argued that the compulsion to repeat an originary psychic trauma across time and in differing circumstances was perhaps the most fundamental human instinct, albeit one that obviates traditional notions of agency and freedom. Indeed, Freud suggested that the feeling of dread experienced by many who undergo analysis may originate from the creeping realization that control lies in something other than the familiar sense of "I": "What they are afraid of at bottom," Freud writes, "is the emergence of this compulsion with its hint of possession by some 'daemonic' power" (30). Compulsion is enacted not by someone, but by some*thing* else here—perhaps not a demon, but, as Burke's passage above suggests, the locus of the compulsion to "plunge on and on" is indefinably located between the human and the "vast technologic grid."

Indeed, one might see the hapless narrator of David Sedaris's *New Yorker* essay "Stepping Out" as an exemplar of the compulsive relationship to technology that Burke-cum-Freud identifies. The essay charts Sedaris's relationship with his Fitbit, an activity-tracking device that digitally measures the number of steps its wearer takes. "To people like . . . me, people who are obsessive to begin with," Sedaris writes, "the Fitbit is a digital trainer, perpetually egging us on. During the first few weeks that I had it, I'd return to my hotel at the end of the day, and when I discovered that I'd taken a total of, say, twelve thousand steps, I'd go out for another three thousand." His dismayed partner asks, "Why? Why isn't twelve thousand enough?," to which Sedaris replies, "Because my Fitbit thinks I can do better." Soon, the narrator finds himself walking more and more, driven by what he refers to as the "master strapped securely around my left wrist": first 25,000, then 30,000, 45,000, and finally 60,000 steps a day. He writes, "At the end of my first sixty-thousand-step day, I staggered home with my flashlight knowing that I'd advance to sixty-five thousand, and that there will be no end to it until my feet snap off at the ankles. Then it'll just be my jagged bones stabbing into the soft ground."

Sedaris's satirical depiction of the human technological compulsion gone haywire is deeply humanist, a contemporary echo of Burke's helpless human in the grip of technology. But its logic of amplification is also recognizably Burkean, pushing through the implicit affordances of digital trainers to an absurd conclu-sion, a rhetorical strategy that highlights this technology's (negative) possibili-ties. In similar fashion, albeit nonsatirically, the British television series *Black Mirror* amplifies contemporary technological concepts. Each episode in the series examines a specific aspect of the relationship of humans to technology, depicting a near-future world where the aspect is amplified and pushed to its logical end. For instance, the episode "Nosedive" depicts a pastel-colored society in which every human interaction is rated on a five-point scale by the humans involved, and each person metonymically becomes their overall rating. It becomes clearer as the episode progresses that these ratings have a material function: when the main character has a testy interaction at an airport and her personal rating drops, she is literally shut out of certain areas, forced to rent a half-broken-down car, and disinvited from an important social event. Through amplification, the episode thus casts a critical eye on several conflated activities: the significance placed on reputation by ranking of consumer goods, the "like" culture of Facebook and other social media platforms, and the opportunities and privileges afforded those perceived to rank more highly by virtue of race, gender, or class.

Technology and the Postanthropocentric Subject

Rather than the inherently fearful humanist frame described above, we might instead detour through thought that characterizes technology not as a force external to but deeply compelling to humans, but as an inseparable component of the human itself. Interestingly, Burke was directly exposed to such views in a 1978 exchange with Father Walter Ong. Ong had sent Burke a letter in which he enclosed his essay "Technology Outside Us and Inside Us," in which Ong cri-tiques instrumentalist notions of technology as "things 'out there,' in front of us and apart from us, belonging to and affecting the world outside consciousness" (190). Rather, Ong argues, we need to consider how technologies also claim our insides, reorganizing our bodies through habit and reshaping our conscious-ness. Ong points out, for instance, that in learning to play, musicians must in a very material sense give themselves over to their instruments in that, as he writes, they "[appropriate] this machine, make it part of [themselves], [interiorize] it, gather it into the recesses of [their] consciousness" (190). Albeit without the language of interior/exterior, Richard Doyle in *Wetwares* similarly articulates the human-technology relationship as a "grafting" that requires a hospitality of sorts to an inhuman form. Such hospitality, writes Doyle, "relies intensely on forgetting; one must be capable of responding to the new action of a body . . . a capacity linked to a forgetting or an undoing of the old arcs of eye, hand, and memory" (5).[1]

In such an understanding of technology, humans don't *use* technologies so much as they are enticed or thrown into alliances with technologies that necessitate a reorganization of their human bodies and consciousness. Repeated encounters between human and technological objects (including the ecologies with which they come bundled), in the light of purpose and scene, prompt bodily reorganization, in the form of new habits of action and perception, as well as new capacities. We might think of the regular Facebook user, for instance, who starts to filter his experiences through the lens of their potential as written or photographic status updates; or the computer word-processing program habitué who, searching for a physical book on a shelf, finds her fingers reflexively attempting to use the Ctrl-F search function; or the Fitbit user who becomes so accustomed to seeing his daily activity as the blinking dots on the device that he observes, like Sedaris, that "walking twenty-five miles, or even running up the stairs and back, suddenly seemed pointless, since, without the steps being counted and registered, what use were they?" This is more than human "use" of technology: in essence, through repeated interaction with the technology, a new virtual body emerges.

A posthuman perspective views technology not as a force external to the human, but rather as one that's inherent—indeed, in such a view the definition of the human is something technological. In *The Posthuman*, for instance, Braidotti argues that the twin forces of globalized capitalism and contemporary technoscience "[strike] the human at his/her heart and [shift] the parameters that used to define *anthropos*" (57). Postanthropocentric subjectivity is neither liberatory (as technophiles like Kevin Kelly and Ray Kurzweil would have it) nor a cause for nostalgic lamentation (as technophobes like Sven Birkerts and Neil Postman would have it). What distinguishes the postanthropocentric subject, according to Braidotti, is "that it becomes an expanded relational self, engendered by the cumulative effect of all these factors. . . . The relational capacity of the posthuman subject is not confined within our species, but it includes all non-anthropomorphic elements" (60).

To push Braidotti's point beyond contemporary technoscience—what Braidotti calls "the four horsemen of the posthuman apocalypse: nanotechnology, biotechnology, information technology and cognitive science" (59)—one might turn to Gilbert Simondon, André Leroi-Gourhan, and even Ong, all of whom were Burke's contemporaries and theorists of the human-technology relationship. Taking different points of intervention, each of these thinkers argues that technology itself is inextricable from the conception of the human. Leroi-Gourhan's ethnoanthropology, as Bernard Stiegler describes it, is an attempt to theorize how "anthropogenesis [corresponds] point by point . . . to a technogenesis" (45). In *Gesture and Speech*, Leroi-Gourhan argues that the human ancestral evolutionary shift to bipedalism prompted the simultaneous emergence of tool use and language, since walking on two feet meant that one no longer had to catch food with one's face: the mouth was freed for speaking, the hands for tool use. Thus, the human is fundamentally and originally inseparable from technology. Likewise, Simondon argues that humans are perpetually supplemental to machines, that "human reality resides in machines as human actions fixed and crystallized in functioning structures" (5). Such a view conceptualizes humans as standing among the machines like a conductor, a "permanent organizer and . . . living interpreter of the relationships of machines" (4), rather than in a master-slave dynamic or, more relevantly to Burke, as a slave compulsively kowtowing to a technological master. A view of humans as co-constitutive with technology rather than as separate—and helplessly caught in its grip— better enables an amplification that positively, rather than negatively, recasts the technological compulsion—in other words, using the comic frame rather than tragic satire.

Amplifying Compulsion: Tweaking Satire as Affirmative Response to Technology

Perhaps because of his humanist conception of the human-technology relationship and the accompanying anxieties about its inevitable, terrible end, Burke failed to secure a truly satisfactory solution to the problem as he defines it. As Rueckert and Bonadonna write, "Burke never developed a final vision beyond defining humans as bodies that learn language, establishing the link between language (symbol systems) and technology, and determining that technology was our entelechy" (272). Judging from the number of apocalypse narratives that currently populate screen, novel, and newspaper, there are many who would agree with Burke's fatalistic vision about the inevitable, tragically perfect end of humanity's current rationally guided course. But I want to suggest that in Burke's notions of entelechy and irresistible compulsion as expressed in his satirical work, there is a compelling framework for "solving" the problem of technology, ironically one that, in the service of a humanist impulse, performatively embraces more posthumanist tenets.

For Burke, because the human relationship with technology was thoroughly bound up with language, symbolic action was the only adequate response to it. But the question remains as to the *type* of symbolic action. Perhaps because, for Burke, technology is so rooted in the idea of entelechy, both Burke and his critics assume that what is necessary to address the technological psychosis is a symbolic *corrective*, something that could serve to block or put the brakes on technology, lest it continue rolling along to its disastrous finale of environmental apocalypse. James W. Chesebro summarizes the essence of this view in his argument that rhetorical critics must adopt a "decisively skeptical" role when it comes to the symbolic constructions of technology; everything must be put on hold until "dramatists have determined how a symbolic perspective can be used to counter technology" (279).

For some, such a corrective could only be grounded in a humanist impulse, guided by human consciousness. For instance, in their introduction to one of Burke's late essays, Rueckert and Bonadonna write, "What you have at the 'end of the line' is a vast human tragedy which might have been averted if humans had paid heed to their own knowledge of what more and more technology might bring. We are not talking about pollution here, but about foreknowledge and the ability or failure to act on it. The other factor is the failure to foresee the consequences of an action or development" (4). With the language of knowledge and foreknowledge, we might hear in Rueckert and Bonadonna's summary the idea that technology is something external to humans and that implicit faith in human consciousness is what might both protect us from technology's disastrous consequences and preserve human freedom—that is, that somewhere in the understanding of technology lies the potential for controlling it. Indeed, the *modus operandi* of much environmentalist rhetoric is to heighten public awareness about the potential harm of technologically induced environmental issues and thus potentially spur them to action.

Consider, for instance, the range of responses by environmentalists to the problem of climate change, a convergence of factors that Burke would certainly have read as the moment before the apocalypse. Most mainstream environmentalist approaches (a prototypical example being Al Gore's *An Inconvenient*

Truth) rely on maximizing consciousness about climate change, the inherent assumption being that if people only understood or had enough information about the problem, they would change their behavior and their voting strategies. And while there's certainly nothing wrong with attempting to combat misinformation, one only need take a quick survey of contemporary American attitudes to see that even if people have the "correct" information, it doesn't mean they'll automatically change their behavior or their beliefs, thanks to factors like identification. Even a cursory glance at the landscape of current public opinion and legislative wrangling over science and technology suggests that mere awareness of problems (or even the provision of mountains of information and evidence) ultimately matters very little when it comes to decision-making or policy creation about environmental matters such as climate change.

Using tactics that are more recognizably Burkean, T. N. Thompson and A. J. Palmiri recommend that rhetorical critics and dramatists develop what they call a "poetic psychosis" in order to counter counter-nature. Psychotic poets would, they say, "exercise the resources and range of symbols, giving wings to 'agitating thoughts' so that they might enlist the action of others" (280) in countering technology. They write, ominously, that "poetic and comic correctives are needed to counter the rapid mutation of counternature before it reaches the 'end of the line'—its perfection—where the merger of mind and machine will leave no need for a poem" (283). But while fighting psychosis with psychosis seems to be a particularly Burkean approach, ultimately Thompson and Palmieri use these tools in the humanist service of preserving the human from the clutches of technology.

To correct the technological psychosis, Burke himself relied more on satire, a form of amplification, albeit one with an inherent frame of rejection. As he explains in "Archetype and Entelechy," satire can reveal the terminological choices that lead to entelechies, but in a way that provides different possibilities for action: "satire can so change the rules that we have a quite different out. The satirist can set up a situation whereby his text can ironically advocate the very ills that are depressing us—nay more, he can 'perfect' his presentation by a fantastic rationale that calls for *still more* of the maladjustments now besetting us" (133). In "Why Satire?," Burke calls attention to the entelechial function of satire—namely "tracking down possibilities or implications to the point where the result is a kind of Utopia-in-reverse" (75). Burke employed this symbolic strategy of amplification in his earliest satire on technology, "Waste—The Future of Prosperity," in which he recommends that people maximally waste as a strategy

for improving the economy—that is, through amplification, Burke calls attention to the very problem that he hoped ultimately to address. In "Towards
Helhaven," he improves upon this amplification strategy by "recommending" an
action proposed by a certain gentleman who suggested that if a lake has been
polluted, rather than turning backward or countering this action by asking how
to undo or mitigate the destruction, to instead "affirmatively" address the issue
by continuing to pollute the lake maximally, ten times as much—thereby, Burke
writes, either converting it to a new form of energy or "as raw material for some
new kind of poison, usable either as a pesticide or to protect against unwhole-
some political ideas" (61). Burke here demonstrates Martin Heidegger's homeo-
pathically tinged point: "But where danger is, grows / The saving power also"
(Heidegger 14). In other words, one must thoroughly understand and come
close to embracing the thing in order to effectively critique it.

However, satire, as Burke himself explained, operates within an inherent
frame of rejection. Taking Burke's use of satire as a cue, I want to argue for a
form of symbolic action that does not critique, but uses this same strategy of
amplification as a frame of *affirmation*—one that says "yes" rather than "no" to
technology. Such a strategy would rely more on Burke's comic frame. To be clear,
I don't mean affirming technology uncritically, in a neoliberal way that suggests
that technology is good and all solutions should be technological, which ultimately is just another type of humanism. Rather, it's an affirmative theoretical
strategy like the one described by Braidotti: "coming to terms with unprece-
dented changes and transformations of the basic unit of reference for what
counts as human. This affirmative, unprogrammed mutation can help actualize
new concepts, affects, and planetary subject formations" (105). Embracing the
human co-constitution with technology activates new possibilities, concepts,
and programs.

Burke's own concept of technology as irresistible compulsion serves as a
candidate for this idea of amplification or pushing through. In other words, we
might take the final words of the Helhaven essay—"No *negativism*. We want
AFFIRMATION—TOWARDS HELHAVEN" (25)—more seriously than Burke
meant them, perhaps not in a directly material, technological sense, like adding
maximal pollutants to a lake, but in a symbolic sense, whereby we amplify the
concept of compulsion to its logical conclusion, by thinking of technology as a
compulsion over which we have no control. What if we literally could not help
ourselves when it came to technology? That we had to, as Burke says, "perpetually tinker" until we blew up the world or sank ourselves in a horrific miasma of

pollution from which only the few lucky rich could escape? How could we use this very idea of compulsion not as a corrective to technology, but as a way to push it through? If nomenclatures, as Burke argues in "Archetype and Entelechy," are "formative, or creative, in the sense that they affect the nature of our observations, by turning our attention in this direction rather than that" (122), then naming and treating technology compulsively will open up certain possibilities for responding to and shut down others.

As an example of an affirmative approach to a technological problem, we might consider approaches to the problem of climate change that literally treat the Western relationship to oil as an addiction. Rather than setting up a frame of rejection, as do typical environmentalist strategies that rely on raising consciousness, amplifications using the metaphor of oil addiction turn attention affirmatively toward particular types of solutions. Those who adopt the nomenclature of oil as addiction can, to use more traditional rhetorical terminology, argue at the stasis of policy rather than via fact or definition. They bring different sets of questions into play—among them, the question of what the most effective way to treat an addiction is—and hence a different set of active programs. For instance, Larry Lapide, the research director of MIT's Supply Chain Management 2020 initiative, argues that most American supply chains are "addicted to oil." The oil-as-addiction metaphor allows Lapide to move past arguments about whether there is a problem and who caused it to more pragmatic issues like identifying the most oil-heavy aspects of supply chains and encouraging businesses to analyze their own supply chains in order to make themselves less dependent on the fraught resource of oil. Lapide relies on a petroleum-based, Pascal's-wager type of argument, recommending what he calls a "no regrets" risk-management strategy when it comes to oil: "Decrease your supply chain's dependence on oil to make it less vulnerable to price increases and supply chain disruptions."

The Transition Network (often simply called Transition), an organization that aims to respond to the realities of climate change, also strategically embraces our technology compulsion. Transition was designed from the beginning around the concept that Western society is literally addicted to oil. In fact, the subtitle of Rob Hopkins's *The Transition Handbook*—a bible of sorts for those who want to start a "Transition Initiative"—is "From Oil Dependency to Local Resilience." In its pragmatic materials for helping towns and other areas begin what Transition refers to as an "energy descent"—decreasing the towns' dependence on oil—the *Transition Handbook* is grounded in metaphors of addiction.

In *The Transition Handbook*, Hopkins argues that, generally speaking, "the environmental movement has failed to engage people on a large scale in the process of change" (84); the argument uses a model well known to addiction psychology called the transtheoretical change model (TTM). The stages of change, as the TTM model is popularly referred to, identify a number of stages such as precontemplation (the awareness of the need to change), action, and maintenance. Addicts incrementally move through these stages in treating their addiction. According to advocates of this addiction-treatment model, understanding which stage one is in offers opportunities for understanding what might be blocking change or, conversely, what pitfalls one needs to be aware of in the treatment of one's addiction. In applying this model to entities beyond an individual, Transition encourages potential Transition Initiative communities to think of themselves as addicts and, like the supply chains discussed above, apply the model to understand the specific nature of their dependence. As the founder of Transition asserts, "Recognising oil dependence makes it easier to understand why it might be difficult to wean ourselves off our oil habit, while also joining us towards proven strategies from the addictions field that might help us move forward" (87). This is a strategy of affirmation; this attitude toward relationships to oil enables a moving forward rather than a blockage or countering.

While they specifically have to do with oil as an environmental issue, the strategic use of an affirmative program used by Transition and others can be characterized by critical theorist Felix Guattari, who in "The Three Ecologies" argues for a logic that "has affinities with that of the artist, who may be induced to refashion an entire piece of work after the intrusion of some accidental detail, a petty incident which suddenly deflects the project from its initial trajectory, diverting it from what may well have been a clearly formulated vision of its eventual shape. There is a proverb which says that 'the exception proves the rule'; but the exception can also inflect the rule, or even re-create it" (140). Like Burke, Guattari here recommends a program of amplification, albeit one that arises from a frame of affirmation rather than rejection (like Burke's satirical maximal pollution of the lake). Rather than moral censure (a frame of rejection), we should seek out and respond to practices that affirmatively remake the world.

Such practices of affirmative remaking seem especially critical now, in the age of the Anthropocene or, as Anna Tsing wryly calls it, "the time of the big human mess" ("Catachresis" 2). Indeed, scientific publicity about the Anthropocene has generated above all else the desire for corrective responses described above: to put on the brakes, to slow down human-caused technology-based destruction. In any case, more than mourning industrial human destructiveness, living in the era requires looking for affirmative ways to inhabit it: new models, new practices, new rhetorics, and generally what Braidotti refers to as the "new conceptual creativity" necessary to "undertake a leap forward into the complexities and paradoxes of our times" (54). Indeed, Donna J. Haraway's concept of the "Chthulucene" and Tsing's notion of "unintentional design" provide models for the affirmative remaking of the "technological psychosis" in the Anthropocene era. Tsing provides examples of "feral biologies" or "disturbance ecologies"— nonhuman creatures that are responding in unexpected ways to disturbed and damaged environments, like coral inhabiting the Great Pacific Garbage Patch or the fungi that repopulate the human remnants of Denmark's brown coal fields ("AURA's"). And Haraway invites us to imagine ways that we can "stay with the trouble" of this era as "mortal critters entwined in myriad unfinished configurations of places, times, matters, meanings" (1).

Burke ultimately could only view his own tragic, humanist vision of technology through a frame of rejection. However, a combination of his notions of compulsion and the comic frame offers a more productive way to reimagine human possibilities for life amid chaos. While his writings specifically having to do with technology may not themselves offer a productive response to technology, considered in a broader context—especially in terms of technology's enmeshment with language and all that it entails in a Burkean sense—I find that they offer a way of thinking around the back door of the technological psychosis, but one that says "yes" rather than "no." We may not be able to "unfuck the world," as one of my graduate students puts it (Brown), but using our imaginative resources, we "bodies that learn language" can invent ways to strategically and joyfully affirm it.

Note

1. Though Ong's description of technology is provocative, he pulls his punch before he reaches the logical conclusion of his argument, which is that, essentially, humans and technology are co-constitutive. In the essay, Ong maintains that even though technology is inside us, it is still also subject to our conscious control, thus affording us mastery over the environment. In his letter to Ong, Burke calls Ong out (if deferentially) about his argumentative sleight of hand, maintaining instead that the inhuman power of technology is too great for the symbol-using, symbol-misused animal to master. What he calls his "troubled attitude" in relation to Ong's essay is the fact that, because of technology's unintended

by-products—especially pollution and waste—and how much more powerful it makes individuals beyond their naked human bodies, no social or political system, no matter how full of self-consciousness, has been developed that can control "the astounding powers of technology" (Burke, Letter). "Hence," Burke writes, "mankind has a tiger by the tail."

Works Cited

Braidotti, Rosi. *The Posthuman.* Cambridge, Mass.: Polity Press, 2013. Print.

Brown, Cody. "Fragments Shored Against Ruin: Towards a Fatalist Ecopoetics." University of Idaho Graduate English Conference. 9 Apr. 2016. Moscow, Idaho.

Burke, Kenneth. "The Anaesthetic Revelation of Herone Liddell." *The Complete White Oxen and Other Stories.* Berkeley: University of California Press, 1968, 255–310. Print.

———. "Archetype and Entelechy." *On Human,* 121–38. Print.

———. *Attitudes Toward History.* 3rd ed. Berkeley: University of California Press, 1984. Print.

———. *Language as Symbolic Action.* Berkeley: University of California Press, 1966. Print.

———. Letter to Walter Ong. 9 Sep. 1978. Walter Ong Papers. St. Louis University.

———. *On Human Nature: A Gathering While Everything Flows, 1967–1984.* Edited by William H. Rueckert and Angelo Bonadonna. Berkeley: University of California, 2003. Print.

———. *Permanence and Change: An Anatomy of Purpose.* 3rd ed. Berkeley: University of California Press, 1984. Print.

———. "Poem." *The Legacy of Kenneth Burke,* edited by Herbert W. Simons and Trevor Melia. Madison: University of Wisconsin Press, 1989. Print.

———. "Realisms, Occidental Style." *On Human,* 96–119.

———. "Towards Helhaven: Three Stages of a Vision." *Sewanee Review* 79, no. 1 (1971): 11–25. Print.

———. "Waste—the Future of Prosperity." *New Republic* 63 (1930): 228–31. Print.

———. "Why Satire, with a Plan for Writing One." *On Human,* 66–95.

Carlson, A. Cheree. "Gandhi and the Comic Frame: 'Ad Bellum Purificandum.'" *Quarterly Journal of Speech* 72, no. 4 (1986): 446–55. Print.

———. "Limitations on the Comic Frame: Some Witty American Women of the Nineteenth Century." *Quarterly Journal of Speech* 74, no. 3 (1988): 310–22. Print.

Chesebro, James W., editor. *Extensions of the Burkeian System.* Tuscaloosa: University of Alabama Press, 1993. Print.

Christiansen, Adrienne E., and Jeremy J. Hanson. "Comedy as Cure for Tragedy: Act Up and the Rhetoric of AIDS." *Quarterly Journal of Speech* 82, no. 2 (1996): 157–70. Print.

Demo, Anne Theresa. "The Guerilla Girls' Comic Politics of Subversion." *Women's Studies in Communication* 23, no. 2 (2000): 133–56. Print.

Doyle, Richard. *Wetwares: Experiments in Postvital Living.* Minneapolis: University of Minnesota Press, 2003. Print.

Freud, Sigmund. *Beyond the Pleasure Principle.* London: Bantam, 1959. Print.

Guattari, Felix. "The Three Ecologies." Translated by Chris Turner. *new formations* 8 (1989). Web. 30 May 2014.

Haraway, Donna J. *Staying with the Trouble: Making Kin in the Chthulucene.* Durham: Duke University Press, 2016. Print.

Heidegger, Martin. *The Question Concerning Technology, and Other Essays.* Translated by William Lovitt. New York: Harper and Row, 1977. Print.

Hill, Ian. "'The Human Barnyard' and Kenneth Burke's Philosophy of Technology." *KB Journal* 5, no. 2 (2009). Web. 3 Jan. 2014.

Hopkins, Rob. *The Transition Handbook: From Oil Dependency to Local Resilience.* White River Junction: Chelsea Green, 2008. Print.

Lapide, Larry. "Is Your Supply Chain Addicted to Oil?" *Supply Chain Management Review* 11, no. 1 (2007). Web. 6 Jun. 2014.

Leroi-Gourhan, André. *Gesture and Speech.* 1964. Translated by Anna Bostock Berger. Cambridge, Mass.: MIT Press, 1993. Print.

Nicotra, Jodie. "Dancing Attitudes in Wartime: Kenneth Burke and General Semantics." *Rhetoric Society Quarterly* 39, no. 4 (2009): 331–52. Print.

"Nosedive." *Black Mirror*, season 3, episode 1, Netflix, 21 Oct. 2016.

Ong, Walter. "Technology Inside Us and Outside Us." *Faith and Contexts: Selected Essays and Studies, 1952–1991*, edited by Thomas J. Farrell and Paul A. Soukup, vol. 1. Atlanta: Scholars, 1992, 189–208. Print.

Rueckert, William H., and Angelo Bonadonna. "Introduction." Burke, *On Human*, 1–10.

Sedaris, David. "Stepping Out." *New Yorker.* 30 Jun. 2014. Web.

Simondon, Gilbert. *On the Mode of Existence of Mechanical Objects.* Paris: Aubier, Editions Montaigne, 1958. Print.

Stiegler, Bernard. *Technics and Time, 1: The Fault of Epimetheus.* Translated by Richard Beardsworth and George Collins. Stanford: Stanford University Press, 1998. Print.

Thompson, T. N., and A. J. Palmieri. "Attitudes Toward Counternature (with Notes on Nurturing a Poetic Psychosis)." Chesebro, 269–83.

Tsing, Anna. "AURA's Openings: Unintentional Design in the Anthropocene." AURA (Aarhus University Research on the Anthropocene) Working Papers, vol. 1. Web. 43–52.

———. "Catachresis for the Anthropocene: Three Papers on Productive Misplacements." AURA (Aarhus University Research on the Anthropocene) Working Papers, vol. 2–10. Web.

7

A Predestination for the Posthumanistic

Steven B. Katz and Nathaniel A. Rivers

Predestination has a history unlikely to resonate with the contemporary project of posthumanism. Understood theologically, predestination denotes the preordination of salvation specifically and of life events generally. Etymologically, the word "predestination" connotes choosing, standing, binding, fastening, and establishing, each of which always occurs ahead of time. Whereas predestination reflects a transcendent determinism, posthumanism represents a commitment to immanent contingency. What *is* emerges across the complex interplay of things, particularly in the posthumanism that emerges from complexity theory. One is that which is already settled; the other is that which is never settled. In the hands of Kenneth Burke, however, predestination becomes more complicated than that.

Almost as an aside in the closing pages of *The Rhetoric of Religion*, which attends, in part, to the power of words to prescribe, Burke performs a dazzling counter-reading of predestination. Rejecting the idea that predestination resides solely in the hands of a transcendent being, Burke imagines instead an immanent predestination wherein what happens in any given moment has been predestined by "the sum total of things" (271). Whenever we try mightily to accomplish anything, our choices rub up against the choices of others. The "combination that results" from this encounter between choices, Burke writes, "is beyond the choice of anyone. Try as you will, the resultant combination will arise 'inevitably'" (272). This double-voiced "inevitably" suggests to us the same sorts of tensions one finds at work in the posthuman, which marks the particular place of the human in relation to "the sum total of things," including bodies, technologies, and environment.

Burke's predestination is complex enough, we argue here, to prove useful in articulating the posthuman. In fact, and in forecasting a distinction important to this chapter, we may find predestination better suited to addressing technology—which we see as folded into posthumanism—than entelechy, the usual Burkean approach to issues of human invention(s) meant to encompass potentiality or agency not demonstrable through scientific causality or the study of mere matter, including technology. This chapter works with Burkean predestination not as a nascent posthumanism—for we will make no claim for Burke as a posthumanist—but instead as possible equipment for posthumanistic living from a thinker who moved around in the milieu of symbols, brains, bodies, and machines, and speculated on their nature and relationships from a multitude of perspectives. Burke's concerns are posthumanism's concerns. Certainly, Burke draws different boundaries, but we show that he does so across the same landscape. In fact, rather than ask what Burke might say about posthumanism, thereby reducing it to the subject of his thoughts, we seek instead from Burke equipment to tell our own posthumanistic stories that privilege combinations.

We begin with a discussion of posthumanism before we describe our particular, Burkean predestination: in some ways, predestination arrives in already-posthuman terms. After articulating posthumanism and predestination, we analyze the documentary film *Fixed* as a form of posthumanistic storytelling that tackles posthumanistic issues of technology in terms of disability studies, body augmentation, and genetic engineering. Expressing the posthuman condition through the lens—the "terministic screen"—of *Fixed*, we show that predestination is a more useful term for importing Burke's concept of rhetoric—rooted as it seems to be in modernist conceptions of the human body—into the project of posthumanism. Key to this particular posthumanistic story is whether we understand the human as it emerges in the film as a function of the tension between the emergent predestination that Burke describes, or the more self-motivated entelechy that he describes. Predestination accounts for a multiplicity of combinations within posthuman ecologies that are never collectively resolved but some of which might appear to reach an end in physical or symbolic action.

Which Posthumanism?

As with Burke, so with posthumanism. Neither is stable and settled, and so much hinges on the point of departure and the attitude of the journey. How does one move from a given starting point? As we risk cherry-picking Burke, we risk charting a course through posthumanism(s) that is too selective and reductive. So we will start by disclosing, as much as possible, our mutual affinity for posthumanism and what we pragmatically take from it. We acknowledge, to begin with, posthumanism's questioning posture toward the human. We acknowledge, as well and relatedly, the blurring of human/nonhuman binaries as well as of the distinctions between individual and environment, inside and outside. These two virtues emerge most strongly in the areas of new materialism. This is the hook for us (the jingle stuck in our heads) and for a Burkean re/approach/ment with the posthumanistic.

Rosi Braidotti's treatment of the posthuman proves uniquely suited to our purposes, inasmuch as she clearly distinguishes posthumanism from other humanisms: traditional humanism, antihumanism, and transhumanism. Her forceful articulation of the posthuman is the perfect launching pad for exploring Burke and posthumanism: "Humanism's restricted notion of what counts as the human is one of the keys to understand how we got to a post-human turn at all" (16). At stake for posthumanism is the definition of and the work of defining the human. It is not so much a rejection of the human (i.e., antihumanism), nor is it an escape from the human (i.e., transhumanism). Posthumanism is a way of unpacking and keeping fluid any definition of the human. Not simply a recent phenomenon wrought by new technologies, posthumanism is a theoretical wedge that we can use to open up and explore the black box that is considered "human." As Judith M. Halberstam and Ira Livingston write in *Posthuman Bodies*, "The posthuman does not necessitate the obsolescence of the human; it does not represent an evolution or devolution of the human. Rather it participates in re-distributions of difference and identity" (10). Posthumanism is, in fact, nothing new; the questions ex/posed by it are quite old. As Cary Wolfe puts it, "posthumanism in my sense isn't posthuman at all—in the sense of being 'after' our embodiment has been transcended—but is only posthuman*ist*, in the sense that it opposes the fantasies of disembodiment and autonomy, inherited from humanism itself" (vx). Posthumanist, or posthumanistic, is how we prefer to refer to this "-ism."

Braidotti offers one of the best junctures for an articulation of rhetoric and posthumanism because she describes the posthumanistic, in part, through our contemporary technological moment. While the "post" in posthumanism, as Wolfe argues, does not so much signal a temporal *after* so much as a dogged pursuit *after*, posthumanistic concerns do emerge in our particular moment in which technology allows for a seemingly infinite range of mediations: bodily, environmental, and informational (both in terms of artificial intelligence and genetic manipulation). "A posthuman theory of the subject emerges, therefore," Braidotti writes, "as an empirical project that aims at experimenting with what contemporary, bio-technologically mediated bodies are capable of doing" (61). The possibility of mediation that emerges through technology presses upon our thinking about being and beings (see Hayles). Our understanding of ourselves as humans—our humanism(s)—comes to resonate with the increasing and pragmatic ways that we can augment ourselves and our environments. Once these realms become recognized as contingent, the terms of our humanity will change. What is compelling, then—in terms of rhetoric generally and Burke specifically—is Braidotti's emphasis on experimenting, which we instinctively read through both Burke's "equipment for living" as well as his call for ambiguity as a resource, both of which are made "manifest" in his book *The Rhetoric of Religion*.

It is also in Braidotti's careful articulation of posthumanism that we feel the pull of various new materialisms, an emerging assemblage of people and ideas that can be broadly understood as posthumanistic. Braidotti writes, "The emphasis on *immanence* [in posthumanism] allows us to respect the bond of mutual dependence between bodies and technological others, while avoiding the contempt for the flesh and the trans-humanist fantasy of escape from the finite materiality of the enfleshed self" (90–91; emphasis added). First, Braidotti's emphasis on immanence stands in contrast to the transcendence implicit in transhumanism. This mutual dependence forestalls our escape to some realm beyond bodies and places. Second, new materialism is a particularly helpful way of thinking through the immanence of the posthuman. Such mutual dependence and immanence also entail rethinking our relation with what we normally consider the nonhuman. And immanence is a mark of predestination as well. Braidotti's use of "mediation" is likewise a way to think through new materialism and predestination. Mediation is the other key term here, and it entails a fully intense form of interaction. Mediation is the point of complex mergers across so-called human/nonhuman boundaries, although even these boundaries themselves are an achievement (see Barad). As Braidotti writes, "This is the 'milieu' of the human/non-human continuum and it needs to be explored as an open experiment, not as a foregone moral conclusion about allegedly universal values or qualities" (80). Therefore, finally, we will see that Braidotti's work helps us think through the relationship between and among people and things such that not only people but things as well are reconceptualized as differentiated yet mutually related, which will lead to social and ethical reconsiderations of both the nature of community and of matter (49).

In their extended introduction to their edited collection *New Materialisms: Ontology, Agency, and Politics*, Diana Coole and Samantha Frost map their "own interests in changing conceptions of material reality and causality and the significance of corporeality, which we see as crucial for a materialist theory of politics or agency" (2). As we will see, both causality and the body are central concerns in Burke's work. Furthermore, Coole and Frost continue, new materialism—and thus, for us, posthumanism—is "post- rather than anti-Cartesian. It attempts to avoid the duality or dialectical reconciliation by espousing a monological account of emergent, generative material being" (8). We will see the importance of this not so much in the conception of material human bodies as in their relations and predestinations, in which dialectical thinking may play a more significant role for Burke. By incorporating natural sciences with new materialism, which is also problematic for Burke, Coole and Frost point out that new materialism

> envisages considerably more indeterminacy and complex choreography of matter than early modern technology and practice allowed, thus reinforcing new materialist views that the whole edifice of modern ontology regarding notions of change, causality, agency, time, and space needs rethinking. . . . New materialist ontologies are abandoning the terminology of matter as inert substance subject to predictable causal forces. According to the new materialisms, if everything is material inasmuch as it is composed of physiochemical processes, nothing is reducible to such processes. . . . For materiality is always something more than "mere" matter: an excess, force, vitality, relationality, or difference that renders matter active, self-creative, productive, unpredictable. . . . [It is] a materiality that materializes, evincing immanent modes of self-transformation that compel us to think of causation in far more complex terms: to recognize that phenomena are caught in a multitude of interlocking systems and forces and to consider anew the location and nature of capacities for agency. (9)

This argument might raise many red flags for Burke. Indeed, one can imagine his rather spirited response that might equal the searing satire he achieved in "Towards Helhaven." Yet few have undertaken a study of what new materialism and posthumanism might mean for the continued relevancy or irrelevancy of

Burke's dramatistic rhetorical theory, in which the pentad is central. More than the well-known inventional and thus misunderstood heuristic of act, agent, agency, scene, and purpose, Burke's pentad is intended to capture the play of human motives as distinct from mere causation (*Grammar*), and therefore seems to suggest that human intention and will are the prime movers of meaningful events. Such intentional and self-contained motives seem very much to depend on human agency and language as the sources of "motion" for symbolic action. And, for Burke, such human agency would seem to require the notion of the human body—in contradistinction to the physical environment and other inanimate machines and objects—as the locus of motivation and self-determination. For Burke, the human body moves in symbols in an entelechy that is willed and fulfilled in—but also beyond—the material world (see Katz).

The relationships that Braidotti and others describe can be thought through in terms of Burkean predestination. This, again, does not mean that Burke would (or needs to) go along with this; it means only that the ambiguity of his predestination becomes a rhetorical resource. Ambiguity, for Burke, is the symbolic space in which humans are pentadically free to create and to will. But again, it is our intention to shift the focus from Burke's discussion of pentad and motives (as expressed in *A Grammar of Motives*) to his discussion of predestination in *The Rhetoric of Religion*, recontextualizing with his own work the concept and scope of "agency" in relation to new materialism and the posthuman. Posthumanistic science, so recognized, thus perhaps presents a particularly difficult barrier to Burkean rhetoric because it represents a "blurring of clear boundaries or distinctions between bodies, objects, and contexts . . . evident in the myriad biotechnological and digital technological developments that are changing the landscape of living" (Coole and Frost 16). Just how much of a barrier it proves to be will depend upon the place that we carve out for Burke's own blurry reading of predestination.

Burke's Blurry Predestination

The glimmer we get of predestination in Burke is of a rhetorical inclination that acknowledges the role—the relational role—that people *and* things have in shaping the emergence of what is to come. Entelechy pushes inward that which is in between and among. Predestination interrupts entelechy. But this is not immediately obvious. It appears that, for Burke, predestination is made possible by symbol systems, regardless of whether those systems be in the logic of language (meaning), or by philosophical systems such as those of Heidegger or Hegel, or by theological systems. At the center of them all for Burke is logology, the study of words. Burke asserts that words, while physical themselves—as sound, as text, as metaphor, and as physiological and psychological processes— exceed or transcend their material referents as symbols, in relation to which language must nevertheless be "discounted" for—as Burke states, significantly— that material reality still remains more powerful (*Religion* 18). It is in this excess of linguistic meaning that different logical (or logological) relations are created and reside, including theological as well as dramatistic systems of predestination.

Interestingly—and problematically, given our discussion of posthumanism—there is an implicit duality in Burke's theory. In fact, Burke makes this implicit duality explicit when he states, "a duality of realm is implicit in our definition of man as the symbol-using animal. Man's animality is in the realm of sheer matter, sheer motion. But his 'symbolicity' adds a dimension of action not reducible to the non-symbolic—for by its very nature as symbolic it cannot be identical with the non-symbolic" (16). Furthermore, and surprisingly, Burke refers to "'nature' in the sense of the less-than-symbolic, or the other-than-symbolic, *the sort of things there would be if all symbol-using animals and their symbol using systems were obliterated*" (18; emphasis added). That is, in *The Rhetoric of Religion*, one of the early moves that Burke makes is—analogically and yet in an ad hoc manner—to erase "nature" and other potentially symbol-using entities, including other animals that use some form of communication and that we therefore presume have not only "language" but also some form of agency. Here, Burke's focus on the symbolic reveals his operation within the human/nonhuman dichotomy, which posthumanism challenges at every level. This is in line with Burke's "Definition of Man," which is far from posthumanistic in its insistence on the distinction in kind between man and animal, as well as the separation from nature created by human technology and its objects.

There's clearly, then, a through line from this definition of the human to Burke's logology in *The Rhetoric of Religion*. At the end of his analysis of Augustine's *Confessions*, Burke states the central problem that does seem to be the antithesis of a posthumanistic perspective:

> A logological calculus inclines to look rather for the *continuities* in the
> development from Western theology to the order of modern accountancy

and modern technology, particularly since such a calculus helps keep us ever on the alert to spot the role of *symbolism* as the motivating genius of secular enterprise. Otherwise, our world looks too purely "pragmatic," whereas its recently much-accelerated dreams of unlimited power and interplanetary empire become so hard to distinguish from paranoia—we should do best to watch for purely symbolic motivations here, despite the undeniable material reality and might of the technologist's engines. (170)

This would seem to confirm the view that Burke's rhetoric is modernist, or postmodernist at best. But Burke is clever if not also prescient. This "despite" does much work here: it begins to bracket off almost entirely what posthumanism takes as its chief area of concern: the discontinuities and unexpected connections that arise when "symbolic action" is placed in the more totalizing context of the physical universe, "the undeniable material reality" in which our machines also live. Burke brackets this for good reason. His critical gaze is focused upon "strict behaviorists, cyberneticists and the like" (188), who are no kin to posthumanism either, which is, again, neither anti- nor transhumanist (Braidotti). Behaviorists can be seen as antihumanist in their claims to be able to boil the human down to simple stimulus-response mechanisms; in cyberneticists of a certain stripe, the human is seen as that which can (or should) be escaped or replaced. However, we say that, despite all that, Burke at the end of *The Rhetoric of Religion* literally "comes to his senses": "Logologically, our design involved an approach to all terminology from the standpoint of Order as an empirical problem, compounded of non-verbal materials which the symbol using animal variously manipulates and to which he is variously related by purposive actions conceived in terms of his symbol-systems" (268).

Yes, having built a logological apparatus—the primary argument of *The Rhetoric of Religion*—that almost romantically (but rationally rather than mystically) places divine love and its empirical equivalent, "human will," as its fairytale center, Burke peeps through the still-open portals of his symbolic house and observes that there is still a world out there that the terms in his *Studies in Logology* (the book's subtitle) continuously point to in their tautology. Divine love and human will are "predestined from the start," says Burke, "yet our way of ranging among them give them a way of unfolding in 'history'" (268). Referencing Heidegger's discussion of our being in the world, Burke adds that "each of us is 'thrown' (*geworfen*) into some one set of situations rather than another" (268). Thus, Burke appears here not (only) to refer to the logological—metaphysical or theological—realms that he has spent a book and, really, a career, (re)build-ing. For at the end of his analysis of the book of Genesis, he asks, "with language being what it is, is not 'predestination' the sum total of things, even from a purely empirical point of view? . . . How can we discuss human eventualities in the large without arriving at some such doctrine? Men may try as hard as they can to shape the future as they would have it to be, but insofar as each person's desires fit and conflict with other people's, the particular combination that results is beyond the choice of anyone. Try as you will, the resultant combination will arise 'inevitably'" (271–72).

It's not just the variety of peoples and their pentadic postures that Burke is alluding to, but also "the purely empirical point of view"—the world of objects and things—and our questionable ability to fully know and represent them (see Barad)—and even the material nature of language itself—a theme that reap-pears in different forms in Burke's work (see Hawhee)—that Burke has come back to here at the end of his soliloquy on the rhetoric of religion: "This is ines-capably true, since it is tautologically true, no matter how earnestly people try to make it seem otherwise. The future will inevitably be what the particular com-bination of all men's efforts and counter-efforts and virtues and vices, along with the nature of things in general, inevitably add up to" (272). And this includes language in which "'predestination' itself is a 'god-term'" like other god-terms, no more, no less; furthermore, "it has its empirical analogue. For however the world is made, that's how language is made" (272).

But, as Burke liked to say in his letters, wait a minute! These few, penulti-mate, unexpected sentences toward the end of *The Rhetoric of Religion* are not only a surprise, but also seeds of a postambiguity. By declaring the empirical an analogue, did Burke just slip back indoors—that is, move away from "the unde-niable material reality" to an entelechy of/in logology, thereby slamming the terministic door of his house of symbols shut to predestination and/as post-humanistic immanence? This is an important question for those who wonder whether we can ever know the world in a way that is unmediated by conscious-ness—who avoid being empirically "naïve" but then reanimate duality—and think we "can't get outside" of our language: hence, Burke uses the phrase "empirical *analogue*." Or did the very last sentence—with its seeming acknowl-edgment that language is "made" of "the world"—leave the door open for other material elements to emerge or immerge? What did Burke believe, and what did he mean? Ultimately, none of us can answer these questions, and perhaps these are not the right questions to ask. For the difference, and the appearance of a new materialistic tendency, a posthumanistic gesture in *The Rhetoric of Religion* that allows for uncertainty and "less-than" or "other-than" symbolism is crucially important in our assessment of Burke's rhetoric and relevance. Entelechy is only mentioned twice in *The Rhetoric of Religion*. For Burke—at least in that book—it is clearly a weaker form of predestination. He states,

> The Aristotelian concept of the "entelechy," as an aim contained within the entity, is essentially a biological analogy. It is the title for the fact that the seed "implicitly contains" a future conforming to its nature, if the external conditions necessary to such unfolding and fulfillment occur in the right order. Were you to think of the circumstances and the seed together, as composing a single process, then the locus of the entelechy could be thought of as residing not just in the nature of the seed, but *in the ground of the process as a whole*. (246–47)

"The ground of the process as a whole"?

Regardless of epistemological issues that might be raised, as we've explored in our discussion of posthumanism, the grounds of a posthumanistic rhetoric would expand beyond the locus of entelechy and in the end, at least in principle, include elements made not only of logology or by the human animal alone, but also other blurry, nonsymbolic objects, entities, and technologies that enter every situation and speech act. So, too, with predestination. Here, perhaps, is the pre-posthumanistic Burke. Here is an opening in what appeared through most of *The Rhetoric of Religion* to be a prohibitive, purely logological formulation. What is admitted into rhetorical theory—curtly, perhaps begrudgingly, in these later, tentative, and uncertain statements—is the recognition of the potential importance of the physical world and its other objects, entities, and machines among which we live. Rather than destroying Burke's dramatistic formulation, it is our belief that allowing all things, forces, and ecologies into pentadic realities strengthens them because they facilitate the recognition, study, and use of new materialisms as integral in rhetorical situations, even as—and because—new materialisms themselves and their effects on the human are not wholly predictable.

Ironically, then, one result of recognizing posthumanism and including new materialisms in Burke's rhetorical theory is a rather higher degree of what we might call "the indeterminacy of motive"—even in predestination—which culminates not only in uncertainty in the social realm of human affairs but also in the physical realm of material being and, thus, necessitates multiple, complementary perspectives (Barad)—or terministic screens—about both the social and the material. Posthumanism calls on rhetoric to consider *all* potential actants, objects, and grounds that could be involved in any rhetorical action. Burke's later analysis in *The Rhetoric of Religion* thus begins to fulfill Braidotti's requirement that posthumanism call into question notions of what counts as a "partial form of accountability, based on a strong sense of collectivity, relationality and hence community building" (49).

The payoff for moving from entelechy (i.e., drive) to predestination (i.e., emergence) is another way to articulate rhetoric and posthumanism. A posthumanistic rhetoric is the combination of the "willing" of people and things with that willing itself (and here we perhaps work against much of Burke's original dualistic formulation) being both "predestined" and at least somewhat indeterminate. Entelechy is the drive to perfection—to complete and flawless fulfillment, to purity, to hierarchy—whereas predestination accounts for imperfection, impiety, and emergence, which are well known to contemporary rhetoric. As Braidotti summarizes, "The important aspect of nomadic vitalism is that it is neither organicist nor essentialist, but pragmatic and immanent. In other words, vital materialism does not assume an overarching concept of life, just practices and flows of becoming, complex assemblages and heterogeneous relations" (171). We could have willed an act, which is where or why we wager rhetoric remains in the mix, or might in fact constitute the mix. For rhetoric is the condition of possibility in complex systems in which neither the sources nor the outcome is established a priori, and in which the whole process that constitutes the complex system may be in flux. This flux is both rhetoric, as the realm of the probable, and the crafting of the possible within a barrage of other objects and forces (willed or caused). Choices are made, intentions are had, purposes are expressed, but what emerges may never be reducible to them. Entelechy, too, imagines or projects too much an independent technology that is separated from the human, which Burke certainly pushes against in more than a few places in trying to account for motive. For entelechy to be the prima facie cause of the unfolding of technology seems to suggest that technology or tools are independent entities, something that posthumanism resists as well. The imbricated quality of human and nonhuman relations means any entelechy never belongs to any one thing. Entelechy certainly seems to emerge, but it is only ever predestined.

In short, entelechy isn't complex enough in its ability to trace the enfolding of persons, things, and technologies to the extent that such distinctions cease to matter or at least become inessential or metaphysical. Entelechial black boxes emerge. Predestination—Burke's predestination—wants to be unpacked, to be traced in and by means of a risky account. But entelechy is simply marked; it is a "force" that explains what happens, an explanatory approach that someone like Bruno Latour rejects methodologically. In addition to the methodological distinctions, there are some attitudinal distinctions to be teased out or to be had if we had time to address Burke's entelechy, about which we would be decidedly pessimistic.

The Fix Is In

Who wants to have a jetpack to fly around in? . . . Who wants to have special robot legs that make you go faster? . . . Who would want another eye? . . . What do you think humans need to improve them?
—*Fixed*

Given the sheer number and force of material and conceptual changes that posthumanistic sciences and technologies pose to a traditional Burkean, we turn to the documentary *Fixed: The Science/Fiction of Human Enhancement*, an independent film released by New Day Films in 2013 and directed and produced by Regan Pretlow Bashear. This one-hour film can be divided into three almost equally timed parts: (dis)ablism, (trans)humanism, and genetic (de)selection. We are drawn to *Fixed* not only because of its multilayered presentation of scientific and technological advances and their implications for a variety of actors, but also because of the film's rich ambiguity, which, as Burke knew of ambiguity generally, can be an opening and a resource for rhetoric (*Grammar*). The documentary's various foci strongly suggest that the posthuman can be productively engaged with an intensified version of Burke's predestination. The world explored by *Fixed* is portrayed as the complex outcome of many things. The New Day website describes the film this way:

Through a dynamic mix of verité, dance, archival and interview footage, *Fixed* challenges notions of normal, the body and what it means fundamentally to be human in the 21st century. . . . Key concepts include:

ableism; access; adaptive technology; bioethics; biomechatronics; bionics; brain-machine interfaces; differing frameworks of understanding disability; disability arts and culture; emerging human enhancement technologies; exoskeletons; eugenics; genetics; health; humans 2.0; innovation; neuro-enhancement; performance enhancing drugs/smart drugs; prenatal screening; science; technology; transhumanism and more. (New)

Beyond the juxtaposition of "chic" or bewildering topics and the number of new fields involved, *Fixed* plays its subject—including "the questioning of technology," which it can't finally answer—in numerous ways. To begin, its subtitle, *The Science/Fiction of Human Enhancement*, with its deconstructivist slash, creates ambiguity where one might expect more certainty. What is science in the film, and what is fiction? What is meant by "science fiction"? Are these terms opposed, or do they chiastically stand in for one another? Thus, "what is real" and "how it is to be read" are immediately put in symbolic flux, static motion. What, if anything, is "fixed," and how, given the several senses of the word "fixed"?

This perhaps "posthuman questioning" is simultaneously carried out visually through the medium. The title, subtitle, and credits are set against imagery and sounds at the beginning and end of the film. The sounds include an original soundtrack by Chris Brierley: a high alto solo voice half-hums and soars over a soft classical guitar track of tragic arpeggios. The image seen is of a presumably "disabled" woman in a wheelchair that has been outfitted for exploring the ocean (with its "other" life forms) through which the woman slowly bobs and floats and flows forward. The imagery is at once fantastical and liberating, but also and oddly almost wholly based on ramshackle technology: a regular wheelchair with two fans and small motors in the back for propulsion, transparent fins on each side (along with her own arms, which she uses to help her swim) for stability and steering, and a diver's mask through which she repeatedly breathes and blows bubbles. Shifts in the fan motors are audible as the wheelchair slightly changes direction or speed. But the woman herself is not in a diver's suit; rather, she wears a loose, everyday dress that fills and wafts around her in the water. The imagery is one of found freedom, despite disability, in a strange new world, but perhaps also vulnerability, because it is temporary, exploratory, and offers no real protection beyond short-term basic survival. But, then, perhaps none is needed in this imaginary/real world; perhaps that is the point.

The questions asked when the documentary starts about how viewers would like to modify or add onto their bodies—answered first by shots of a seemingly ordinary family eating hamburgers and fries at one of a thousand nondescript malls—are questions that are apparently asked throughout the film. We say "apparently" because viewers only get answers—albeit at fairly regular intervals—through scenes of a variety of individuals or small groups of people from all ages and walks of life. These answers present one set of unified and technologically affirmative positions in the film. The aesthetics of original music and breathtaking choreography performed by disabled or "extra-enabled" dancers—on prosthetic stilts, in wheelchairs, with Down syndrome—create another demographically affirmative and moving set.

However, most of the answers by the public are zany. Someone who loves photography would like an eye that's a camera. Another person would like fingers that could produce pasta from their tips. A surfboarder expresses a desire for ninja abilities. Women say they would like to be able to fly, or teleport, or have an extra (i.e., hidden) arm to swat unwanted advances away. The answers given in the film are quotidian, funny, cute, and meant to be so, meant to give us another, more general or ordinary perspective about the very serious subject of the film without undermining it. These zany yet positive statements balance the more critical or negative clips of interviews and debates by disability scholars, ethicists, and writers who question or critique the practical, financial, social, political, or historical wisdom of augmenting or selecting our bodies; but the zany, positive statements also and ironically "balance" the optimism of high-end technomedical innovators and biolabs already working on "the front lines" with a disabled woman with limited mobility whose official job title is "Test Pilot" and whom futurists in the film call a "first adopter." The counterpoint of such optimism is the technological evolution proclaimed by transhumanists as the destiny of humanity.

In this carefully crafted, multidimensional film, what is actually, aesthetically, and structurally undercut—yet preserved and becomes *immanent* in the film—are highly divergent questions, assumptions, images, positions—assenting and dissenting opinions, arguments, debates—about the relations and effects among humans and machines. Most of these questions and assumptions seem to imply individual agency—the type of *potentia* (i.e., power, and future possibility) that Burke would consider applicable to the human animal and, thus, to be subject to entelechy. Most presume control and self-determination, even as the film layers in questions and doubts about the advantages, effectiveness, cost, history, and potential effects on humans as individuals, as civilization, and as a species. Thus, whether the subject is ableism, transhumanism, or genetic selection, *Fixed* as a whole calls into question not only (the loss of) control of technologies and the unreliability of human decision-making and dangers of human choices, but also larger issues of individual free will and collective self-determination. Not all of the interviewees or television celebrities are disabled, but they all admit to being integrated to varying degrees with technology—a posthumanistic condition—rather than separate from it. For example, even a less technologically minded personage in the film admits to using drugs to enhance performance, and another to loving her motorized wheelchair even though it breaks down all the time.

This is not entelechy, then, in the narrow sense, although the motive toward determinism still very much exists in these speakers, in this film, and in us. Rather, the message and effect of the film seem much closer to the cusp of Burke's emerging communal cup of posthumanistic predestination in *The Rhetoric of Religion*: the ongoing ambiguity of the relation of the human and nonhuman, and the emergence of the "non-location" (more dispersed in posthumanism) of agency and thus will and power. Throughout the film, the "pervasiveness" of disability at the levels of the personal, social, and species is stressed and shown in images, music, dance, historical facts, and statistical figures provided by various interviewees. According to Sylvia Yee, an attorney and disability rights advocate, approximately "62 million Americans have some level of basic functional impairment . . . and then within that of course there are people with multiple impairments" (*Fixed*). In another segment of the film, Yee states that "anyone can join the ranks of people with disability at any time, and as we age, are likely to, even if it is only temporarily." The film thus illuminates the "everydayness" of the human-machine continuum, in which we are all both disabled and enabled, even as the filmmakers question the relation of both; but the machines, too, are already disabled in a positive negation of the condition of being human, just as Burke says that language, although transcendent, is a positive negation *in relation to its material referents* (*Religion* 18).

What we see and otherwise feel in screening *Fixed*, then, is a unique disclosure of posthumanism by technologies and techniques at play in an already-complicated understanding of the human. The debates in the film concerning (dis)ability, (trans)humanism, and genetic (de)selection—and the problems, progress, and promise of the technologies involved—are joined by dis/extraenabled interviewees who wholly embrace research and development and even transhumanism (viewers are shown shocking and even moving examples of how unbelievably far medical technology has progressed), as well as by dis/extraenabled interviewees who question if not outright reject the problems, progress, and promise of these technologies. Most notable in this latter group is Dr. Gregor Wolbring, a biochemist who rejects both transhumanism and the concept of the "disabled," arguing that society's species-specific norms must change. He says that he is not "impaired" but "a variation," and as much as Hugh Herr, whose legs were amputated after a hiking accident on Mt. Washington, prefers his artificial legs, Gregor prefers to crawl: "crawling is in, walking is out" (*Fixed*). Gregor and others in this latter group fear the possible spiraling competition among (trans)humans to have the best body, to be the most improved human being; the inevitable breakdowns of technology that we already experience when it is further integrated with flesh; and the instantiation of the unsolved social issues of race, poverty, access, and affordability to health care will only intensify and be further institutionalized by high-end medicine and technology.

Fixed, then, is not just an argument for or against technology, but also about what it means to be human in a posthuman age. Herr, an engineer who designs his own legs, believes it's what's between his ears that defines the human. As the film moves from person to person, from machine to machine, and from medical intervention to technological revolution, the humans at the center of the documentary seem less and less "fixed," and so the very idea of being fixed is brought in for serious questioning, or "discounting," to use Burke's term for the basic premise of logology. And so the documentary, too, appeals to us in the same way that Burke and posthumanism do: via the productive move away from fixity toward immanence. That is what connects them, and this link poses an important question: if not fixed, then *how formed?* The lack of fixity doesn't necessarily indicate the lack of form. It doesn't mean that things don't take shape, that they aren't settled or decided. But the questions of just who decides and how decisions happen make the lack of fixity a chiefly rhetorical concern, as the present collection posits.

And so Burke, our link to rhetoric, comes in. There's a rhetorical mechanism at work here: how do certain bodies, certain forms, emerge complexly? There is the general movement in the film from disablism to ableism to "extra ableism," from correcting to augmenting to enhancing the human body, from coping to equaling to surpassing the ordinary body via transhumanism. But that is too simple, too entelechial, too self-centered. For there is a necessary social and ethical dimension in posthumanism that must, too, arise out of the indeterminacies if humans, whatever they are, are to survive. Near the end of the film, Yee presents a rather stark choice between utopian ideals—namely, social equality and justice versus technological equality and justice, both of which are undercut by questions of practicality, cultural preference, past political action (e.g., euthanasia and exterminations), social inaction, and by questions of whether humans are able to control their own destiny as individuals or a species, with or without technology. Neither choice is the correct one. And so what emerges in the film are not only issues about disabled or unenabled or enabled or extraenabled humans and their relationship with technology, but also issues of social undecidability in the face of the "collective" need for decision-making and "communities" that include people, objects, buildings, and machines. As Braidotti explains, "the critical posthuman subject with an eco-philosophy of multiple belongings [is] a relational subject constituted in and by multiplicity, that is to say a subject that works across differences and is also internally differentiated, but still grounded and accountable" (49).

Fixed works with and against itself in moving away from entelechy toward predestination. Given all the widely and wildly differing opinions held—some totally opposed—as well as the inventions and interventions of technologies not even conceived of yet, the outcome of the many debates can only be partially foreseen and is hardly at all under human control. It is not only binary ratios that reduce human action to dualities of inner and outer, body and environment, human and machine that posthumanism seeks to transcend, but also the consequential action of objects—the emergent effects of the direct interface of a human brain and computers that already and really exist. One of the "rhetorical functions" of *Fixed*, then, is to point out and perform a central problem in our notion of communal living, of rhetoric, and perhaps even our mutual survival (see Morton): the unresolved and seemingly unresolvable interactions of humans and machine-things. *Fixed* confirms the multiple differentiations—of terms, conditions, people, positions, machines, and things—but also raises issues that remain when the film ends and the shock and awe wear off—namely, how we regard (or don't regard) and treat each other and our already-damaged world through increasingly complex and crucial social and ethical decisions (such as in ableism, transhumanism, and genetic selection) when the criteria, variables, and answers are not knowable (see Braidotti 49).

What *Fixed* does, from the menu screen forward, is overwhelm the viewer with images of technology folded around and into human beings: a wheelchair under water, synthetic legs, corneal implants, a mind-computer interface, and menus of already-possible genetic modifications. Folded into all of this as a compelling caveat are people in various levels of opting in and opting out as well as a host of qualifications and complications. The film frames a certain type of posthumanistic conversation, not just a conversation *about* posthumanism but a posthumanist conversation. As Wolfe writes, "posthumanism in my sense isn't posthuman at all—in the sense of being 'after' our embodiment has been transcended—but is only posthuman*ist*, in the sense that it opposes the fantasies of disembodiment and autonomy, inherited from humanism itself" (vx). There is only the hint of disembodiment in *Fixed*—although it is strongly implied by the most ardent transhumanists who speak in the film—but the embodied interviews, for which there is no narrator, are only part of the film, which is visually rich and layered with voices that aren't usually in harmony. *Fixed* performs convergences in our current posthumanistic moment, which can frequently and not always incorrectly be understood as transhuman (Braidotti), as posthumanism is in fact far more emergent and distributed than it first appears.

It is in the complexity and polyvocality of the film that predestination does more than entelechy in coming to terms with posthumanism. In short, there is not a drive here so much as a convergence without a source or independent cause(s), either external or internal. As Burke himself concedes, predestination accounts for the "particular combination of persons and things, only an infinitesimal fraction of which will express our particular wills except insofar as we happen to have willed what will be" (*Religion* 272). Read speculatively, there is something productively posthuman*ist* here, provided we casuistically stretch it somewhat further beyond even the entelechy that Burke grants technology, to imagine that the will of things is likewise exceeded.

Fixed doesn't catalyze posthumanism but is itself already a function of a posthuman*ist* way of thinking through the human. Braidotti explains that "the posthuman predicament enforces the necessity to think again and to think harder about the status of the human, the importance of recasting subjectivity accordingly, and the need to invent forms of ethical relations, norms and values worthy of the complexity of our times" (186). A reconsideration of Burke's concept of predestination as contained in *The Rhetoric of Religion* and applied and exercised by us in our analysis of the film *Fixed* may render Burke's theories of rhetoric, including pentadic ones, to be relevant to posthumanism insofar as they can include both human and nonhuman elements, objects, ecologies, and such as agential in the world in which we find ourselves today, and thereby describe the Anthropocene.

Fixed is here a posthuman*ist* story. It is a parable designed to address a (newly) recurrent situation, an emergent reality, which we call posthumanism. Our reading of *The Rhetoric of Religion* is also a posthumanistic one. Posthumanism isn't (or doesn't propose) a certain type of human being. It is a posture, an attitude, in the face of the very question of the human. It's a mode of telling the human story. Predestination is equipment for telling such stories. What other posthuman*ist* stories can we tell, and how can "non-fixed" predestination amplify such equipment for posthuman living?

Works Cited

Barad, Karen. *Meeting the Universe Halfway: Quantum Physics and the Entanglement of Matter and Meaning*. Durham: Duke University Press, 2007. Print.

Braidotti, Rosi. *The Posthuman*. Cambridge, Mass.: Polity Press, 2013. Print.

Burke, Kenneth. *A Grammar of Motives*. Berkeley: University of California Press, 1950. Print.

———. *The Rhetoric of Religion: Studies in Logology*. Berkeley: University of California Press, 1970. Print.

———. "Towards Helhaven: Three Stages of a Vision." *Sewanee Review* 79, no. 1 (1971): 11–25. Print.

Coole, Diana, and Samantha Frost. "Introducing New Materialisms." *New Materialisms: Ontology, Agency, and Politics*, edited by Diana Coole and Samantha Frost. Durham: Duke University Press, 2010, 1–43. Print.

Fixed: The Science/Fiction of Human Enhancement. Directed by Regan Pretlow Bashear. New Day Films, 2013. DVD.

Halberstam, Judith M., and Ira Livingston, editors. *Posthuman Bodies*. Bloomington: Indiana University Press, 1995. Print.

Hawhee, Debra. *Moving Bodies: Kenneth Burke at the Edges of Language*. Columbia: University of South Carolina Press, 2009. Studies in Rhetoric/Communication. Print.

Hayles, N. Katherine. *How We Became Posthuman*. Chicago: University of Chicago Press, 1999. Print.

Katz, Steven B. "Burke's New Body? The Problem of Virtual Material, and Motive, in Object Oriented Philosophy." "Rhetoric as Equipment for Living," edited by Kris Rutten, Dries Vrijders, and Ronald Soetaert, special issue, *KB Journal* 11, no. 1 (2015). Web.

Latour, Bruno. *Reassembling the Social: An Introduction to Actor-Network-Theory*. Oxford: Oxford University Press, 2005. Print.

Morton, Timothy. *Hyperobjects: Philosophy and Ecology After the End of the World.* Minneapolis: University of Minnesota Press, 2013. Print.

New Films. "Fixed: The Science/Fiction of Human Enhancement." *New Day Films.* Web. https://www.newday.com/film/fixed.

Wolfe, Cary. *What Is Posthumanism?* Minneapolis: University of Minnesota Press, 2009. Posthumanities 8. Print.

8

Emergent Mattering | Building Rhetorical Ethics at the Limits of the Human

Julie Jung and Kellie Sharp-Hoskins

Who, after all, decrees what we shall call a separate event? Why must I call crops one thing and sunlight something essentially different, particularly when I have so much evidence to indicate that one can *become* the other?
—Kenneth Burke, *Permanence and Change*

By some accounts of the interdisciplinary relationship between rhetoric and posthumanism, the focus on the future emphasized by the latter participates in a well-established trajectory of rhetoric (see, for example, Hawk; Muckelbauer and Hawhee; Rickert). Indeed, rhetoric itself is a future-thinking enterprise, the art of anticipating future contexts and building effective arguments for them. The oft-cited renaissance figure of the open hand representing rhetoric suggests that it is a field open to invention, connection, change. Thus, although much rhetorical activity centers on description, explanation, and analysis (ostensibly focused on extant arguments), this activity serves the project of the future, motivated by building the future itself. From this perspective, posthumanist thinking acts as rhetorical invention par excellence, expanding its scope and loci, epitomizing its ethics. As Cary Wolfe explains, posthumanism names "a historical development that points to the necessity of new theoretical paradigms" (xvi). Its relational ontologies, for example, displace the centrality of the Western autonomous human subject and thus require different ways of understanding relations and ethics. For Rosi Braidotti, such an understanding—what she terms a "sustainable ethics for non-unitary subjects"—"rests on an enlarged sense of inter-connection between self and others, including the non-human or 'earth' others, by removing the obstacle of self-centered individualism on the one hand and the barriers of negativity on the other" (190). Yet posthumanism also recognizes that such theories are themselves "open both to question and to what is to come" (Badmington 10). Posthumanist thinking, then, in recognizing and contesting boundaries while remaining open to other possible futures, energizes the open hand of rhetoric, multiplying its connections and propelling it toward new inventions.

This invention/multiplication is particularly salient in scholarship in new materialist theory, a category of posthumanist inquiry that examines constitutive relations of discourse and matter for purposes of "return[ing] to the most fundamental questions about the nature of matter and the place of embodied humans within a material world" (Coole and Frost 4).[1] Such a return demands a rethinking of matter as something other than a "massive, opaque plentitude"; rather, new materialists argue that matter is "indeterminate, constantly forming and reforming in unexpected ways" (10). In short, matter *becomes*, with "becoming" conceived as "the opening up of events into an unknown future" (Gries 37), a process in which any given thing, better thought of as a multiplicity, "changes in nature as it expands its connections" (Deleuze and Guattari, qtd. in Gries 31). Accordingly, a new materialist approach to rhetoric both attends to objects and sees those objects anew as dynamic matter participating actively in the world's becoming.

While the future-oriented focus of becoming remains important in both posthumanist and rhetoric studies, such a focus can discount the significance of *mattering*—that is, how matter comes to matter, for whom, and why. In this chapter, we attend to mattering in order to develop a new materialist rhetorical methodology capable of sponsoring interventions in present worlds such that more-just worlds become possible. To do so, we posit that mattering is a rhetorical phenomenon, one in which a materialized object embodies a conferral of value, and, by virtue of having value, enacts the capacity to effect change. To investigate this phenomenon and further explore the value of making a distinction between "becoming" and "mattering," we turn to Karen Barad's concept of "agential cut" and demonstrate its affordances in the scene of scholarship in feminist technoscience. Importantly, this demonstration enables us to foreground the politics of *differential* mattering—namely, how and why objects come to matter differently—and thus the need to tarry with these differences rather than bypass them completely in the heady rush to see them becoming otherwise. We then explain how our methodology, which we term "emergent mattering," attends to histories of mattering and asymmetries of value for the purposes of bringing into being interventions that confer value differently. We specifically examine how this framework hinges on Kenneth Burke's articulation of irony, which, as we explain below, can both recognize consubstantiality and intervene in practices of knowing. When brought into conversation with Barad's work, Burkean irony enables us to theorize emergent mattering as a politics and ethics of radical interdependency.

As a note on our own research method, we use this chapter itself both to argue for a methodology of emergent mattering *and* to perform it, which requires extensive review of and work with transdisciplinary texts adequate to confer value *differently*. In other words, we aim to make apparent how our argument emerges and matters in relation to a range of scholarship that examines the dynamics of differential mattering. It is precisely this relationality that grounds our argument that scholarly orientations participate interdependently to make some knowledges to the exclusion of others and, thus, that new materialist rhetoricians are ethically obligated to investigate our selected methodologies and foci of inquiry as temporarily determinate objects interacting with, changing, and being changed by others. Given our own ethical and political commitments, we have selected to interact here with transdisciplinary texts that examine issues of gender, race, and colonialism, thereby working to expand the circumference of what matters in posthumanist and Burkean rhetorics.

Methodological Objects

To make a distinction between becoming and mattering—and, further, to study the effects of its having been made—is to wage a confrontation with time. Specifically, the distinction calls on us to wrestle with new materialism's spatio-temporal paradox and its implications for rhetoric. In her discussion of the differences between linear, sequential "clock time" and the "timescapes of network society," in which "information—conceived as flow—converges toward simultaneity with no past or future" and "duration . . . is eradicated . . . in favor of an eternal present" (30), Gries captures this paradox well. Clarifying her use of the term "constant," she writes: "*Constant* refers to the fact that 'now' is not a static moment in time but rather is a 'now' always undergoing a process of transformation" (54n9). Gries's clarification points to the limits of language in the intellectual space of simultaneity: shared meaning that makes understanding possible simultaneously, and ironically, undermines a writer's efforts to communicate what she intends.

Beyond the sentence level, at the level of methodology, rhetoric scholars also find ourselves struggling to develop complex frameworks capable of attending to the doubleness of "now," temporarily identifying an object of inquiry in the present that is in the unpredictable process of becoming something *else*. The issue, as we see it, is one of selection. In the complex space of simultaneity, scholars must make selections about which "chronotopic layer of activity" (43) deserves our attention. Gries begins her inquiry, for example, with the selection of an Obama campaign image that went viral, underwent multiple transformations, connected diverse elements in unpredictable ways, and effected various types of change. To select an object of inquiry like the Obama image is to enact what Barad terms an "agential cut," whereby some apparatus, such as a methodology, makes a distinction between—and therefore renders *temporarily* determinate—the object of observation. Apparatuses, Barad explains, "*are the material conditions of possibility and impossibility of mattering;* they enact what matters and what is excluded from mattering. Apparatuses enact agential cuts that produce determinate boundaries and properties of 'entities' within phenomena . . . It is only through specific agential intra-actions that the boundaries and properties of 'components' of phenomena become meaningful" (*Meeting* 148).

Gries's selected methodology—a new materialist approach to visual rhetorics—makes the Obama campaign image intelligible as a knowable rhetorical entity *worth knowing about,* while some other flow of information, one that perhaps did not go viral and undergo such obvious transformation, was excluded from mattering. Of course, such distinctions between subjects and objects in scholarly research projects emerge from intra-actions through which certain theories, epistemological assumptions, and other systems of value come to matter. The methodological selections we make, then, are not freely chosen, but neither are we freed of responsibility for choosing them, as the objects they select help some worlds unfold and not others. At issue here, then, is something more complex than accounting for our situatedness as researchers. As Barad argues,

> The point is not simply to put the observer or knower back in the world (as if the world were a container and we needed merely to acknowledge our situatedness in it) but to understand and take account of the fact that we too are part of the world's differential becoming. And furthermore, the point is not merely that knowledge practices have material consequences but that *practices of knowing are specific material engagements that participate*

in (re)configuring the world. Which practices we enact matter—in both senses of the world. Making knowledge is . . . about making worlds. (*Meeting* 91)

In the remainder of this chapter, we examine existing methodologies of mattering that align with this Baradian ontoepistemology in order to develop and demonstrate the affordances of a theory of emergent mattering. As we do so, we understand "mattering" as involving the study of how an object's materialization, its intelligibility as determinate matter, functions rhetorically in two key ways: (1) it articulates a *prior* system of value—namely, the object's existence evidences the beliefs and commitments of both those who made it and those who study it—and (2) it enacts a selection—specifically, a "chronotopic layer of activity" (Gries 43)—that reconfigures the world.

A Brief Case Study: Making the IUD Matter

An exemplary study of mattering as we conceptualize it is Chikako Takeshita's *The Global Biopolitics of the IUD*, which deploys a feminist technoscientific methodology to examine how the IUD has historically materialized in conjunction with different constructions of its implicated user and corresponding modes of governance—namely, the sometimes centralized yet more often than not dispersed techniques of power that manage real users' bodies. Takeshita uses the term "biopolitical script" to describe the entangled co-constitution of these three elements (i.e., technology, user, and mode of governance), and it is through such scripts, she argues, that specific material realities become intelligible as both possible and good.

For example, in one of her early chapters, Takeshita focuses on the IUD's development in the 1960s, examining how the IUD materialized as a "technological solution to what was widely viewed as a population problem" (31). Specifically, she explains how the IUD was configured as a geopolitically appropriate technology, one capable of quelling the perceived threat of overly fertile women in the global South who could not be trusted to regulate their own fertility. This configuration was co-constituted with neo-Malthusian population policies that relied on colonial tropes of Western supremacy and non-Western primitivism such that the mass insertion of IUDs among women in the global South emerged as a justifiable approach to fertility control. As Takeshita explains,

"Rather than considering fertility control as a complex social practice involving individuals, families, communities, and the state, [Population Council chairman Dr. Alan E. Guttmacher's] vision for reducing population size privileged the consecutive insertions of a device in machine-like bodies," a type of "gynecological Taylorism" that reduced the complex lives of women in the global South to a standard uterus that, once colonized, could help ensure world order (34). The design of early IUDs materializes this colonizing mindset: developers' speculation that it was necessary to "[fill] up" the uterus (46) in order to prevent pregnancy generated designs that aimed to "occup[y] the uterus in some ideal way" (44). When IUDs failed, "developers . . . often explained that the uterus was rejecting the insertion of the foreign body. Sometimes they described expulsions as the ring 'escaping' the uterus. . . . However, scientists more commonly attributed the expulsion problem to the act of an 'angry uterus' that was 'sending a message' by contracting itself and expelling the device" (50).

As a methodology for the study of mattering, Takeshita's biopolitical script makes apparent how a materialized object embodies a conferral of value and effects changes that correlate with that value. In the case of this "Population" script, co-constitutive relations among *implicated users* (imagined by developers and population policy-makers as the standardized uteruses of excessively fertile women in the global South), *technology* (an object that occupies the uterus and has a low failure rate because individual women do not need to be trusted to manage it), and *modes of governance* (neocolonial mindsets, eugenics, and the "problem" of overpopulation) render certain types of practices (mass insertion of IUDs) intelligible as both possible and good. It is precisely this intelligibility, which authorizes practices that affect real users' bodies, that signals a key onto-epistemological shift: from an object's becoming to its mattering.

Of course, the IUD, like all matter, is also (and simultaneously) in the process of becoming, "through its constant production through time and of space" (Gries 24). And focusing on this becoming can reveal how its "potential to alter reality and reassemble collective life is constantly materializing via [its] multiple and distributed encounters" (32). A methodology that is centered on becoming would thus multiply possible futures by destabilizing our imagination of the present, revealing its contingency, indeterminacy, and constant emergence. Takeshita's methodology, on the other hand, makes a cut that renders the IUD temporarily *determinate.* In so doing, it not only corroborates the importance of studying matter as a consequential force but also discloses *how the IUD has come to matter* and, furthermore, *makes it matter differently.* Following Takeshita's book-length study, for example, the IUD can no longer signify as a neutral object or medical device, but neither is it only in the process of becoming. Rather, Takeshita's methodology articulates a particular shape and ethos of the global biopolitics of the IUD, which reveals their implication in colonialism, capitalism, and eugenics. Her "cut," her "specific material engagements[,] . . . participate[s] in (re)configuring the world" (Barad, *Meeting* 91) by reconfiguring what matters to us as researchers.

In short, we take Takeshita's methodology as exemplary for new materialist rhetorical work because it enacts a particular selection in order to intervene in matter's becoming, performing Barad's claim that "we too are part of the world's differential becoming" (91). Taking cues from Takeshita, we argue that rhetoricians interested in progressive futures must work to *recognize* matter's becoming and build theories and methodologies that intervene in this becoming by calling into relief not only the fact of matter's emergence but also *how* it emerges, *how* it materializes, *how* it matters. Only then, we contend, can we contribute to its mattering (differently).

Burkean Irony and Mattering Differently

Mattering differently poses problems for the emergent-minded rhetorician who, in the words of Gries, "perceives reality as change, as mobility" (29), for we are proposing a temporal—even if temporary—perspective that is grounded in determinacy. It is this seeming paradox that induces us to turn to the work of Burke, who articulates a conceptualization of irony that embraces contradictions for the purposes of helping humans become more pliant thinkers. Given the new materialist framework within which we're working, and especially its attendant focus on ontological becoming, it might seem an odd move for us to turn to Burkean irony, which plays a key role in enacting Burke's epistemology of "perspectival knowledge" (Tell 41). Edward Schiappa, for example, argues that Burke's four master tropes "function in *all* discourse as an irreplaceable means of making sense of 'reality'" (404). Hans Kellner likewise emphasizes the epistemological and discursive (and, therefore, human-centric) nature of Burke's master tropes when he argues that together they constitute "a system, indeed *the* system, by which the mind comes to grasp the world conceptually in language" (17). And Burke's own description of synecdoche as the "'*representation*' of certain material conditions" (*Grammar* 507; emphasis added) similarly suggests that the epistemological focus of his tropology is ill suited to posthumanist inquiry.

We argue, however, that Burke's unlikeliness as a candidate for theorizing a new materialist rhetorical methodology actually sponsors interventions in emergent matterings otherwise unthinkable. More than supplying a handy heuristic, Burke's concept of irony intercedes in practices of knowing, shifting our attention from the known to the emergence of knowing and the split that constitutes such a difference. This shift does not concern itself with *only* knowing, however, since Burke's complex tropology, like Barad's agential realism, theorizes the inseparability of epistemology and ontology. As Jeffrey W. Murray explains, Burke's "primary concern with [the tropes is] not with their purely figurative usage, but with their role in the discovery and description of 'the truth.' . . . Truth is, for Burke, a rhetorical product as much as a rhetorical precursor. Hence, the tropes function not only *epistemologically* in the discovery of truth, but also *ontologically* in the very constitution of truth. Burke's subsequent discussion of metaphor, metonymy, synecdoche, and irony illustrates how each trope functions *dramatistically* to make, and to make known, the world" (22). That Burkean tropology might offer a theory of rhetorical ontology is further suggested in the holism of Burke's poetic orientation, which sees "the universe as a *Making* rather than as a *Made*" (*Permanence* 260). Burke selects this orientation over a mechanistic one that views the universe as a composite of autonomous elements, an orientation that "lacks the symphonic quality whereby the notes of coexistent melodies can at the same time both proclaim their individual identity and function as parts in a whole" (249). Unlike a mechanistic orientation, Burke's poetic orientation does recognize parts as contributing to some whole, a "larger process" in which they all participate (260).

In "Four Master Tropes," Burke further explicates this relation between whole and part via his conceptualization of irony as an emergent property of contributory parts: "Irony arises when one tries, by the interaction of terms upon one another, to produce a *development* which uses all the terms. Hence, from the standpoint of this total form (this 'perspective of perspectives'), none of the participating 'sub-perspectives' can be treated as either precisely right or precisely wrong. They are all voices, or personalities, or positions, integrally affecting one another" (*Grammar* 512). Because all the subcertainties constitute "successive positions or moments in a single process" (*Rhetoric* 187), each is "neither true nor false, but *contributory*" (*Grammar* 513). It is this contributory integration that implicates each subcertainty in the fulfillment of the principle that unites them: each is accountable for the actions and attitudes the principle authorizes. As Burke explains, "Where a part is implicated in the whole, any given selection from the whole may be discussible as either the cause or the result of the rest" (*Permanence* 259). The shared accountability constitutive of Burkean irony thus works to reconfigure the violence of scapegoating into the vulnerability of interdependency.[2] This is why Burke describes dialectical irony as "humbling," for it "is based upon a sense of fundamental kinship with the enemy, as one *needs* him, is *indebted* to him, is not merely outside him as an observer but contains him *within*, being consubstantial with him" (*Grammar* 514).

We argue that Burkean irony's capacity to recognize consubstantiality points to its potential as a new materialist rhetorical methodology that takes as given the inseparability of matter and meaning, yet also acknowledges its own role in making distinctions that constitute some matterings to the exclusion of others.[3] To make this argument, we begin by explaining in more detail the function of irony in Burkean tropology, paying particular attention to how the material excesses made possible by metonymic reduction produce a resistance that, when recognized as such, suggests possibilities for mattering otherwise.

Key to Burkean irony is the interaction between metonymy and synecdoche. Burke defines metonymy as a reduction, a downward conversion whereby "some higher or more complex realm of being" is reduced "to the terms of a lower or less complex realm of being" (506). The "basic strategy" of metonymy, he continues, is "to convey some incorporeal or intangible state in terms of the corporeal or tangible" (506). As an example, Burke explains how a map (e.g., a topographical map of the United States) functions metonymically by reducing a concept (e.g., "United States") to a tangible form. Burke defines synecdoche as representation, an upward conversion that directs attention toward an *understanding of the whole*, of which the part is perceived to be integral (507). In the example of the map of the United States, a topographical map of the country induces a particular understanding of "United States" (metonymy) by representing it in terms of its diverse landscapes (synecdoche). A metonymic reduction is, thus, "a special application of synecdoche" (509), because "a reduction is a *representation*" (507). Irony's importance in Burkean tropology is tied to its ability to challenge a given representation's inducement to *certain* understanding. Indeed, "United States" is more than just its physical landscape. By making us aware that alternative understandings are possible, irony reminds us that the world is always more complex than our language tries to persuade us to believe.

Such a remembering is enabled by irony's bidirectional movement from whole to part *and* part to whole, which emphasizes "a *relationship* or *connectedness* between two sides of an equation, a connectedness that, like a road, extends in either direction" (509). The first move—the metonymic reduction from whole to part—Burke terms "adjectival synecdoche," in which the key element "embod[ies] one of the qualifications necessary to the total definition" of the whole (516). The second move—the synecdochic representation from part to whole—Burke labels "substantial synecdoche." Here, rather than describing a key element of the whole (i.e., adjectival synecdoche), the part is the "summarizing vessel" that "[represents] the *end* or *logic*" and "embod[ies] the conclusions of the development as a whole" (516). Irony emerges via the simultaneous interaction of these two functions—adjectival *and* substantial.

Using the opposition of disease versus cure as his example, Burke explains that when the two terms are reconfigured as "reversible pairs" in a development that uses them both, we can "'ironically' note the function of the disease in 'perfecting' the cure, or the function of the cure in 'perpetuating' the influences of the disease" (512). In terms of a contemporary example, we might consider some parents' resistance to immunizing their children against diseases like the measles. In such a drama, a complex phenomenon named *vaccine* could be metonymically reduced to "an injection that prevents disease," thereby adjectivally embodying one of the qualifications necessary for defining what a vaccine is. This same definition, however, when simultaneously viewed as representing the end or logic of the development as a whole, induces an understanding of vaccine as the eradication of disease. Applying the "over-all ironic formula" that "what goes forth as A [vaccine] returns as non-A [disease]" (517), we can note how both vaccine and disease contribute to a larger drama in which parents decide not to immunize their children because the disease appears not to exist—which in turn creates the disease, which in turn creates the vaccine, and so forth. When the bidirectional movement is not simultaneously engaged, however, we encounter the type of hubristic oppositional logic that authorizes scapegoating. Indeed, doctors and public health officials remain baffled by parents' refusal to immunize their children: the existing empirical evidence proving the causal relationship between vaccines and decreasing occurrence of disease should be enough to persuade.

But it isn't. And Burkean irony suggests how doctors and public health officials might go about persuading otherwise. It does so by introducing the concept of recalcitrance, which can inaugurate revision as it helps identify the terms by which such revision is possible. In brief, Burkean recalcitrance refers to materials (including discourses) that a given orientation excludes as being factual or meaningful, which, as Lawrence J. Prelli, Floyd D. Anderson, and Matthew T. Althouse explain, renders Burkean recalcitrance and orientation inextricable: "There is no recalcitrance without a disclosing point of view, nor is there a point of view that does not disclose recalcitrance" (102). In the example of parents' resistance to having their children vaccinated, data supplied by doctors regarding the effectiveness of vaccines are recalcitrant materials disclosed by an orientation that does not recognize such data as meaningful (e.g., a faith orientation that disavows the authority of Western medicine). But recalcitrant materials can also refer to forces in the physical world and "the resistance that is offered by reality against our symbolic constructions" (Murray 26). In *Permanence and Change*, Burke offers one such example when he observes that the statement "I can safely jump from this high place" requires the addition of the words "with the aid of a parachute," a change that occurs "after one had taken the recalcitrance of this material adequately into account" (255–56). The first statement, which voices the perspective of human omnipotence, excludes gravity and human fragility, yet once recognized as facts that matter, these factors call forth the corrective supplied in the second statement, "with the aid of a parachute." Here, then, the two statements that might have been regarded as oppositional— humans versus nature—emerge instead as contributory via a larger orientation interested in the dynamics of safe human flight. In such instances, recalcitrant materials function as correctives to faulty or incomplete interpretations. They also, as Murray argues, spark a confrontation through which a humble irony can emerge. As Murray puts it, "A particular way of seeing becomes ironized when it is called into question by another way of seeing" (29). In place of "another way of seeing," however, we substitute "another way of being," conceptualizing recalcitrance as a material resistance that has the potential to bring into relief the contingency of synecdochic representation and the understanding it sponsors.

In tropological terms, we can say that understanding begins with metaphor, an orientation toward some complex phenomenon that renders it an object of inquiry, something to be known. Metonymy reduces that object to a material form (i.e., it becomes matter) that in turn induces, through synecdochic representation, a particular understanding (i.e., it has come to matter). The irony sparked by synecdochic reversal makes apparent the material excesses that a particular orientation both discloses and excludes.[4] It is the recalcitrance introduced by this excess that makes possible shifts in perspective and thus changes in the world (i.e., the object comes to matter otherwise).

Of course, there is no guarantee that a confrontation with recalcitrant materials will necessarily produce a humble irony that motivates orientational revision. Indeed, these materials can be integrated in ways that shore up an existing perspective (see Prelli et al. 102). Nevertheless, as Prelli et al. argue, it remains the case that the "evo[cation] of incongruous points of view . . . , at least partially, [opens] the universe of discourse by enabling expression of a wider range of voices that—through revising, reshaping, rephrasing, and correcting—could ultimately yield a more mature, more encompassing, and less reductive orientation toward a situation" (117). And although irony can be ignored or subsumed by an orientation that rejects another way of seeing or being, Burke reminds us that "our interpretations themselves *must* be altered as the universe displays various orders of recalcitrance to them" (*Permanence* 256; emphasis added).

To return to our vaccine example, we can consider as the system's excluded material excess those bodies with depressed immune systems for whom *vaccine* means not an injection that prevents disease but rather the life-threatening *introduction* of it. When doctors and public health officials talk about vaccines only as injections that prevent disease, however, they fail to acknowledge these bodies; in so doing, they help sustain a lay understanding of vaccine as the *eradication* (rather than *the judicious use*) of disease. This in turn keeps them from seeing how they are implicated in sustaining the very problem they seek to solve. Disclosed by an orientation interested in the health and well-being of all, bodies with depressed immune systems thus offer a confrontation with recalcitrance. Specifically, via Burkean irony, we can begin to see how public health policy might revise *vaccine* and thereby not only increase vaccination rates but also protect the lives of those for whom vaccination is not an option; it can more pointedly define vaccine in terms of the disease it *contains within*.

Burke + Barad → Emergent Mattering

By making manifest the radical interdependency of being, knowing, and being-knowing otherwise, Burkean irony disrupts the subject/object distinction that Barad argues is a product of "intra-actions," or the "*mutual constitution of entangled agencies*" (*Meeting* 33). Unlike the more conventional "interaction," which "presumes the prior existence of independently determinate entities" (170),

Barad's concept of intra-action "recognizes that distinct agencies do not precede, but rather emerge through, their intra-action" (33). Clarifying the relationship between intra-action and the constitution of subjects and objects, Barad explains, "It is through specific agential intra-actions that the boundaries and properties of the 'components' of phenomena become determinate and that particular embodied concepts become meaningful. A specific intra-action (involving a specific material configuration of the 'apparatus of observation') enacts an *agential cut* (in contrast to the Cartesian cut—an inherent distinction—between subject and object) effecting a separation between 'subject' and 'object'" ("Posthumanist" 815). Accordingly, through Barad's theorization of intra-action, we can think through with complexity the co-constitution of objects and their agencies of observation—including those human agencies rendered intelligible as such by prior intra-actions—who participate in making objects matter. In other words, it is via intra-actions among viruses, organs, cells, policies, practices, conventions, narratives, decisions, and a host of other matter(s) that *vaccine* emerges as a distinct object that matters, distinct from not only the disease it exists to eradicate but also those who study, administer, advocate for, and receive it (or not). To remind us that these distinctions are only temporarily determinate—and thus revisable—is where Burkean irony steps in. Indeed, it is this irony—or rather, the *recognition* of irony—that can spark an ontological revision for all knowers: we "too are part of the world's differential becoming" because *how* we know now participates in creating a world in which some objects matter more than others (Barad, *Meeting* 91). Our ethical responsibility as knowers thus resides in the realization that "the world is materialized differently through different practices," which requires that we take "responsibility for the fact that our practices matter" (88).

In the case of reservations regarding vaccination, a doctor's unwitting part in spreading disease can *become* witting when she recognizes her participation in the larger drama of public health. But this is not a recognition that merely emerges with good intentions; good intentions support and defend the synecdochic representations that we use to make sense of the world (e.g., doctors who try to stop the spread of disease, or parents who try to protect their children). And this is also not a recognition that emerges *in general*. As discussed above, the general recognition that matter matters does little to affect how matter matters or how it can come to matter differently. Again, what can spark the recognition of the radical interdependency that prompts revisionary practices and differential participation in systems of materialization and mattering (read: what can spark an ironic perspective) is the material excess excluded by synecdochic representation. A doctor whose own embodied experience of, for example, living with a suppressed immune system materially flouts the synecdochic equation of vaccine with eradication could use such an experience to reimagine the terms by which vaccine becomes intelligible. This rupture of representation makes the doctor's body matter differently, makes vaccines matter differently, and allows the doctor to conceptualize the system and his participation in it differently.

Taken together, Burkean irony and Baradian intra-action produce an emergent rhetorical ethics, one that suggests how we can productively combine the radical interdependency of subject and object with the concomitant responsibility to intervene, to "breathe life into ever new possibilities for living justly" (Barad, *Meeting* x). Such an ethics directs us away from thinking that matter's inevitable becoming renders that becoming immune to intervention. It further punctuates the importance of *recognition*: it is through recognizing material excess as a potentially revisionary recalcitrance, recognizing how matter has mattered, that we can intervene in becoming and participate in creating the conditions of possibility for how matter can come to matter (differently).

To demonstrate the affordances of and the need for such an ethics, we turn to Sara Ahmed's research on institutional diversity work/ers, which provides a compelling example of how the material recalcitrance of embodied experience can intervene in boundary-making practices that sustain injustice. In *On Being Included*, Ahmed investigates the promises of inclusion touted by diversity policies, wherein "the language of diversity is often exercised in institutional response to reports of racism" (143). While diversity policies focus on including diverse bodies in institutional life and granting them institutional recognition, Ahmed explains, such inclusion begins and ends with the *arrival* of diverse bodies: "If your arrival is a sign of diversity, then your arrival can be incorporated as good practice" (150). But understanding this arrival as good practice—as a "solution" to the "problem" of institutional racism—conceals *how* bodies arrive and are included (as so-called beneficiaries), under what conditions (of scrutiny or suspicion), and with what expectations (to be model minorities: careful, compliant, happy, submissive). Indeed, Ahmed argues, inclusion is premised on "those who in being included are also willing to consent to the terms of inclusion," which include "protecting whiteness" (163) by folding minorities into existing institutional (and racial) hierarchies where race is a problem that has already been solved (147).

It is not, then, the language of diversity but the embodied experiences of persons of color, Ahmed argues, that reveal the interdependency of diversity policies and racism: "If we start from our own experiences as persons of color in institutions of whiteness, we might think about how those benevolent acts of giving are *not what they seem*: being included can be a lesson in 'being not' as much as 'being in.' The 'folding into life' of minorities can also be understood as a national fantasy. . . . We come up against the limits of this fantasy when we encounter the brick wall; we come up against the limits when we refuse to be grateful for what we receive" (163). This experience of coming up against a wall—against the limits of inclusion—is sponsored by the material excess of bodies and feelings. Persons of color "encounter the brick wall" when their embodied experiences of conditional inclusion are met not with gratitude, guilt, or compliance but with anger, outrage, or indignation. Such feelings not only reveal the inadequacy of diversity language to eradicate racist practices, but also implicate diversity language in perpetuating racist practices. This experience of recalcitrance can thus spark interventions in the synecdochic logic of institutional diversity by instantiating the recognition of *how* bodies have mattered (under the sign of inclusion) and suggesting how they might matter differently.

As this example suggests, however, whereas material excess is the by-product of synecdochic representation, recognition of such is neither automatic nor guaranteed. In institutional diversity work, it is the experiences of marked bodies, excluded bodies, the bodies that come up against a wall (named inclusion), that seem to precipitate recognition. These experiences (of oppression) are distributed asymmetrically: they materialize for some bodies based on histories of racism, colonialism, heterosexism, and ableism. But can we *seek out* the material excesses that will lay bare the logics that produce irony? Again Ahmed is instructional as she tracks the material excess and attendant experiences that are available to privileged bodies. For those who occupy white bodies, she explains, "the proximity of the black body is experienced as 'forcing' (onto individuals, onto the institution) and is experienced as forcefulness" (159). While it would be easy to *deny* such a feeling, persons who *acknowledge* the embodied experience of "proximity to black bodies as forcefulness" can also begin to recognize the inadequacy of the language of diversity to eliminate racism. In short, Ahmed affirms the possibility that an embodied experience of "going against" or "coming up against" can be intentionally pursued as a way to call into question synecdochic mattering: "The body who is 'going the wrong way' is the one experienced as 'in the way' of a will that is acquired as momentum" (186).

Ahmed thus suggests that to experience on an embodied level "going in the wrong way"—to orient ourselves to the world otherwise—is to participate in intra-actions capable of making matter matter differently. Explaining how Ahmed conceptualizes the relationship between orientation and mattering, Julie Jung notes that, "according to Ahmed, our history of repeated interactions with objects that occupy the spaces we inhabit orients us to similar *kinds* of spaces, and our habituated contact with certain objects in said spaces makes those objects *matter* to us." To make matter matter otherwise, then, necessarily requires that we "develop new embodied habits by engaging in repeated kinds of actions with objects in different kinds of spaces" (Jung). Jung is careful to note, following Ahmed, that histories of who and what matters render some spaces more accessible to some bodies than others. We posit this ontological fact as the exigency for ethical action in a posthuman world—namely, the fact that in some spaces my body matters more than others confers a privilege that obligates me to move into spaces where I can experience my body as mattering otherwise. Viewed in these terms, emergent mattering as a methodology calls on us to remake the world by moving into spaces where we not only experience our bodies moving in the wrong direction but are also, crucially, *open to recognizing our bodies moving as much.* Such openness is crucial because it mitigates against the colonizing impulse to consume and incorporate the "strange." Instead, it is committed to sustaining relations of difference as it anticipates that difference coming to matter otherwise.

One study that models and demonstrates the affordances of this research ethic for rhetoric studies is Phaedra C. Pezzullo's *Toxic Tourism: Rhetorics of Pollution, Travel, and Environmental Justice.* Toxic tours, Pezzullo explains, are organized and hosted by local community members who are motivated by their "collective desire to survive and to resist toxic pollution through active participation in public life" (6). As appropriations of commercial tourism, toxic tours offer a persuasive example of the inventional possibilities—the possibilities for mattering differently—that emerge when tourism is made to matter differently through environmental-justice activism. By pairing the history of tourism—that is, how it has come to matter via associations with "vacation, leisure, and picturesque beauty" (1)—with an explicit social-justice mission, it can matter differently. Perhaps more significant, however, is how people and land can come to matter differently to those who participate in the tours. As Pezzullo explains, because

> toxic assaults tend to occur in or on communities that historically have been segregated from elite centers of power. . . . There exists . . . both a psychological and geographical distance between dominant public culture and the cultures of those who live in places where both waste and people are articulated together as unnecessary, undesirable, and contaminating. The creation of these "separate areas of existence" enables our culture more readily to dismiss the costs of toxic pollution because the waste and the people most affected by the waste appear hidden within their proper place. (5)

By going on a toxic tour, one experiences, momentarily, the collapse of this distance. And it is precisely this collapse, this temporary contact, that renders participation in toxic tours a potentially risky undertaking.

Indeed, in the first lines of her introduction, Pezzullo hails her (most likely academic) readers to imagine themselves as potential participants. She begins with the following epigraph:

> Before the judicial body here makes a decision, we strongly urge that you come to our city and meet with us and see where we live and see what we're exposed to. Right now, I'm offering that invitation. I would very much like an answer.
> —Zulene Mayfield, on behalf of Chester Residents Concerned for Quality Living, in her remarks to the Pennsylvania State Environment Hearing Board

Immediately thereafter, Pezzullo addresses her readers directly: "Would you accept Zulene Mayfield's invitation? Can you imagine traveling to a place that local residents claim is polluted by toxins to witness the bodies and landscapes that supposedly have been affected? Would—or could—you risk exposing your own body? Or would you refuse, given the chance that the smells, sounds, contagions, and stories would be too much?" (1). This too-much-ness is what Pezzullo posits as the basis for some readers' logical refusal to participate in toxic tours: the risk of collapsing subject and object is too great. Yet, via the framework of emergent mattering, it constitutes the material excess capable of remaking the boundary that separates my community here from yours way over there. Hearing testimony, smelling decay, seeing seepage, and feeling shame puncture the synecdochic logic that bodies are safe when toxicity is geographically distant. And such experiences can intervene in emergent relations between the tourists and the land. Relations grounded in denial or indifference can be revised when the tourist's embodied experience sparks recognition of her implication in toxic practices and radical interdependency with her environment. With her own body at risk, the toxic tourist might begin to imagine that (her) consumption and disposal practices do matter, that the proximity of bodies to toxicity does matter, that environmental justice must matter.

Unlike the immunosuppressed doctor discussed earlier, however, whose body *demands* an intervention (for self-preservation), the researcher who participates in a toxic tour recognizes, via a history of prior intra-actions, the need to seek out contact with her presumed object of inquiry. Pezzullo describes this motivation to make contact with a place in terms of *presence*. But presence— which "suggests that the materiality of a place promises the opportunity to shape perceptions, bodies, and lives"—involves "more than simply 'showing up'" and "coexisting with another in a particular place and time" (9). Instead, for Pezzullo, being present refers to a "*structure of feeling* or one's *affective* experience when certain elements—and perhaps more importantly, relationships and communities—in space and time appear more immediate to us, such that we can imagine their 'realness' or 'feasibility' in palpable and significant ways" (9). Participants' affective experiences thus emerge as being especially significant for rhetoricians who are working to advocate effectively for causes that we care about. In the specific case of toxic tours, Pezzullo explains that a "sense of presence or willingness to feel connected to the people and places toured is particularly important to the political efficacy of the practice" (31). It is the "political efficacy of the practice," we submit, that gives Pezzullo's work an ethic of emergent mattering. Indeed, understanding toxic tours as an activist methodology— as a type of "embedded rhetorical research" (McHendry et al. 303)—suggests how "interested others" can become committed allies in the work of social justice. By engaging the former in experiences that change them on an embodied level, toxic tours effect Burke's ironic formula: what goes forth as A (a tourist) returns as non-A (an ally of those who live there).

More than a Feeling: Becoming Researchers and Other Future Matters

As we have demonstrated through our examples, a research ethic of emergent mattering can take a number of forms and focus on diverse methodological objects. Such an ethic need not explicitly invoke Burke or Barad. As our first example of Takeshita's work with the IUD demonstrates, participation in differential mattering does not require a disciplinary or lexical investment in Burkean tropology or new materialism. Common to each of the examples we cited, however, is the insistence that *what* matters is premised on *how* it matters, that what matters has a history (i.e., it has been made to matter), and that what matters can matter differently. We further contend that a research ethic of emergent mattering is more than a passive or passing feeling. An ironic recognition of radical interdependency capable of motivating intervention and revision requires seeking contact, pursuing moments of forcefulness, and "develop[ing] new embodied habits" (Jung). These embodied habits can intervene in the future of rhetoric and possibilities for rhetorical futures writ large. But we also submit that they can intervene in the present by presenting us with perspectives that challenge how we understand and interact with the matter we study and of which we are a part.

We strove to make one such intervention in our own decisions about which research examples to include in this chapter. Taken together, these examples are arguments for the type of work that we think is needed in posthumanist rhetorics now—namely, the political efficacy that Pezzullo offers as a potential effect of toxic tours, which we posit as an exigent future, one toward which new materialist rhetoricians can and should strive. Among other things, this means that as researchers we should seek out and accept invitations to move into spaces where activists are already engaging in practices that draw boundaries that divide "them" from "us" otherwise.[5] As Pezzullo's work makes clear, doing so can help generate new rhetorical theories, new ways of persuading others to act with respect to issues that concern us. But the call of political efficacy also suggests that we consider moving *with humility* into spaces that don't hail us or that we find uninteresting, and in doing so become open to the unpredictable matterings that emerge.[6] Far from abandoning the future-oriented work of new materialism, posthumanism, or rhetoric, then, we suggest that theories and methodologies that focus on *presence*—what has come to matter and how in our temporary articulation of *the present*—can intervene in *which* futures emerge. Because while a new materialist sensibility may persuade us that "information . . . converges toward simultaneity with no past or future" and "duration . . . is eradicated . . . in favor of an eternal present" (Gries 30), we cannot forget the political and ethical power—nay, the necessity—of the now in materializing what can become.

Notes

1. "New materialism" is a title sometimes used to group together various strands of post-humanist inquiry in order to foreground the shared project of decentering the human subject by attending to the agency of matter. Ehren Helmut Pflugfelder, for example, categorizes object-oriented ontology (OOO), Jane Bennett's thing-power, and Karen Barad's agential realism all as "new materialisms." While we recognize the rhetorical affordances of this type of titling, and while we do situate new materialism as a category of posthumanism, we recognize important differences between OOO and feminist approaches to new materialism— particularly the tendency of the former to posit a flat ontology that discounts the significance of differential embodiment within the category of the human. Our adoption of a new materialist approach is intended to highlight these differences by demonstrating how mattering is differential and therefore political. It is also intended to demonstrate that conscientious uptakes of new materialist theory can contribute to work in feminist rhetorics. For a discussion of differences between feminist new materialism and other theories of materiality, see Micciche. For a thoughtful discussion of similarities and differences between OOO and new materialism, see Rivers.

2. Elizabeth Galewski similarly suggests that Burkean irony can productively grapple with the tensions of ontological contingency: "Dialectical irony . . . emerges out of [an] abyss of infinite possibility in order to draw a new profile for the world to see. As such, dialectical irony holds open a perspective that deviates from the norm even as it seeks to recover the possibility of mutual understanding. It demonstrates faith in the world's ability to inaugurate new realities and preserve collective meanings at the same time" (99).

3. On the role of projection in scapegoating, Gregory Desilet and Edward C. Appel argue that Burke "emphasizes the comic frame and its inducement of humble irony as the model for human relations and conflict because within this frame scapegoating remains internal, never escaping through projection to the external victimage of others. From within comic framing of conflict, each person identifies the internal blindness before it reaches the volume of emotion that might trigger the escalation to victimage and tragic scapegoating" (349).

4. We are indebted to Chris Mays for introducing us to this conceptualization of "excess" as the condition of possibility for both temporary stability and possible change.

5. Gabriela Raquel Ríos models what moving in such spaces might look like in her 2015 article "Cultivating Land-Based Literacies and Rhetorics." Drawing on her research, indigenous concepts of relationality, and her participation in farm-worker activism, Ríos shows that "the land *and* working with the land has taught . . . [the activists] how to organize and build coalitions" (64). Her work not only calls attention to settler-colonial logics of (alphabetic) literacy but also shows how moving in such spaces makes literacy, the land, and farm workers themselves matter differently.

6. Taking cues from Ahmed, for example, white scholars attending the Conference on College Composition and Communication could seek out panels on race, seek out the experience of allowing scholarship on race to matter to them. Or scholars who do not identify as feminist could read the CFPs to the Feminisms and Rhetorics Conference as an invitation to reconsider how that conference—and the bodies that tend to populate it—might matter differently.

Works Cited

Ahmed, Sara. *On Being Included: Racism and Diversity in Institutional Life*. Durham: Duke University Press, 2012. Print.

Badmington, Neil. "Introduction: Approaching Posthumanism." *Posthumanism*, edited by Neil Badmington. London: Palgrave, 2000, 1–10. Print.

Barad, Karen. *Meeting the Universe Halfway: Quantum Physics and the Entanglement of Matter and Meaning*. Durham: Duke, 2007. Print.

———. "Posthumanist Performativity: Toward an Understanding of How Matter Comes to Matter." *Signs: Journal of Women in Culture and Society* 28, no. 3 (2003): 801–31. Print.

Braidotti, Rosi. *The Posthuman*. Cambridge, Mass.: Polity Press, 2013. Print.

Burke, Kenneth. *A Grammar of Motives*. Berkeley: University of California Press, 1969. Print.

———. *Permanence and Change: An Anatomy of Purpose*. 3rd ed. Berkeley: University of California Press, 1984. Print.

———. *A Rhetoric of Motives*. Berkeley: University of California Press, 1969. Print.

Coole, Diana, and Samantha Frost. "Introducing New Materialisms." *New Materialisms: Ontology, Agency, and Politics*, edited by Diana Coole and Samantha Frost. Durham: Duke University Press, 2010, 1–43. Print.

Desilet, Gregory, and Edward C. Appel. "Choosing a Rhetoric of the Enemy: Kenneth Burke's Comic Frame, Warrantable Outrage, and the Problem of Scapegoating." *Rhetoric Society Quarterly* 41, no. 4 (2011): 340–62. Print.

Galewski, Elizabeth. "The Strange Case for Women's Capacity to Reason: Judith Sargent Murray's Use of Irony in 'On the Equality of the Sexes' (1790)." *Quarterly Journal of Speech* 93, no. 1 (2007): 84–108.

Gries, Laurie E. *Still Life with Rhetoric: A New Materialist Approach for Visual Rhetorics*. Logan: Utah State University Press, 2015. Print.

Hawk, Byron. "Reassembling Postprocess: Toward a Posthuman Theory of Public Rhetoric." *Beyond Postprocess*, edited by Sidney I. Dobrin, J. A. Rice, and Michael Vastola. Logan: Utah State University Press, 2011, 75–93. Print.

Jung, Julie. "Systems Rhetoric: A Dynamic Coupling of Explanation and Description." *enculturation* 17 (2014). Web. 1 Aug. 2015.

Kellner, Hans. "The Inflatable Trope as Narrative Theory: Structure or Allegory?" *Diacritics* 11, no. 1 (1981): 14–28. Print.

Mays, Chris. "From 'Flows' to 'Excess': On Stubbornness, Stability, and Blockages in Rhetorical Ecologies." *enculturation* 19 (2015). Web. 8 Jan. 2016.

McHendry, George F., Jr., Michael K. Middleton, Danielle Endres, Samantha Senda-Cook, and Megan O'Byrne. "Rhetorical Critic(ism)'s Body: Affect and Field on a Plane of Immanence." *Southern Communication Journal* 79, no. 4 (2014): 293–310. Print.

Micciche, Laura R. "Writing Material." *College English* 76, no. 6 (2014): 488–505. Print.

Muckelbauer, John, and Debra Hawhee. "Posthuman Rhetorics: 'It's the Future, Pikul.'" *JAC* 20, no. 4 (2000): 767–74. Print.

Murray, Jeffrey W. "Kenneth Burke: A Dialogue of Motives." *Philosophy & Rhetoric* 35, no. 1 (2002): 22–49. Print.

Pezzullo, Phaedra C. *Toxic Tourism: Rhetorics of Pollution, Travel, and Environmental Justice*. Tuscaloosa: University of Alabama Press, 2007. Print.

Pflugfelder, Ehren Helmut. "Rhetoric's New Materialisms: From Micro-Rhetoric to Microbrew." *Rhetoric Society Quarterly* 45, no. 5 (2015): 441–61. Print.

Prelli, Lawrence J., Floyd D. Anderson, and Matthew T. Althouse. "Kenneth Burke on Recalcitrance." *Rhetoric Society Quarterly* 41, no. 2 (2011): 97–124. Print.

Rickert, Thomas. *Ambient Rhetoric: The Attunements of Rhetorical Being.* Pittsburgh: University of Pittsburgh Press, 2013. Print.

Ríos, Gabriela Raquel. "Cultivating Land-Based Literacies and Rhetorics." *LiCS* 3, no. 1 (2015): 60–70. Print.

Rivers, Nathaniel A. "Deep Ambivalence and Wild Objects: Toward a Strange Environmental Rhetoric." *Rhetoric Society Quarterly* 45, no. 5 (2015): 420–40. Print.

Schiappa, Edward. "Burkean Tropes and Kuhnian Science: A Social Constructionist Perspective on Language and Reality." *JAC* 13, no. 2 (1993): 401–22. Print.

Takeshita, Chikako. *The Global Biopolitics of the IUD: How Science Constructs Contraceptive Users and Women's Bodies.* Cambridge, Mass.: MIT Press, 2012. Print.

Tell, David. "Burke's Encounter with Ransom: Rhetoric and Epistemology in 'Four Master Tropes.'" *Rhetoric Society Quarterly* 34, no. 4 (2004): 33–54. Print.

Wolfe, Cary. *What Is Posthumanism?* Minneapolis: University of Minnesota Press, 2009. Print. Posthumanities 8.

9

What Are Humans For?

Nathan Gale and Timothy Richardson

First introduced to the world in 2008, the Fitbit activity tracker promises greater control over health through data about our bodies that was previously difficult to access. Fitbits and other trackers record information such as the number of steps we take in a day, the qualities of our sleep, and our frequency of activity versus stillness, and then upload this data to home computers, to the cloud, or both. The data can then be parsed by doctors, shared with friends, or simply collected as a record.

Gathering and sorting data is also, of course, big business, and it is a business that we are all involved in to a greater or lesser extent. As the types of devices that record our lives become increasingly ubiquitous and discrete, the types of data that they privilege become valuable beyond what they say about an individual, and the collection of information becomes a goal, not a means. At the same time, privileging certain types of data may encourage behaviors that might not occur otherwise. A Fitbit user marching around her kitchen island in order to reach ten thousand steps, for instance, may be an innocuous example of machine-persuaded behavior, but the fact that the user's data is collected, represented, and aggregated with other users' data indicates a larger relationship between humans and technology. That she chooses to be persuaded by her Fitbit—that she has "bought in" to the ecosystem of data-driven assessment and sharing—suggests how open we are (and may always have been) to networks and collection. We have always used and been used by our technologies, but our increasing networkability reveals to a much greater extent how enmeshed with technology, and how potentially interchangeable we are as data with and within our relationships with new technologies. *We become data* in all the manifold ways that we might parse this turn of phrase.

In responding to our titular question—"What are humans for?"—with a description of the above scene, we seek to participate in longstanding conversations about the relationships between and boundaries among humans and technology that excite, incite, and worry scholars across a range of disciplines. More specifically, in this chapter we work through Kenneth Burke's oft-cited "trouble with technology" (Giamo), which seems to pit Burke's thought against posthumanist thinking. This trouble, however, doesn't doom Burke's thought to obsolescence. Rather than reject Burke's engagement with technology, we argue that what Burke calls "pure persuasion" is at work in much contemporary, data-driven technology. Technological devices, like literary devices, make demands beyond the uses to which they are put by users and authors. To articulate these demands, we turn to Kevin Kelly's notion of the *technium* and to his suggestion that technology *wants*. Building from Kelly, we introduce Burke's pure persuasion alongside our discussion of wearables. Ultimately, we merge Kelly's evolutionary, and somewhat optimistic, account of the technium with Burke's own admittedly pessimistic treatment of Big Technology. From this emerges what we call technolistic screens, which fully frame the stakes of this posthuman moment.

Burke's Definitions of *Humanity*

It is well known that Burke distrusted new technologies: he gave them the ominous god-term Big Technology. Nevertheless, he defined humanity in part as a being unique in its usage of technology. First in *The Rhetoric of Religion*, later in the article "Definition of Man" (written for the *Hudson Review*), and then in his *Language as Symbolic Action*, Burke defines "man" [*sic*] according to the following four clauses:

1. Man is "the symbol-using animal."
2. Man is the "inventor of the negative."
3. Man is "separated from his natural condition by instruments of his own making."
4. Man is "goaded by the spirit of hierarchy." (*Rhetoric of Religion* 40)

While all four deserve attention (including the later-added "rotten with perfection" clause), for our purposes only numbers one and three are of immediate interest. This is not to say that all of Burke's clauses are independent of each other; this selection is simply a way for us to focus our reading of Burke on the specific relationship between technology and the "symbol-using animal." It is the link between clauses one and three—in this network between symbol usage and tool usage—that Burke defines humans as animals that *use* both language and technology (or "instruments of [their] own making"). If we take each of these four as *conditions* for humanity (i.e., that man *is*) rather than as definitions, we are presented with a view in which technology must be (at least) consubstantial with humanity—namely, that it must be brought into that which we consider *human*. This reading of Burke's "Definition of Man" opens the human subject to possibilities beyond action in the symbolic and into a network of actants that includes both humans and technology. This is, broadly, the definition of the posthuman condition for which our close reading of Burke allows.

Assuming contemporary mechanical/digital ubiquity—an assumption that we feel is not only justified but somewhat obvious—we propose that perhaps, despite Burke's anxiety regarding technology, he nonetheless offers a fruitful way to describe the posthuman transcorporal situation as one of pure techno-logical persuasion. While initially requiring language to exist prior to any form of human technology, Burke's understanding of the relationship between humans and technology is complicated by the vast, intricate networks of machines readily seen in our cars, in our homes, and in and on our bodies. Using wear-ables as a primary example allows us to argue that technology is not always an explicit form of human domination or a builder of counter-nature, but perhaps something into which we are willing to buy. In order to advance this argument, we first carefully work through the relationships of the human with language and technology according to Burke's own definition of "man" in order to better recognize both the limits of Burke's perspective and, through a posthuman lens, the nuance that his position allows. Next, in an attempt to better understand what makes up "technology," we turn to technologist Kelly and his notion of the technium, a complex organism of various human and nonhuman networks that includes not only machines but the patents for those machines. This expansion of technology seems to best represent our reading of Burke's conditions, if not his attitude toward new technologies. That is, drawing on Kelly's work, we pro-pose an expansion of the definition of technology that understands it not as mere "things" that have motion but as an organism with desires of its own. We then work through this expanded definition of technology by looking at wear-ables, arguing for a type of what Burke, in *A Rhetoric of Motives*, calls *pure per-*

suasion, wherein all data is contemporary data *for itself*. What we might usually count as human, motivated action is transmuted—in its encounter with the technium—into perpetual, atemporal motion. This sets up our final argument— namely, that technology exists consubstantially with humanity (a condition that Burke only allows with language). There is, of course, a necessary, ethical tension between pure persuasion and consubstantiality. Big data is both for itself at the same time that it is substantially with us. Ultimately, we discount Burke's well-known "terministic screens," or the set of terms we use to define a specific reality, by shifting the focus away from its other aspects. Instead, we submit that terministic screens become among the many technolistic screens that shape human reality through various forms of technology.

Burke's Conditions for Humanity

One of the distinguishing differences in defining the human for Burke is humanity's use of and relationship to technology. That is, as much as Burke's early works deal with the human body and its connection to rhetoric,[1] his later writings seem to wrestle with technology's place in human symbolic actions. To that end, Burke elaborates on his third clause by stating that "it concerns the fact that even the most primitive of tribes are led by inventions to depart somewhat from the needs of food, shelter, sex as defined by the survival standards of sheer animality. The implements of hunting and husbandry, with corresponding implements of war, make for a set of habits that become a kind of 'second nature,' as a special set of expectations, shaped by custom, comes to seem 'natural'" ("Definition" 503). This second nature is beyond animal survival standards. Technology, then, is what humanity has in addition to its animality. Humans are not only the symbol-using animals, but also the "tool"-using animals. And for Burke, the symbol systems seem to come first.

What interests us here is that when technology arrives, it appears to lead the human animal toward a second (human) nature. Human nature initially seems to exist on par with animalistic survival instincts, while inventions lead us to our humanity. Burke finds that, as with language, technology has a "reflexive" or second-level aspect to its usage, too, because "animals do not use words about words (as with the definitions in a dictionary), and though an ape may even learn to put two sticks together as a way of extending his reach in case the sticks are so made that one can be fitted into the other, he would not take a knife and deliberately hollow out the end of one stick to make possible the insertion of the other stick" (504). Here, Burke directly aligns language with technology. Marking the difference between humanity and animality, Burke likens technology to language in that both require a second-level or reflexive attitude in which we think about other things, whether words or objects.

However, Burke also feels strongly that language is not like other forms of technology because language is a necessary condition for technology. Instead, Burke maintains that technology is born through language. He argues that "even if one views the powers of speech and mechanical invention as mutually involving each other, in a technical or formal sense, one should make the implications explicit by treating the gifts of symbolicity as the 'prior' member of the pair" (505). Technology—though apparently similar to the instrumental nature of language—*needs* language in order to grow. We have to define a tool as a certain type of tool (a symbolic action) in order to improve on it (a technological improvement), which necessitates having previously defined it. We cannot make a better phone unless we first define something as "a phone."[2] And as Ian Hill indicates, even in terms of the communication of information, machine communication, for Burke, lacks the "poetic sensibility to react to changing conditions with altered symbolism," since language comes before technology.

Burke spends much of the six paragraphs devoted to this third clause in "Definition of Man" discussing how language is not really a form of technology and, better, how his third clause cannot be reduced to another form of his first clause. In lieu of a definition, he offers a loose explanation of what he means by this "second nature" when he states that we often depart from our "survival standards," or what we might understand as—simply—nature itself (503). But, while this departure is guided by our "inventions," Burke offers few illustrations of how this takes place or what our first and second "natures" feature. Instead, one of the few technological examples he does give in describing how humanity is separated from its natural condition by instruments of its own making focuses on how machines communicate information: "'Information' in the sense of sheer motion is not thus 'reflexive,' but rather is like that of an electric circuit where, if a car is on a certain stretch of track, it automatically turns off the current on the adjoining piece of track, so that any car on that other piece of track would stop through lack of power. The car could be said to behave in accordance with this 'information'" (504). Though this example might explain electrical current and how "information" is passed along such tracks, it does very little in helping us understand how technology separates humanity from some "natural condition."

And nowadays, it is quite easy to think of newer technologies that go beyond simply "reading" electricity, such as IBM's Watson computer, or a Fitbit.

Even earlier in the same essay, after defining the purpose of this third clause, Burke gives us the following observation in a parenthetical: "(I recall once when there was a breakdown of the lighting equipment in New York City. As the newspapers the next day told of the event, one got almost a sense of mystical terror from the description of the darkened streets. Yet but fifty miles away, that same evening, we had been walking on an unlit road by our house in the country, in a darkness wholly 'natural.' In the 'second nature' of the city, something *so natural as dark roadways* at night was weirdly 'unnatural')" (503; emphasis added). Here, Burke seems amused at the urbanites' reliance on technology such that they find it so disconcerting when it breaks. But this recollection, set off from the main paragraph through parentheses, invites a question for us: *what counts as technology for Burke?* He mentions the lighting equipment but then later refers to the entire city as a "second nature," explicitly contrasting the city with country (as if one human dwelling is natural and the other is not). This contrast prods us to pose additional questions: While the darkness of the country in which Burke was walking might be wholly natural, what about the unlit *road* by his house? Or, even, his *house?* Ultimately, the passage seems to demonstrate Alan Kay's notion that "technology is anything that wasn't around when you were born" (Greelish). From this perspective, prior technology such as roads and houses is natural. Our point is that Burke perhaps extols language and is anxious about technology because his definition of technology is directed at particularly oppressive or exploitative or even grand deployments of technology.

His argument that language is a condition for technological change indicates a temporal, developmental model of technology (as old country roads lead to the city). But from these examples, technology also seems to be both the electrical grids and sheer motion-operated machinery—like the electric cars and their pieces of track, or, as we see elsewhere in his work, "world empire" itself (*Attitudes* 357). It is no wonder, then, that technology seen on such a grand scale would cause Burke to label forms of human instrumentation as "Big Technology."

Big Technology

Burke's opinion of technology is, in our view, a little dour, and his ideas about Big Technology are wrought with dread and anxiety. As much as Burke's understanding of the nature of technology seems fraught, we agree with Hill that "beyond mere 'instruments,' Burke's concept of technology referred to complex technologies and techniques, like television, gene-splicing, and atomic bombs. Complicated systems of human behavior, such as the 'technology of money as motive,' also contributed to what Burke called the creation of the 'technological empire' that 'establishes . . . the conditions of world order.'" Big Technology, as a term (used by Burke in "Definition"), includes not only the objects and inventions used to separate ourselves from our "natural condition," but also "systems" that maintain and advance these relationships. As such, Big Technology aligns with Kelly's *technium*, a term he coins to encompass every technology ("radar or plastic polymers") and also to include the networked conditions for their creation. As Kelly puts it in *What Technology Wants* (the most posthuman title we can imagine), "*technologies* can be patented, while the technium includes the patent system itself" (12).

Like Burke, Kelly sees technological innovation as practiced via the human intellect. But unlike Burke, he is happy to include language and culture in the list of technologies that make up the technium. Kelly explains, "We tend to think of technology as shiny tools and gadgets. Even if we acknowledge that technology can exist in disembodied form, such as software, we tend not to include in this category paintings, literature, music, dance, poetry, and the arts in general. But we should. If a thousand lines of letters in UNIX qualifies as a technology (the computer code for a web page), then a thousand lines of letters in English (*Hamlet*) must qualify as well. They both can change our behavior, alter the course of events, or enable future inventions" (10–11). This passage represents a significant and, we suggest, necessary departure from Burke's representation of the relationships between humans, language, and technology. Whereas Burke's definition disambiguates language from technology, thereby distinguishing nature from "second-nature," Kelly's explanation—in effect—rejects that very distinction.

In this way, Kelly both changes and *broadens* the traditional categories from which language and technology work, including a variety of objects and animals previously unaccounted for. Despite this marked shift in the perspectives about technology afforded by Burke and Kelly, however, Burke's technological anxiety echoes through Kelly: "After 10,000 years of slow evolution and 200 years of incredible intricate exfoliation, the technium is maturing into its own thing. Its sustaining network of self-reinforcing processes and parts have given it a noticeable measure of autonomy. It may have once been as simple as an old computer program, merely parroting what we told it, but now it is more like a very complex organism that often follows its own urges" (12–13). This sounds like a sinister possibility, one that evokes all sorts of Skynet scenarios. Kelly, though, understands it as generative. He argues that technology predates the human and that we (have) coevolve(d) with it. We are symbiotic with the technium even while we generate new cooking gadgets, write new novels, and fight "natural" darkness with the blue light of our screens. It is both a biological and rhetorical relationship; technology can change behavior, enable invention, and influence audiences (to use Burke's word, technology *leads* us). Or, as Rosi Braidotti situates it, the "analogue function that machinery fulfilled in modernity, as an anthropocentric device that imitated embodied human capacities, is replaced today by a more complex political economy that connects bodies to machines more intimately, through simulation and mutual modification" (89–90). Technology exists, then, *not apart* from humanity as an invention that separates (as posited by Burke), but *with* humanity as an economy (as per Braidotti) or (using Kelly's term) a technium.

So while Burke sees Big Technology as anxiety-provoking Second Nature, Kelly's technium is old and natural, and might be understood as a (co)formative (eco)system, a reef of individual technologies and social conventions and even language that exist and move individually but perhaps act together. The technium, Kelly claims, "extends beyond shiny hardware to include culture, art, social institutions, and intellectual creations of all types. It includes intangibles like software, law, and philosophical concepts. And most important, it includes the generative impulses of our inventions to encourage more tool making, more technology invention, and more self-enhancing connections" (11–12). Everything that, for Burke, makes us *human* animals would then count as technology. And while language may be more than a spoon or a golf cart, it would still be part of the technium as Kelly describes it.

Where Burke fears the possibilities afforded by technology (i.e., what it may do to us), Kelly recontextualizes technolog*ies* as particular, temporal manifestations of a consubstantial technium that includes language. Kelly's key points are compelling in part because they work so nicely with Burke's and yet avoid the tendency to fear the machines he cannot drive.

Given the emerging complexity of the technium and what he considers its burgeoning autonomy, Kelly asks very early on what the technium could possibly want. Of course, assuming that the technium could want anything brings to mind that corresponding Burkean anxiety, because we are bound to read the question as about what the technium wants *from us*. Kelly's first answer also reframes the question and is worth quoting in full:

> The technium wants what we design it to want and what we try to direct it to do. But in addition to those drives, the technium has its own wants. It wants to sort itself out, to self-assemble into hierarchical levels, just as most large, deeply interconnected systems do. The technium also wants what every living system wants: to perpetuate itself, to keep itself going. And as it grows, those inherent wants are gaining in complexity and force.
>
> I know this claim sounds strange. It seems to anthropomorphize stuff that is clearly not human. How can a toaster want? Aren't I assigning way too much consciousness to inanimate objects, and by doing so giving them more power over us than they have, or should have?
>
> It's a fair question. But "want" is not just for humans. Your dog wants to play Frisbee. Your cat wants to be scratched. Birds want mates. Worms want moisture. Bacteria want food. The wants of a microscopic, single-celled organism are less complex, less demanding, and fewer in number than the wants of you or me, but all organisms share a few fundamental desires: to survive, to grow. All are driven by these "wants." (15–16)

Several things are interesting here. First, to defend against the pathetic fallacy, Kelly turns to nonhuman animal examples. Where Burke makes his distinction when contrasting the human and the machine, Kelly takes the same distinction and moves the technological to the side of the nonhuman animal via metaphor.

Second, Kelly argues for a different, smaller type of want. (In another idiom, this would be called drive: he says that organisms are driven, and this is the right way of phrasing what he calls fundamental desires, which aren't properly desires but pulsions, impulses.) These wants, though, add up among the countless technologies (past and present) such that the "millions of amplifying relationships and countless circuits of influence among parts push the whole technium in certain unconscious directions" (16).

To tamp down Kelly's optimism, we should admit here that Burke's anxiety about Big Technology may easily be refigured in terms of an anxiety about the spread of unchecked capitalism (capital being, per Kelly, a technology, too). The hazards of industrial expansion in the service of capital is a common theme in Burke's early work, and very often his discussion of the dangers of technology coincide with his resistance to the expansion of unchecked capitalism (Giamo).

Burke was his own type of progressive, to be sure, but he was always writing and thinking in a time when there were living, if flawed, real-world alternatives to capitalism.[3] If we imagine that now, following Mark Fisher (whose acknowledged debt to Fredric Jameson is vast), "it's easier to imagine the end of the world than the end of capitalism," the ubiquity of technology—and especially the technology of capital and the capitalization of technologies—has every potential to sustain that impression (8). By the 1980s, Burke saw "the counternatural innovations of Technology in the aggregate as a vast 'creatively' destabilizing clutter, a bureaucratization of ingenious imaginings that takes on truly eschatological dimensions, powerful, pervasive, wasteful, pollutant, and challenging its human inventors to somehow round out the technical developments by developing a political bureaucratization competent to control them" (*Attitudes* 401). Given our broader definition of technology, then, we might understand Burke's anxiety as a recognition of the tension between industrial (and eventually digital) self-perpetuating systems that have a material (what Hill refers to as "counter-natural") agency and a political commitment to wrestle with them.

That the political reins Burke hoped for have now frayed (or even broken) is currently evident. As Steven Shaviro and others have recently shown, public resources like water, land, and education are increasingly being privatized, and the "entrepreneurial spirit" means treating oneself as both commodity and capital (8). This is true for the least vulnerable of us, for those of us already invested in late capitalism as a system beyond government, and for those who can enjoy the global economy while being enjoyed by it. But for many, as Braidotti indicates, "the bodies of the empirical subjects who signify difference (woman/native/earth or natural others) have become the disposable bodies of the global economy. Contemporary capitalism is indeed 'bio-political' in that it aims at controlling all that lives, as Foucault argues, but because Life is not the prerogative of humans only, it opens up a zoe-political or post-anthropocentric dimension. *If anxiety about extinction was common in the nuclear era, the posthuman condition, of the anthropocene, extends the death horizon to most species*" (111; emphasis added). In terms of catastrophe, where the humanist anxiety of Burke is a critical reaction to the hierarchies of technological and political power "in the nuclear era," the posthuman turn marks an extension and diffusion of our debt to other species (111). This is terrifyingly magnanimous. In relation to the technium, the posthuman "human" is instrumentalized, commodified, while being a consumer at the same time. Again, Braidotti realizes that "the effect of global financial networks and un-checked hedge funds has been an increase in poverty, especially among youth and women, affected by the disparity in access to the new technologies. The status of children is a chapter apart; from forced labour, to the child-soldier phenomenon, childhood has been violently inserted in infernal cycles of exploitation. Bodily politics has shifted, with the simultaneous emergence of cyborgs on the one hand and renewed forms of vulnerability on the other" (112). The hierarchies that Burke resisted have become diffuse, microlevel cooperations not only between technologies but among bodies that are vulnerable to both extreme and subtle forms of exploitation or, as we will see next, bodies that are privileged enough to willingly take those forms up.

Wearables and "Pure Persuasion"

Burke defines humans against animals and machines by positing humanity as a site for the other two: animals are poor in human language, and machines are poor in animality (or the corporeal form needed for rhetorical/artistic re-actions). Yet one form of current technology actually relies on our animal bodies to fully function. In a nutshell, wearable technologies (or simply, wearables) are any type of informatic or communicative technology that a user can wear on her body.[4] They take the form of glasses, hoodies, watches, bras, and even sex toys. The goal of most wearables, however, is to allow for easier access to certain forms of data not otherwise recorded. Most wearables track fitness-like data, allowing users real-time access to information such as how many calories they've burned, the number of steps they've taken, and their heart and breathing rates.

Wearables straddle the divide between stand-alone devices and networked, connected parts of a larger collective. Often they can be programed to measure human body data, issue calendar reminders, play music, and even tell the time. Always, though, wearables depend on access to a network at some point. Body data is uploaded to the cloud for archiving, calendars are synced across devices and services, and music is streamed. Wearables emerge from their boxes telling the time in Cupertino, California. Included in this network are the corporations (i.e., Google, Apple, Microsoft, etc., themselves a type of technology) that manipulate, store, share, and sell the collected data.

In most cases, small, separate bits of data from individual humans are of little use to corporations. Google may use information from someone's Gmail account to advertise to her, but she is not the only person to whom they are serving those ads; she is part of a demographic, or maybe even several demographics. The aggregation, sorting, and parsing of her data with everyone else's can indicate trends and concerns and offer marketing possibilities. Just like separate technologies in Kelly's reckoning, then, the individual matters less than the quantification and amplification that happen when her data is fragmented and thrown in with everyone else's and she becomes part of a demographic in which she, as whole, registers instead as parts.

Perhaps this is what Jay Timothy Dolmage picks up on when, in his *Disability Rhetoric*, he points to a general discomfort in recognizing the world and our bodies as already fragmented through technology and prosthetics:

> The idea of a relationship with the world mediated by technology might be acceptable, but the idea of the *incorporation* of technology as part of this process is less easily accepted. We resist the idea that we may allow technologies to trespass beyond the boundaries of our bodies; we will not admit that we all extend ourselves through our relationships with others and our use of tools. We will not admit that our knowing of the world is fragmented because our knowing of our bodies and therefore ourselves is fragmented—or, rather, relies on constant augmentation. (110)

For Dolmage, this inability to think of the incorporation of technology into our world is seated in an assumption of the *normate*, or the "organic unity and autonomy of the body," as a default way to think about our bodies and their environments (111). In the inability or refusal to think of our bodies as already fragmented, we see ourselves as wholly "human," without this essential relationship with technology. And yet, technology's desires are continuously fragmenting our bodies—if not in terms of ability and disability, then in terms of data that is reconfigured for aggregate bodies. Burke's original anxiety may have a new object, then, in the dispersion of the human subject in a flat sea of data.

But if we (qua data) can be used so easily, what do we get out of it? What does the instrumentalization of the individual human subject do for that individual subject? Dawn Nafus and Jamie Sherman attribute the Quantified Self movement to Kelly and Gary Wolf: "Wolf and Kelly felt that the explosion of personal tracking technologies, both software and hardware, opened up new questions about what these devices meant for individuals," and so the Quantified Self movement began to ask "what it means to think of data 'as a mirror' and what kinds of reflection, learning, and personal insights might emerge" (1787).

So while advertising companies might be lining up to sift through our data, the quantifiable self is supposed to make users aware of the hidden data in and of our lives. However, what is our relationship to this new data? Or, again, what are humans for?

Let us once again consider a Fitbit user who marches around her kitchen island just before bed in order to reach her goal of ten thousand steps for the day. (Or perhaps she marches in order to feel her Fitbit buzz against her wrist once she has passed ten thousand steps, or to share the achievement with other users via social networks.) Her sleep is monitored, too, as is her heartbeat throughout the day. Via separate applications on her phone, she is able to track the calories ingested at each meal and map and store the route she took on her morning run. And so on. Synecdochically, each of these bits of data stand for her, and, as they are gathered together and parsed via other applications, compared with data from other people (some friends, against whom she "competes" for the largest number of steps each day), a potentially more complete understanding of her health at any given moment may emerge. Of course, and synecdochically, just as a container can stand for the contained, she represents all of this data.[5] It is entirely possible that, over time, she may be able to take the data collected and, with help from her doctor, use it to make better decisions and improve her health. As final causes go, that is a pretty good one. The specific, daily pieces of data mean almost nothing on their own. Their aggregate potential, though, depends on developing habits and faith in that cause. There is a goal (being healthy and being in heaven are roughly correlates), but there is also a reliance upon ritual, and ritual is almost always also *for itself*.

Burke gets at ritual via artistic performance and argues that performing ritual is "a symbolic getting, not a real one. Hence, it could exist only by prolonging or delaying the act. . . . This element is so intrinsic to the ritual act that, even without the class motive, you could derive it. All purely ritual getting is also a not-getting" (*Rhetoric of Motives* 273). While ostensibly in service to the goal or final cause, the daily *performance* of data resists closure (i.e., final meaning) and perpetuates the action for itself. The repeated activity resists the very closure it is intended to bring about and, as ritual, becomes what Burke calls *pure persuasion*, as, "in any device, the ultimate form (paradigm or idea) of that device is present, and is acting. And this form would be the 'purity'" (273–74). Synecdochically, each act also indicates—stands for—a perpetually deferred end by calling it *into the present*. And this present is therefore also perpetual insofar as the ultimate form is repeated in every act. So whether the data eventually becomes part of a personal triumph or failure, part of an algorithm or advertising campaign, the motive of the wearable remains the same: "use my data now." As Burke remarks regarding another form of technology, pure persuasion "can arise out of expressions quite differently motivated, as when a book, having been developed so far, sets up demands of its own, demands conditioned by the parts already written, so that the book becomes to an extent something not foreseen by its author, and requires him to interfere with his original intentions. We here confront an 'ultimate' motive (as distinct from an 'ulterior' one)" (269). Data as ritual becomes an ultimate motive of technology and our relation to it. Contra an understanding of the relationship between humans and technology in which one *uses* the other, attending to data as ritual muddies the distinction between humans and technology, undermining the idea that one is prior to, in service to, or even separable from the other. This data, because of its ritual input, collection, and usage, becomes unending, perpetual, or atemporal, and the humans and technology become mere input: pure persuasion.

If human motive becomes transmuted by the technium so much so that there is a constant recursive back and forth between the human and the machine, then dramatism is in need of a revision: it needs to account for ever more *devices*. By and with which devices, both semiotic and material, are we motivated?

Technolistic Screens

Though Burke includes both language and technology as defining characteristics of humanity, he maintains language's primacy and the power it alone has to change our worldview. In his "Terministic Screens," Burke argues, "Even if any given terminology is a reflection of reality, by its very nature as a terminology it must be a selection of reality; and to this extent it must function also as a *deflection* of reality" (*Language* 45). For Burke, language has the ability to alter our realities not physically, but by moving our attention to one area and away from another. Terministic screens can reattune our perspectives. To clarify, he provides the following technological example: "When I speak of 'terministic screens,' I have particularly in mind some photographs I once saw. They were *different* photographs of the *same* objects, the difference being that they were made with different color filters. Here something so 'factual' as a photograph revealed notable distinctions in texture, and even in form, depending upon which color filter was used for the documentary description of the event being recorded"

(45). Here, the color filters allow certain characteristics of the objects to be seen over others, changing the focus and attention of the viewer. In this way, language, like the color filters, both broadens and focuses our worldviews and changes our reality by moving us *away* from certain terminologies and *toward* others in order to talk about our world. And, for Burke, recognizing the terministic screens in which we work is essential for our work in rhetoric and for understanding our relationship with technology.

And yet, it has been our argument that contemporary technology always acts in the same way as Burke's terministic screens regardless of these original terminologies. Technology (like language and precisely like the color filters) has the ability to persuade us into differing worldviews, so much so that if the machine and the human subject are, via synecdochic clustering, interchangeable, then it becomes difficult to distinguish between the motion of machines and the action of bodies or, indeed, between machines and bodies. Tracking and reporting become actions for their own sake (as moments of "pure persuasion"). Contemporary data is data for itself. What we might usually count as human, motivated action is transmuted—in its encounter with the technium—into perpetual, atemporal motion. Because of this, and because of the ubiquitous nature of technology, it is our view that, just as language is and has always been part of the technium (and not, as it is for Burke, an exception or first), the terministic screen should be considered a subset of a broader category that we call the technolistic screen. Like terministic screens, technolistic screens force us to question our dealings (not only with language, but also) with the technium. Technolistic screens not only acknowledge the human's physical relation to technology but also how that technology shapes and attunes us to what counts as human.[6]

Take the following as an example: At the time of this writing, a fundraising campaign has begun through the crowdfunding site Kickstarter for a product called Doppel. The campaign demonstrates both the presentness of data and the rhetoricity of rhythm promoted by Burke. Doppel is a machine and application bundle that purports to help manipulate one's attitude. Using rhythms similar to musical beats, Doppel provides haptic feedback to a user in order to simulate a "natural" body tempo. According to product and company cofounder Jack Hooper, Doppel "can be used to keep you going through a really long meeting, help you stay calm during a presentation or wind down at the end of the day. It gives people more control over how they feel" (Lomas). Much as the Internet changed our relationship to information and communication, Doppel has the potential to change how we relate to our surroundings and to each other.

As Burke points out, "the state of technology itself provides the conditions which open up avenues of 'pure' speculation. Instruments and methods are like images in suggesting new sets of implications" (*On Human* 285). For Burke, these "sets of implications" are always housed in their own precisely linguistic, terministic screens. Read through a technolistic screen, however, Doppel not only physically (and physiologically) alters one's perspective about reality, but could also potentially change the way we approach events that would otherwise leave us anxious, nervous, or unsettled.[7] Like the pure persuasion of language and its effects on the body, every instance of technology is rhetorical—that is, technology is contingent. "As a result of the contingency of rhetoric on technological behavior," Hill explains, "the potentially transformative function of both rhetoric and technology intermingle to either correct our technological problems or facilitate our probable doom."

For both Burke and Hill, anxieties about Big Technology can only be quelled by *expanding* symbolic action, because the invention of technology itself is already "a type of symbolic action" (Hill). It is when seen through the lens of posthumanism, however, that technology exists as its own organism, which means that we may not be able to approach it solely through linguistic means. Current technology, as Debra Hawhee argues, works through touch, rhythm, and sensation as well as symbols: "Sensation needn't become encased in language to be known . . . and needn't be so attached to meaning. Other attachments matter for rhetoric—political, bodily, technological, and sensory—and these intermix and move recursively" ("Rhetoric's" 13). By including technolistic screens with our terministic screens, we might not only understand humans as both symbol-using and technology-using animals, but also, more importantly, understand technology (like language) as using us.

Yet the question is not simply whether technolistic screens exist. Burke seems to admit the possibility when he points to the irony that he finds in the relationship between the human and technology (*On Human* 302). And in his later writings, especially "Variations on 'Providence,'" Burke progressed his terministic screens such that technology seemingly loses the tinge of its terministic birth, moving from the terminology that we use to discuss our world to the "institutions of 'technology'" that guide it (158). Hill puts this another way when he states that, for Burke, "people mold technology, technology molds the situation, and people utilize rhetoric to induce remolding technology to transform society." Part of what Hill means by this is that eventually, for Burke, after its initial terminological "molding," technology is seemingly imbued with its own "creative force that motivates human behavior by determining, in part, the scene in which humans act" (Hill). So it would seem that even though Burke begins with the actions of the symbol-using animal, he ends up in a place reminiscent of Kelly's technium, where these machines create "a universe of their own" ("Variations" 158).

Building on these posthuman murmurs in Burke's work, we argue that technolistic screens have always intersected and even *overwritten* human symbolic actions, making us turn left at the next street or check in at our favorite restaurant without seriously thinking about it. Complicating Hill's suggestion that Burke understood "technological materialization [to] embod[y] the *terminological* thrust of human inventiveness," we draw on Burke's articulation of "pure persuasion" to propose a recognition of technology as a material system in its own right, as an (habitual) actor with its own symbolic, ritual actions, which are not mere extensions of our own. Because technology keeps us marching around our kitchen islands until we have reached our ten thousandth step, we find a need for a revision to Burke's humanist definition of our relationship with technology. Technology has reached an easily identifiable point beyond creating a second nature or "Counter-Nature" to our (prime/primal) humanity, to being recognized as its own symbol-using entity that influences, persuades, and possibly loves.

Rather than Burke's dystopic vision of technology, Kelly suggests a more coevolutionary future:

> In the future, we'll find it easier to love technology. Machines win our hearts with every step they take in evolution. Like it or not, animal-like robots (at the level of pets, at first) will gain our affections, as even minimally lifelike ones do already. The internet provides a hint of the passion possible. Like many loves, it begins with infatuation and obsession. The global internet's nearly organic interdependence and emerging sentience make it wild, and its wildness draws our affections. We are deeply attracted to its beauty, and its beauty resides in its evolution. (324)

Technology is not (or perhaps won't remain) a simple extension (or perversion) of human symbolic action. Technolistic screens cannot be reduced to the human even though they come to in-form the human. The Fitbit user marches around her kitchen island. As organism, though, the technium offers a new actor in the scene, one that we have always worked *with*. Kelly's vision of love presents a rhetorical challenge that Burke would recognize and intensify. To love is to be identified with, which is to be consubstantial with. But identification isn't easy; love is hard. The work of remaining with is a constant march.

Notes

1. See Debra Hawhee's *Moving Bodies* for an expanded perspective on this. In that book, Hawhee traces Burke's fascination with the human body through both his early rhetorical texts and his early fiction.

2. In a way, this marks a confusion of formal and final cause, as the formal appellation "phone" begs for development toward an ideal, even as that ideal changes; phones can now be "smart."

3. See Benedict Giamo for a review of Burke, Marxism, and technology, and Stacey Sheriff for a compelling account of Burke's early commitment to communism as a response to, in his words, "the unsoundness of the capitalist method" (282).

4. See also the issue of *Rhetoric Society Quarterly* 46, no. 3, devoted to wearables.

5. The technological relationship of part to whole may be read as synecdochic. In *The Philosophy of Literary Form*, Burke proposes a form of clustering that takes synecdoche as its dominant form, and as one way of understanding the influence of motion on action. In synecdoche, the part can sometimes become representative of the whole, "the whole for the part, the container for the thing contained, the cause for the effect, the effect for the cause, etc.," or, put simply, "'twenty noses' for 'twenty men'" (25–26). Clustering—identifying what goes with what—by way of synecdoche requires a different approach to things and people. If a person's material property can become representative of that person as a whole, Burke's strict distinction between what "moves" and what "acts" must be reexamined.

6. "Somatechnics, a constellatory critical neologism cognisant of the mutual enfleshment of technologies and technologisation of embodied subjectivities," is a relatively recent formulation of this sense of the relationship of bodies and technology (O'Rourke and Giffney xi). It arose at the intersection of gender studies and disability studies from the recognition that "body modification" and other similar terms presuppose preexisting bodies to which technology does things, separating the body from the rest of the world and its processes.

7. Yoga or meditation might do this, but technology allows us to outsource our discipline.

Works Cited

Braidotti, Rosi. *The Posthuman*. Cambridge, Mass.: Polity Press, 2013. Print.

Burke, Kenneth. *Attitudes Toward History*. 3rd ed. Berkeley: University of California Press, 1984. Print.

———. "Definition of Man." *Hudson Review* 16, no. 4 (1963): 491–514. Web.

———. *Language as Symbolic Action: Essays on Life, Literature, and Method*. Berkeley: University of California Press, 1968. Print.

———. *On Human Nature: A Gathering While Everything Flows, 1967–1984*. Edited by William H. Rueckert and Angelo Bonadonna. Berkeley: University of California Press, 2003. Print.

————. *The Philosophy of Literary Form.* 3rd ed. Berkeley: University of California Press, 1974. Print.

————. *A Rhetoric of Motives.* Berkeley: University of California Press, 1969. Print.

————. *The Rhetoric of Religion: Studies in Logology.* Berkeley: University of California Press, 1970. Print.

————. "Variations on 'Providence.'" *Notre Dame English Journal* 13, no. 3 (1981): 155–83. JSTOR. Web. 19 Sep. 2016.

Dolmage, Jay Timothy. *Disability Rhetoric.* Syracuse: Syracuse University Press, 2014. Print.

Fisher, Mark. *Capitalist Realism: Is There No Alternative?* Washington: Zero Books, 2009. Print.

Giamo, Benedict. "The Means of Representation: Kenneth Burke and American Marxism." *KB Journal* 5, no. 2 (2009). Web. 12 Jul. 2015.

Greelish, David. "An Interview with Computing Pioneer Alan Kay." *TIME.com.* Web. 8 Jul. 2015.

Hawhee, Debra. *Moving Bodies: Kenneth Burke at the Edges of Language.* Columbia: University of South Carolina Press, 2012. Studies in Rhetoric/Communication. Print.

————. "Rhetoric's Sensorium." *Quarterly Journal of Speech* 101, no. 1 (2015): 2–17. Print.

Hill, Ian. "'The Human Barnyard' and Kenneth Burke's Philosophy of Technology." *KB Journal* 5, no. 2 (2009). Web. 6 Jul. 2015.

Kelly, Kevin. *What Technology Wants.* New York: Penguin Books, 2011. Print.

Lomas, Natasha. "Doppel Is a Wearable That Puts a Pulse on Your Pulse." *TechCrunch.* Web. 8 Jul. 2015.

Nafus, Dawn, and Jamie Sherman. "Big Data, Big Questions| This One Does Not Go Up To 11: The Quantified Self Movement as an Alternative Big Data Practice." *International Journal of Communication* 8 (2014): 1784–94. Print.

O'Rourke, Michael, and Nancy Giffney. "Originary Somatechnicity." *Somatechnics: Queering the Technologisation of Bodies,* edited by Nikki Sullivan and Samantha Murray. Queer Interventions. Farnham: Routledge, 2009, xi–xiii. Web. 20 Sep. 2016.

Shaviro, Steven. *No Speed Limit: Three Essays on Accelerationism.* Minneapolis: University of Minnesota Press, 2015. Kindle.

Sheriff, Stacey. "Resituating Kenneth Burke's 'My Approach to Communism.'" *Rhetorica* 23, no. 3 (2005): 281–95. Web. 19 Sep. 2016.

10

A Sustainable Dystopia

Casey Boyle and Steven LeMieux

But in any case, let there be no turning back of the clock. Or no turning inward. Our vice president has rightly cautioned: No *negativism*. We want AFFIRMATION—TOWARDS HELHAVEN.

ONWARD, OUTWARD, and UP!

—Kenneth Burke, *On Human Nature*

Kenneth Burke writes that *"Man is the symbol-using animal"* as the first of five clauses in defining the human (*Language* 1; emphasis in original). The well-known statement also, ironically, figures man as technological, as tool-using if we understand language and symbols themselves to be technological. We do. It is at least a little surprising, then, that Burke often held antagonistic views toward technology. But who could blame him? Experiencing the same cultural and historical moments—world wars, genocide, massive industrial upheavals—that forged the most ardent technological determinists, such as Thorstein Veblen and Jacques Ellul, Burke himself responded to those visible technological developments with suspicion if not outright disdain. Burke could not turn away from the negativity that was integral to emerging technology. Perhaps such integral negativity is best framed by Paul Virilio, who proclaimed that "[t]o invent the sailing ship or the steamer is *to invent the shipwreck*. To invent the train is *to invent the rail accident* of derailment. To invent the family automobile is to produce the *pile-up* on the highway" (10). Burke saw similar problems in and around high-paced technological development, and his writings often sought to sift out those interweavings.

These problems for Burke were not just the visible spectacles of automobile collisions or train crashes, but also the more pervasive ways that technological change shaped social conditions through our minor interactions. For instance,

Burke comments about how our increasingly technologically dependent activities compel each of us to specialize our knowledge, making our democracy not a society of equals discussing shared concerns, but a space wherein we take turns being subservient to our technological needs: "Under technology the division of labor requires a society of specialists serving one another. The garage man is the dishwasher's servant, and the dishwasher is the garage man's servant, an 'invidious' relation made 'democratic' by money and by the constant reversal of roles. Recalling the festival of the Roman Saturnalia, where master and slave changed places, we could describe our democracy as a kind of permanent but minute Saturnalia, with constant reversal in the relation between up and down" (*Rhetoric* 224).

This "constant reversal" between "up and down" betrays a source of unlikely anxiety for Burke and offers a type of short-circuiting of his typical, dynamic approach. This anxiety should be read as out of context for Burke, given his own repeated attempts to develop techniques and concepts that make social order more fluid and less fixed. For instance, in *A Grammar of Motives*, Burke turns to the very dissolution of his drama and its roles as a necessary step in preserving sociality (440–41). In those efforts, Burke presents the case for considering his work as not completely tied to the humanist tradition that might be more committed to conserving a particular social order. While we might not immediately attribute the anxiety in our oscillating relations with one another, it is here where we can see why Burke is taken to be a more humanist than posthumanist thinker. Given Burke's apparent disdain for technology, we might read further and realize that what makes such reversals "invidious" for Burke is that we have become objects for our objects. Burke welcomes fluidity and nonfixity in our social systems when those systems are reduced to those actions that take place between humans, but the Saturnalia offered in the above quotation involving humans and technical objects demonstrates anxiety when we expand what we mean by "the social." The above passage's phrasing of "garage['s]" man or the "dishwasher's servant" subordinate us not only to one another but to one another's possessions. Actually, it might be worse, because the dishwasher and the garage are themselves subservient to yet more of our possessions, dishes and cars. So our service to one another becomes further abstracted and distances us from one another through our things' things. Elsewhere, Burke responds to such conditions by writing that "while recognizing the tremendous motivational importance of all the new properties which modern technology has produced" an "ideal terminology must be designed . . . to perceive how man's relation to his properties is *symbolically constituted*" (*Permanence* 289; emphasis in original). When cast together, both passages position technological advance as causing "constant reversal" and necessitate that rhetoric respond by designing terminology for perceiving this "permanent but minute" change we experience. That is, Burke wants to make visible the invisible technological and infrastructural surrounds that motivate our actions, making his project, on many levels, very much an enterprise framed by humanism's aims for organized categorization.

It is this vision of technology, a negative vision concerned with reversals and service, that we wish to engage here. We embrace Burke's sensitivity to the "permanent but minute" reversals, but, instead of making these technologies more visible and thus avoidable, we seek to leverage those reversals, despite not knowing how exactly to define and categorize them. Such a reversal for rhetoric— which usually seeks to define, categorize, and use—is intended to activate its pragmatic potentials for generating and enacting change. This reversal also turns over a humanist rhetoric (again, one that would seek to know through definitions and critique) into a posthumanist rhetoric that would incorporate definitions and knowledge as part of—but irreducible to—a wider system of relations than the symbol or its definitions that rhetoric helps to shape.

Responding to what she calls a "posthumanist predicament," Rosi Braidotti argues for an affirmative politics as a key component for an ethics of a posthuman age. A traditional humanist orientation might categorize and hold separate *the* human as distinct from the machinations in which we are now inextricably entangled, but a posthumanist orientation leverages categorical uncertainty as a feature for inventing anew. This is not to say that posthumanism leaves the perils of technology unchecked. Indeed, the posthuman orientation is one often articulated as being brought on by the shame of having ravaged a planet through industrialization and unbounded technological drive. Far from eliding or ignoring the pitfalls that Burke warns about, Braidotti notes that "it is important to stress that affirmative politics, as the process of transmuting negative passions into productive and sustainable praxis, does not deny the reality of horrors, violence and destruction" (122). Braidotti argues we have entered a necro-politics in which the propensity toward harnessing life for capitalist gain that we once found in biopolitics is giving way to a necropolitics that forecloses on that very life through overuse and exhaustion. Furthermore, Braidotti proposes that an "affirmative ethics is based on the praxis of constructing positivity, thus propelling new social conditions and relations into being, out of injury and pain" (129). Again, we find another helpful reversal here in that Braidotti wishes to leverage injury and pain to compose new social conditions and new possibilities of being and for becoming. In fact, Braidotti eventually orients posthumanism itself toward affirming the inevitability of death—not just inevitable but as already having happened—and toward enacting "multiple practices of dying" (122). These practices would affirm our own deaths, and they would exercise that inevitable event according to a situated ethics of relation. In a posthuman ethics, our striving to live well is synonymous with dying well.

We seek here to put these two thoughts into unlikely conversation. In response to the problems of upheaval and the promise of upending, we offer a proposal for understanding our posthuman predicament through Burke—the inimitable humanist—as an opportunity to engage reversal as an affirmative mode of becoming. We first engage Burke's staunch humanism through his dystopian portrayals of unsustainable technological advancement, and then we present a case for creating an ongoing production of becoming other-wise. Second, in place of a rhetorical tendency to define and place phenomenon, we engage rhetoric through displacement. Swerving around *topoi* as an organizing strategy (via Burke's use of terminological frames and circumference), we introduce *dystopoi* as a material tactic for dis/organizing bodily practice. Finally, we offer material proposals for enacting *dystopoi* in a series of corrupted keyboards whose designs frustrate but do not interrupt one's practices. Our hope is that, by reversing Burke and traditional rhetorical practice, we contribute or—to put it better— extend rhetorical practice and Burke toward adjacent avenues of inquiry.

Seeking Safe Harbor in Helhaven

Man is the "*inventor of the negative,*" Burke claims (*Language* 9; emphasis in original). In addition to and in concert with symbols, the human is that being who, against natural order, concerns itself with what ought not to be. We traffic in the negative, especially as we use those symbols that stand for things not present; furthermore, we create technologies to stand in for our absence. We compose ideals that we then impose onto our worlds, regardless of whether they fit the given circumstances. Given this claim, we might consider Burke's aversion to technology in two ways. The first is that Burke defines human beings as indi-cations of the inventors of the negative and casting tools and systems as indica-tions of advanced stages of this negativity. Mechanisms, like symbols, take the place of what is not there. A factory takes the place of a thousand artisans; a car takes the place of a troop of comparatively less effective feet. We might also view

Burke's claim about man inventing the negative as an acknowledgment that humanity's creations negatively contribute to its environments. Of great concern for much of Burke's later writings is how technological change offers what Burke termed a counter-nature that worked against a prior, more ecologically balanced environment. Of course, neither of these excludes the other, so together they construct, for Burke, the negative as something of a persistent presence. A poetic problem, no doubt.

It should be no surprise, then, that the most persuasive piece that Burke offers against accelerated innovation revels in its stylistic flourishes concerning what might seem to be the negative aspects of technological change. Having written about humanity's propensity to invent the negative, Burke leverages that negativity into an affirmative embrace of certain ruin. In what is considered his "Helhaven" project, Burke, through three separate essays, presents technology's promise paradoxically through its propensity to produce waste through three separate essays. The first lays out a "techno-logic" of production that takes waste into account; the second offers a satirical portrayal of a moon colony constructed to affirm all technological development, especially its wasteful nature; and the third essay reflects back and comments on the use of satire for persuasive ends. Taken together, the "Helhaven" essays embrace the qualities of dystopia in that they portray the disastrous effects that will unfold if a current techno-logic is not reversed.

While it was not collected later along with the other two "Helhaven" essays, Burke begins the first salvo of the project with an article titled "Waste—The Future of Prosperity," which he wrote before but published after the 1929 stock market crash. The article extolls the seemingly limitless capacity for humans to produce waste, and Burke observes in the essay that much of that waste is accomplished in our engagement with and through technological living. Burke writes, "The more we learn to use what we do not need, the greater our consumption; the greater our consumption, the greater our production; and the greater our production, the greater our prosperity" ("Waste" 228–29). Tacking technology to the larger culture of production and consumption, Burke's logic is difficult to combat, despite its self-defeating effects. It has become our nature to consume, so we realize our *potential* when we somehow make our consumptive practices productive.

In the first of the two proper "Helhaven" essays, "Towards Helhaven: Three Stages," Burke satirically responds to the "irreversible change" wrought by "*Hypertechnologism*" and sketches a dystopic vision of progress left unchecked. In this fun and funny essay, Burke amplifies his past writing about waste and lambastes technology's inevitability by *affirming* its wasteful and wasting nature as integral to progress itself. In commenting on our culture as fundamentally a culture of waste, Burke proposes that "in order to ensure maximum production, hence maximum prosperity, all that we needed to do was to keep on wasting and a constantly accelerated pace—and we could look forward to a permanent bull market" (*On Human* 54–55). Recasting waste, then, as a positive development of technological innovation, Burke writes that "we are sick of Lamentation. What we want is affirmation," and that we must "stoutly affirm: We must not turn back the clock. We must continue what made us great" (56–57). The essay goes on to argue against looking to some nostalgic past in which humanity, for instance, rehabilitates a polluted body of water but instead uses that poisoned pond as a pesticide. Burke asks, "If there is a drive, why not drive with it, towards an ideal end?" (61). Above all, affirmation.

Here, we can imagine Burke premediating a response to Virilio by not seeking to eliminate the train crash but to profit from it by selling tickets to the catastrophe. And why not? In this first essay, Burke engages affirmation with sarcasm, hoping that the logic of the drive will exhaust its reader from even thinking of starting the journey. Burke goes on, in the essay's final section, to build an entire world as a result of wasting a planet: "In any case, now that the Irreversible Change is on the way, get in on the ground floor. Buy shares for yourself or your family in Helhaven, the greatest apocalyptic project this side of Mars" (62). In a faux marketing guise, he writes, "HELHAVEN, the Mighty Paradisal Culture-Bubble on the Moon" (62). The lunar colony will be a work of complete ease where "each such area will be kept in proper climatic balance," but, just in case things get too easy, Burke proposes that several "Chambers of Discomfort" be erected since "too orderly a mode of existence can itself become a source of personal disorder" (62). Again, we find the human as the inventor of the negative and, in this case, it is legitimate negativity that is desired for contrast. Taken together, the "Helhaven" world is one that feeds on itself.

In the latter of the three essays, Burke pulls back the curtain on the project and explains his method for deploying satire, arguing that "reduction to absurdity of the already quite absurd idea that cultural 'progress' is to be equated with the ever mounting development of 'new needs'" (69). Burke goes on to reveal his overall approach in the "Helhaven" project: "the satiric foretelling would be motivated devoutly by the hope that, in the world of facts, such a trend is *not* inevitable" (80; emphasis in original). The satire works because "*in principle* the Helhaven situation is 'morally' here already" (80 ; emphasis in original). That is,

Helhaven as a dystopia is a comment on the present despite also being an attempt to build a future-oriented separate world. Burke, then, reverses course again and makes dystopia not a future to avoid but a present to change.

In effect, Burke presents us a delayed dystopia through logical absurdity. Appropriating and "affirming" the wasteful effects of contemporary culture, Burke builds a world that feeds on its own environment until it is only able to consume its own exhaust. In place of minimizing waste through technological efficiency, Burke reverses course and situates techno-logic to consume itself. The reader then fills in the rest of the argument and understands that any system that feeds off its own environment is a system contributing to its inevitable demise. Burke's solution to the "irreversible change" that technology has wrought on our planet and culture is to "envision an apocalyptic development whereby technology could of itself procure, for a fortunate few, an ultimate technological release from the very distresses with which that very technology now burdens us" (61). The "Helhaven" project "will have been made possible by the very conditions which made it necessary" (62)—namely, exhaust, by-product, and waste.

Helhaven presents us with a situation in which dystopia is employed for a rhetorical aim. The illogical logic of embracing waste as productive achieves the highest point of negativity. Such is the logic of dystopias. They persuade through negative portrayals: "DO NOT ENTER." "HERE BE MONSTERS." To portray the negative, dystopias usually go one of two ways. They are either violent and oppressive, or they are pleasurable and atrophic. In the first, we are presented with a harsh, violent world whose technological advance is turned outward toward surveillance and repressive control. George Orwell's 1984 might be the best example of this style through its portrayal of a world built and sustained through oppressive media practices that intertwine through each human relationship. On the other side of the spectrum, the dystopias often offered are worlds of extreme pleasure brought about by technological innovation. Bypassing pesky intellects, the entertainment in Aldous Huxley's Brave New World reaches in and affects the citizen—that is, both the characters and the reader— at the level of sense, avoiding all friction and obstacles by ensuring that social order, above all, is maintained. Not unlike Helhaven, Huxely's world is built on the ideas of Fordist production. In fact, Helhaven, as another brave world, is that world where strife must be employed as recreation.

We think that strife could be used for more than mere recreation. Burke's dystopic lampooning as a response to the "irreversible change" of technology possibly did not go far enough. We propose to push Burke's satire further, toward sincerity, so that a new, productive line of inquiry concerning technology and/as rhetorical practice may be inaugurated. That is, just as Marshall McLuhan and Eric McLuhan have written that a reversal occurs when a medium has been pushed to its limits, we wish to push and accelerate Burke's dystopia and, with it, his definition of the human toward its own limits and reversals.

Worldbuilding

Burke's understanding of the human is that being which is *"separated from his natural condition by instruments of his own making"* (*Language* 13; emphasis in original). In a sense, then, the human is only ever inventing worlds to inhabit. Burke's "Helhaven" essays are an attempt at worldbuilding. By establishing a logic, sketching a world, and explaining that world in three separate essays, Burke offers readers a persuasive escape not from their current world but from a possible world that should be avoided. In that sense, Burke's dystopias are, as are most dystopias, cautionary tales. In that, though, they are not unlike our technologies. Our instruments, according to Burke, are always building "second natures" whose habits, customs, and practices come to be known as *natural*. Through language and, now, increased technological change, Burke sees such development as an ongoing, irreversible separation from our *natural* environments. In moments like these, we find Burke to be his most humanist and resistant of the social dynamisms that he otherwise extols for relations that constitute the human drama. Understanding technology use as separating us from *natural* conditions not only sustains a divide between the human and the nonhuman, but also inaugurates another divide between the human and something that comes after.

In service of exploring how our natures might be separated from our present conditions, hallmarks of our posthuman predicament, we turn to yet another dystopia, Kurt Vonnegut's short story "Harrison Bergeron." Vonnegut's story offers a slight but productive difference from our archetypical dystopia stories. In place of the extremely repressive dystopia found in *1984* or the debilitating paradise found in *Brave New World*, Vonnegut strikes a balance that strives to level all human capacities to an equal measure. In the story, each person is separated from a distinctive ability by being assigned a "handicap" that they experience via some external device. For those who are intelligent, earpieces and headphones are attached to blast noise that disrupts contemplation; for those who are strong or dexterous, metal frames and weights are attached to their bodies so that they are weighed down and encumbered. The story's imprisoned title character, Harrison Bergeron, is described as both a genius and an athlete, so it is noted that "nobody had ever borne heavier handicaps" (11). In addition to Harrison—who breaks out of prison to become an "emperor" and find his empress—an unnamed ballerina is described in the story as being in need of a debilitating mental handicap as well as a hideous mask to cover her "blindingly beautiful" face (12). In the story's climactic scene, Harrison and the unnamed ballerina drop their handicaps and come together in dance on live television. They move so well that, "in an explosion of joy and grace, into the air they sprang!" (13). They soar such that "not only were the laws of the land abandoned, but the law of gravity and the laws of motion as well" (13), until they are brought back to earth by the Handicapper General's shotgun. So it goes.

The theme of this dystopic story is traditionally understood to be that, without determinative constraints, Harrison's and the ballerina's natural talents can shine forth, and their full potentials can be expressed. Indeed, Vonnegut puts much work into describing the handicapping apparatuses as heavy burdens and, furthermore, Harrison as "under-handicapped," despite still being weighed down by handicaps heavier than all others. According to this traditional—now commonplace—interpretation, the story tells of the dangers of enforcing equality at the expense of distinction. However, we wish to offer an alternative reading. Perhaps instead of reading the spectacular dance as the result of losing determinative constraints, we might read instead that the ability to soar and transcend apparent physical laws, separating oneself from a sedimented nature, followed from having to wear the restraints in the first place. That is, the restraints and handicaps did not prevent additional capacities but instead afforded new capacities to form. Much as the rigid structure of a sonnet requires different and new imaginations, Vonnegut's characters determine their natures by submitting to the cruel pedagogy of enforced handicaps; their constraints have afforded a new relation with gravity. What "Harrison Bergeron" shows us, then, is that we are not negatively determined by our constraints; we affirmatively determine what comes next through constraint.

Burke is not too far removed from these thoughts. For instance, in the Helhaven dystopia, the need to invent strife in the form of "Chambers of Discomfort" is invoked solely because total pleasure and ease would be impossible without some friction. If the human is that being who separates itself from its natural conditions, then what ends might that human eventually determine if it might not even be bound, in the commonplace sense, by being human? With this question in mind, we move now toward a rhetoric that might be best understood as applied science fiction.

Architectural theorists Madeline Gins and Shusaku Arakawa echo Burke with their own provocative claim toward irreversible change: that architecture can enable its human inhabitants to *reverse* their mortal destinies and live forever. They write that "architecture is the greatest tool available to our species, both for figuring itself out and for constructing itself differently" (xx). They propose architecture that challenges the body by making it "live uphill." Their imagined space is by no means a utopia but, rather, utilizes dystopia in that its main purpose is to provide manageable strife in place of ease. We understand this project as arguing for leveraging the available means of exercising a body's tendencies as a way to create new capacities for living in and through an architectured experience. Where Burke might have seen technological advance as evidence of a counter-nature—pulling the human away from its more fitting environs—Gins and Arakawa instead seek to counter fate by pushing our nature past its limits, reversing destiny.

While their proposal may be grand (even preposterous), its impetus and operations are architectonically rhetorical (McKeon). That is, we consider rhetorical living—especially in a posthuman mediascape—as offering occasions for ongoing rhetorical training, an education that is executed by undertaking its process as always "learning uphill." In more traditional architectural discourses, we could compare the architectural body and this "learning uphill"—one that incorporated the human and the nonhuman architecture as one body—to a similar design in the "oblique function" as developed by Virilio and Claude Parent, who played with the production of inclines, moving up and moving down as a way to dismiss the staticness of strict horizontal and vertical architectures. They sought to displace a building's inhabitants by making them both work and strive to stay still. In this way, the strife and striving compelled by these architected environments differ from our prior examples of dystopia because these environments are designed not to exhaust themselves but to be sustainable.

Alongside the worldbuilding done through fictional dystopias and the grand architectural designs offered above, we look to user-experience design—a profession whose practitioners seek to make efficient and pleasurable interfaces between users and tools—as a space that can be reinvented for producing what we are calling *sustainable dystopias*. These interface spaces, both physical and digital, would be those situated assemblages designed to nudge and prod a user and her surroundings toward novel compositions through manageable strife. Whereas Burke embraces the literary dystopia for persuasive ends, we embrace literal dystopia for productive experience. In further exploring a notion of "learning uphill" as a posthuman rhetoric, we draw from interaction designer Dan Saffer's notion of microinteractions. Saffer defines microinteraction as "a contained product moment that revolves around a single use case—a tiny piece of functionality that only does one thing" (2). Such design elements are not major features of a product—a switch, a button, a slider—but are part of the minute, minor interactions that occur, for the most part, just below the user's conscious awareness. Working from Saffer's microinteraction and toward a sustainable dystopia, we propose "microruptures"—the amplification and inversion of microinteractions—as a vital method for habituating technology use differently. While rhetoric is often thought to be an art of rendering implicit assumptions consciously explicit, our project leverages nonconscious practices as available material for rhetorical experience. For instance, what we are calling microruptures—have been found to be productive uses of friction in interface design in the neighborhood-focused social network Nextdoor. In response to a problem—namely, that Nextdoor enabled racial profiling when some of its users responded to the presence of minorities in a neighborhood as possible "suspicious activity"—the designers of the Nextdoor interface went against design practice, which usually calls for fewer steps, by instead creating additional steps to slow down users' reports. According to several popular-press accounts of the redesign, the social network was able to reduce the number of unwarranted reports of suspicious activity considerably and thus reverse the habits and structures of implicit bias (see Rhodes). While not explicitly calling any user's implicit bias to the fore, the frictional redesign compelled users to trudge through a series of microruptures that then persuaded users to counter their habits and not report activity on the basis of a person's race. Microruptures, as seen in the Nextdoor example, offer a singular example of how friction can be a productive social practice. This particular example, along with the concept of microruptures in general, is not entirely like what Burke says about "pure persuasion," which Burke describes as the "apparent" furthest reaches of rhetoric and persuasion in the traditional sense of, for instance, trying to gain advantage in a debate; instead, it is better understood as "education" (*Rhetoric* 268). Burke further notes that the "indication of pure persuasion in any activity is in an element of 'standoffishness' or perhaps better *self-interference*" (269; emphasis in original). For Burke, what would make an occasion for persuasion pure is the joy that one would get out of the act of saying just words, an experience of intrinsic joy. Microinteractions and microruptures are those interactions that help inform an experience without wholly governing the experience. That is, microinteractions and microruptures cannot be reduced to an identity of a user experience, but they nonetheless reform that experience. Microrupture shares with pure persuasion's self-interference function that displaces any aim for effectual advantage from having said something to be enveloped by the joy of the having said (269).

Our proposal for sustainable dystopias through microruptures are not without precedence.

Technology can be designed to separate us from our sedimented activities, as seen in the example of Nextdoor. Techno-logics shape an ongoing ethical comportment of displacement (or standoffishness, as Burke might say) that, we argue, is rhetorically productive. In addition to traditional technology that works to enhance or assist—in a disability-studies sense—Sara Hendren, in "Towards an Ethics of Estrangement," proposes a techno-logic whose chief function would be to "interrogate the assumptions and ideas about the body, its capacities, and disabled-ness itself" (59). Furthermore, "tools for estrangement," Hendren proposes, would "leave open questions about the liberations and limitations of our extended machine-body-selves" and "disrupt our easy notions of technical efficiency and utility" (59). These tools are not unlike the *standoffish* "self-interrupting" mechanism in Burke's articulation of "pure rhetoric." By dislodging a body's typical experience—especially if just a little—the bodily practices must adjust and make up for multiplicity of minor missteps by exercising new possibilities of going on.

Dystopias may persuade someone to take an alternate course, but we are persuaded that dystopias can do more. Although worldbuilding is often undertaken for the sake of gathering in place, we wish to engage dystopia (and the examples of worldbuilding in this section) as a way to displace. In a humanist rhetoric, the *topoi* or commonplaces are those places where we share consensus. These are the repeated sayings, beliefs, and customs that bind us. In their binding capacities, the *topoi* are not different from the ways that "circumference" or "terministic screens"—as Burke describes them—help constrain a discourse to certain repeating features and functions. In response, we invoke Gins and Arakawa's desire for the "circumjacent" (the potential tendencies and capacities not yet informed by the landing-sites that one inhabits) that the architectural body strives to compose. In explaining the "circumjacent," they write that, "similarly to how she flexes her muscles, a person flexes her surroundings—both are with her and of her always. Landing-site dispersal and a flexing of the circumambient determine and describe the world that lies within one's ambit of the moment" (40). This place is not the shared bounds of circumference and *topoi*, but the leveraging of bad places (*dystopia*) to move to an adjacent place. In concert with and against traditional *topoi*, and in conversation within and through the circumjacent, we propose *dystopoi*. As a new rhetorical *technē*, the *dystopoi* are formalized assemblages, body-machines, that incorporate a series of microruptures as a way to constrict and thus compel movement through *self-interference*. They compose events for learning uphill.

The Uncommonplace of *Dystopoi*

The human is "*goaded by the spirit of hierarchy*" and "*moved by a sense of order,*" according to Burke (*Language* 15). We find this hierarchy being reversed to and fro through constantly changing social statuses and, as mentioned in the introduction, through technological engagements. Burke gestures toward examples of how hierarchy and order move us by immediately pointing to "the grotesque fictions of Franz Kafka [as] marvelous in this regard" (16). We agree and turn to another example from Kafka that might further substantiate Burke's claim. In a letter to his friend Oskar Pollak, Kafka described a world we are all familiar with: the writing desk. His desk, however, may be less familiar to the comfortable writing environments that we have built for ourselves: "You see, it's a respectably minded desk meant to educate" (3). Kafka further describes the desk: "Where the writer's knees usually are, it has two horrible wooden spikes," which is fine, provided that "you sit down quietly, cautiously at it, and write something respectable" (3). Kafka explains to his friend that, as might be the case, "if you become excited, look out—if your body quivers ever so little, you inescapably feel the spikes in your knees, and how that hurts" (3). He concludes with a lesson: "Don't write anything exciting and don't let your body quiver when you write" (3). Kafka's writing desk localizes the architectural body to the writing body that is composed of the writer, the desk, writing materials, and, above all, the relations therein. It is, he claims, "meant to educate"; it is meant to lead one out of and into ethical comportments.

Bruno Latour renders explicit what is implicit in Burke and excruciating in Kafka about how our technological structures help shape our moral and ethical engagements. Latour claims that "at first I thought we would take a giant step forward if only we would recognize that a substantial part of our everyday morality rested upon technological apparatuses" (252). The example he offers—the world of the writing desk—is that "for reasons unknown to me, the maker of my desk prevents me from opening a drawer without the two others being carefully and completely shut" (252). Furthermore, "to the super-ego of tradition we may well add the under-ego of technologies in order to account for the correctness, the trustworthiness, the continuity of our actions" (253). Although we hesitate to delve into morals, we read what Latour discusses here as ethics cast in a pragmatic sense. In this, we follow Gins and Arakawa's advice that "the effort to counter mortality must be constant, persistent, and total. The wish and will to do this must be in the air we breathe, having been built into the places within which we live and breathe" (xv). Latour's "under-ego of technologies" that helps maintain the continuity of our actions is not unlike the "living uphill" offered by Gins and Arakawa's conceptualization of the architectural body, or Parent and Virilio's "Oblique Function," or Hendren's "tools of estrangement." All of these places are what we call *dystopoi*. They are, as Kafka says of his desk, "meant to educate." They function as pest machines that furnish us with occasions to learn uphill, reincorporating a body with and through its environs with each and every microrupture. In this, we affirm again Gins and Arakawa's claim that "the body, a complex organism that is always in the process of reading surroundings, needs to be defined together with that within which it moves" (xx). In favor of defining the human as separate from its environments, we embrace the posthuman as defined with its surroundings, and as those elements change so, too, does what might have been thought of as *human*.

Burke establishes "the doctrine of technological progress [as] the 'higher standard of living'" to be a misconstrued ethical pursuit that reinscribes "the human body as vile and depraved" while celebrating every new piece of technology (*Rhetoric* 307). For Burke, this pursuit instills a "mind-body dualism, with the equivalent of 'mind' now being the corpus of mechanical inventions (born of intellect)" (307). The body, not only subordinate to the mind, is now subordinate to "mechanical devices" (307). The machines that we'll engage here reverse the fundamental assumption of Burke's doctrine of technological progress. Rather than producing a higher standard of living—an easier time of it—they do the opposite. They rely on the mediation of technological entanglements, and rather than reaffirm a mind-body dualism, they resist it by leveraging mind and body as one substance.

Whereas Virilio drew causation between the invention of new technologies and their corresponding, eventual disaster, and Burke satirically saw profit margins in technologically assured destruction, the three *dystopoi* that we describe below—*Reticence*, *Resistance*, and *Reluctance*—are invented disaster. Rather than figuring which disaster follows a "higher standard of living," we instead ask which affordances emerge from the deliberately invented shipwreck, derailment, or pile-up. These *dystopoi*, rather than leapfrogging embodied relation for an end product, present themselves as pure mediation in Burkean pure persuasion. For Gins and Arakawa, "a territory of mediation gets described or suffuses or flourishes in/as place through movements and activities," and these machines mediate "for a person much of what hitherto existed for her as a procedural or unconscious" (56). Part of Braidotti's posthuman ethics concerns a similar resituating of the human; she writes that "the human organism is an in-between that is plugged into and connected to a variety of possible sources and forces" (139). Braidotti continues by stating that we can consider the human to be a machine, "simultaneously more abstract and more materially embedded" than purely utilitarian (139). These body-machines are structured through *dystopoi* as "an embodied and affective and intelligent entity that captures processes and transforms energies and forces" (139). They produce—by attending to mediation—body-machines and create environmentally bound entities. As such, "an embodied entity feeds upon, incorporates and transforms its (natural, social, human or technological) environment constantly" (139). But feeding upon one's own environment does not necessarily lead to the demise that Burke envisions in Helhaven. Braidotti is clear that "being embodied in this high-tech ecological manner" is dangerous; the "inhuman aspects entail multiple forms of vulnerability" (140). But this vulnerability does not spell disaster; it demands that "we need to experiment with new practices" that tease out different possibilities for relating (140).

Gins and Arakawa refuse the certainty of death. Braidotti refuses the certainty of life: "Life is at best compelling, but it is not compulsive" (134). For Braidotti, "the ethical life is life as virtual suicide. Life as virtual suicide is life as constant creation. Life lived so as to break the cycles of inert repetitions that usher in banality. Lest we delude ourselves with narcissistic pretences, we need to cultivate endurance, immortality within time, that is to say death in life" (135). We need to learn uphill. In offering the *dystopoi*—in three specific devices and other related examples—we are proposing sites for generating and cultivating endurance and distinction, for reincorporating the body by asking what it can do. Two of the following three material *dystopoi*—*Reticence* and *Resistance*—were designed and constructed by Steven. They, along with several other digital and physical pieces, are part of an ongoing project that interrupts normative writing and reading practices through embroiled material relations that create feelings of both stupidity and indigestion. Casey and Steven codesigned *Reluctance* as a third *dystopos* that blends physical and digital processes. All three of these materially situated writing machines function as *dystopoi*, as sites whose aim is to provide an experience of microruptures as a way to build up greater capacities.

In *Reluctance* (fig. 10.1), we are afforded an opportunity to work with delayed production. This machine relies on an Arduino-powered device that mediates between the keyboard and computer. Its function is to vary the speed with which text appears on the screen after having been typed on the keyboard. The dystopic function here is achieved through the seemingly immaterial obstacle that estranges, to use Hendren's term, physical and digital connections. This distancing, done through variable speeds, imposes a feeling of reluctance on the act of writing. Whereas in typical circumstances a writer might be able to read

Figure 10.1 | *Reluctance* intercepts and alters the signal between keyboard and computer by assigning delays for when entered text appears on the screen. Photo: Casey Boyle and Steven LeMieux.

what she writes while she writes it, writing with *Reluctance* compels a user to question what she has written, to constantly wait for her own words to appear so that she might find out what has been written. Latour "[rails] against" the rigid constraints that his writing desk saddles him with, but he "[gets] on it" because he "is bound by it," and there is little else he can do if he is to remain part of that body-machine (253). *Dystopoi* are both voluntary and binding. Gins and Arakawa's description of the architectural body runs along similar lines: it is communal and cooperative, it "mediates the body proper and the architectural surround" (70–71). Neither is prior to the other. By mediating and thus separating writing from reading, *Reluctance* disassociates a writer from her writing and resituates the process as fundamentally communal. A user reluctantly writes and reluctantly reads.

In *Resistance* (fig. 10.2), a line of rubber bands stretching across the keyboard's expanse invites the user to interact with a pre-interface before the interface. To use the machine—the combination of keyboard, computer, and word processor—the user must position her fingers precisely within each individual band. For someone who is proficient with touch-type, this can require a degree

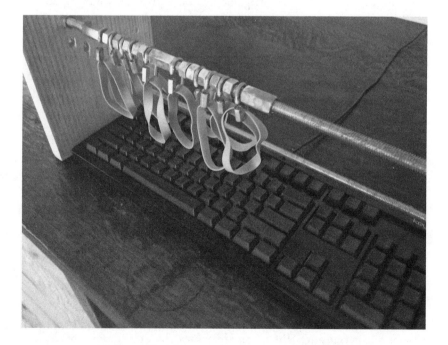

Figure 10.2 | *Resistance* compels a user to actively work against it to write. Photo: Steven LeMieux.

of hand-eye concentration akin to early days of finding the home row. To type, a user must have both hands simultaneously positioned within the machine. In order to fully situate herself, a user has to meticulously position each finger within each band. This preparatory layer both focuses a user's attention on the placement of each individual digit and foreshadows the layered entanglements that writing emerges from. *Resistance*—because it inserts itself directly between a writer and her keyboard—becomes a form of prewriting, a deliberate dystopic introduction to the writing process.

Once a user begins typing, each keystroke takes a considerable amount of effort. It's important to distinguish this physically demanding machine from something like a manual typewriter, which requires noticeably more effort than a modern keyboard. Modern keyboards, too, have their eventual disaster. To invent the keyboard is, as Virilio might write, to invent carpal tunnel syndrome. With both manual typewriters, modern keyboards, or even pens and pencils, discomfort—for an experienced user—occurs after a significant duration. But the *Resistance* strives toward immediate mediation; here, there is intense physical exertion from the beginning. Each letter is worked for at a different level of intensity. Hitting a "G" or "D" is significantly easier than a key near the edge of the keyboard, which requires further reach with a weaker finger. Deleting anything or making corrections becomes very labor-intensive; the backspace key is a definite stretch. Because both hands are suspended within the rubber bands, maneuvering around the screen also becomes difficult; a user only has the arrow keys, accessible only by her little finger, at her disposal. All of this upends a typical writing experience and a typical writing body, and things slow down considerably as a user labors toward any particular key, or she stops and rests while determine the best fingers to use to hit particular keys.

Finally, the *dystopos* offered by *Reticence* (fig. 10.3) has screws attached to each key. None of the screws are sharp enough to break the skin, but the pressure required to push any given key induces pain. This machine does not cause any lasting harm—there's no blood involved. Instead, every keystroke leaves a definite impression, an embodied memory of having written. Furthermore, a user has to aim her fingers for any given spike; because the screws displace the point of contact, and because they frustrate without wholly disturbing, the keyboard resists familiarization and encourages displacement. In the short term, rather than becoming accustomed to the pinprick of the keyboard, the user becomes hypersensitive. The longer she writes, the more prominent the keyboard becomes in the relationship, and the slower writing becomes. As with

Figure 10.3 | *Reticence* warrants trepidation even before use but obliges caution during use as well. Photo: Casey Boyle and Steven LeMieux.

Kafka's writing desk, *Reticence* enforces a particular discipline. And while his desk demanded bourgeois restraint by physically punishing a writer for excess emotion, this spiked keyboard demands bodily attention with a material presence that resists familiarization. As with *Resistance*, the writing process slows to a crawl as the user hesitates about pressing any given key even while she actively aims for it. And, again, as with *Reluctance*, it's important that this isn't a pain that develops after extended periods of writing. From the very first, each letter written with *Reticence* is made through a painful encounter. While learning uphill, "persons need to be rescued from self-certainty, but they also need to put their tentativeness in precise order in relation to works of architecture" (Gins and Arakawa 50). *Reticence* operates at a similar point of mediation. Because each keystroke is delivered so slowly, each stroke a microrupture, the user writes in her head, she has time to rewrite—tentative but deliberate, uncertain but structured.

These physical keyboards are fierce manifestations of a range of other user-experience environments offered by digital interfaces. Over the past few years, an array of software applications related to typing and writing instruments has offered writers opportunities to experience what we call *dystopoi*. One case, the Prisoner's Keyboard, designed by Nick Barr, is an application based on a particular Oulipian writing game called the prisoner's constraint (fig. 10.4). The prisoner's constraint imagines a prisoner who attempts to write a note in the most compact manner possible. To accomplish this, the prisoner only writes words that contain neither ascenders nor descenders, letters in the Latin alphabet that rise above or below the main body of the letter (e.g., q, t, y, i, and p in the first row of the QWERTY keyboard). This game constructs elaborate lipograms, pieces of writing in which particular letters are excluded. Barr's Prisoner's Keyboard streamlines the prisoner's constraint by erasing the excluded keys from the iOS visible keyboard. But the prisoner's constraint is only its starting point. With this application, users can modify their keyboards however they please and so can create their own constraints and subsequent lipograms. It demands, rather than acquiesces to, particular writing. Georges Perec, writing about the history of the lipogram, states that "a lipogram may not be remarked; most of the time the omission must be announced in its title. A lipogram that did not advertise itself as such . . . would have every chance of being overlooked" (106–7). Barr's Prisoner's Keyboard, like the physical keyboards above, is focused almost entirely on the user's experience during the event of writing. The writing that these machines produce denies textual trace. The constraints, though, leave a trace on the writer herself. Unlike the other *dystopoi* described above, this keyboard doesn't turn the user's attention toward her embodied relations. Instead, she must constantly exercise her relation to the alphabet, to words that she's both familiar and unfamiliar with. It demands attending to the subject of writing as afforded by particular sets of letters. What change does a move from the definite article "the" to the indefinite "a" produce?

A related application, Flowstate, will erase all the words written during a timed writing session if the writer stops or slows before the timed session is complete (fig. 10.5). Flowstate works on a different register than the previous four devices. Rather than slowing writing to a crawl, Flowstate speeds everything up. It's a runaway rather than derailed train. Once a writing goal is set, if the user stops writing long enough to reread a paragraph, check a quotation, or decide which homonym is needed, her text vanishes. The physical machines described above estrange a writer's relationship with the mechanical devices of writing, and the Prisoner's Keyboard performs a similar estrangement with alphabetic language; this application more broadly interferes with the relationship between writing's experiential process and the purpose of any particular writing. Writing—writing anything—becomes more important than writing something particular. Flowstate is described as "emphasiz[ing] the distinction

Figure 10.4 | The Prisoner's Keyboard is an iOS application that provides users an alternate keyboard on their iOS device that is constrained by letter assemblages. The app was created by Nick Barr.

Figure 10.5 | Flowstate is a completely contained, pressured writing environment. The app was created by Overman LLC.

between writing and editing" ("Flowstate"); we might further say that Flowstate flattens the hierarchy of activity and situates the mechanical and intellectual process of writing alongside any other craft requiring hand-eye coordination. Flowstate paradoxically demands both speed and patience. Only after a user has met her goal—writing for, say, one to one hundred eighty minutes—is she given the chance to edit what she's written.

In each of these *dystopoi* that we have presented, a series of reversals occurs through microruptures in the space that is beneath an ability to upend an entire process but just above being insignificant. While our prior examples of dystopias were written as science fiction, our *dystopoi* write us through science friction. In place of commonplaces, instead of holding to a circumference, *dystopoi* enact the circumjacent, goading users toward engaging with and reversing hierarchies, simultaneously moving and equipping users to press forward.

Equipment for Dying Well

We have presented a case for leveraging Kenneth Burke's humanist tendencies toward the posthuman. Following Burke's lead, we have embraced *dystopia* as a productively persuasive mechanism for engaging our posthuman predicament. Instead of using *dystopia* as a cautionary tale, as a constraint to avoid and keep at bay, we argue instead that *dystopia* is something to labor in, to live through, to die with. *Dystopoi*, as mechanisms for invention in a posthuman rhetoric, do not seek to place everyone on the same page—as the function of *topoi* or common-places might—but to incorporate missteps, mistakes, and misshapenings. These *dystopoi* explode rather than reduce possibility. Beyond their specific applications, the above *dystopoi* provide a method for reading Burke's humanism differently. The editors' introduction to this volume calls attention specifically to Burke's brand of humanism. He positioned humans as different from animals not merely by degree but by kind. Beyond symbol use, he called out what he saw as a unique propensity toward cruelty, that "we are something special, endowed with the ability to be the unkindest kind of all" ("Revival" 488). This cruelty, alongside with the specific violences that Burke lists in the lead-up to his proclamation, can be taken up productively as the cruel pedagogy of *dystopoi*. Humans might not be uniquely, exceptionally unkind, but humanism, as a constraining *dystopos* within his work, is. The *dystopoi* are ways to die a little bit over and over so that one never has to die a lot. As Gins and Arakawa proclaim, "Once people realize that the human race has not yet availed itself of its greatest tool for learning how not to die, they will cease being defeatists in the matter" (xiii). We shall enact a reversal of the ultimate medium, life itself, when we realize that the manageable strife offered by *dystopoi* offers us equipment for living forever by dying well. In concert with Burke's claim that the human is *"rotten with perfection"* (*Language* 16), we propose the posthuman is *ripe with imperfections*.

Works Cited

Barr, Nick. "The Prisoner's Keyboard." *Medium*. 8 Jun. 2014. Web. 28 Jul. 2014.
Braidotti, Rosi. *The Posthuman*. Cambridge, Mass.: Polity Press, 2013. Print.
Burke, Kenneth. *A Grammar of Motives*. Berkeley: University of California Press, 1945. Print.

————. *Language as Symbolic Action: Essays on Life, Literature, and Method.* Berkeley: University of California Press, 1966. Print.

————. *On Human Nature: A Gathering While Everything Flows, 1967–1984.* Edited by William H. Rueckert and Angelo Bonadonna. Berkeley: University of California Press, 2003. Print.

————. *Permanence and Change: An Anatomy of Purpose.* 3rd ed. Berkeley: University of California Press, 1984. Print.

————. "Revival of the Fittest." *Equipment for Living: The Literary Reviews of Kenneth Burke,* edited by Nathaniel A. Rivers and Ryan P. Weber. Anderson: Parlor Press, 2010, 486–89. Print.

————. *A Rhetoric of Motives.* Berkeley: University of California Press, 1969. Print.

————. "Waste—The Future of Prosperity." *New Republic* 63 (1930): 228–31. Print.

"Flowstate." *Overman.* http://hailoverman.com/flowstate. Web. 11 Feb. 2016.

Gins, Madeline, and Shusaku Arakawa. *Architectural Body.* Tuscaloosa: University of Alabama Press, 2002. Print.

Hendren, Sara. "Towards an Ethics of Estrangement." *Cyborgs and Monsters* 3 (6 Dec. 2011): 52–63. https://organseverywhere.com/pdf/OE_3_Cyborgs-and-Monsters.pdf. Web. 22 Apr. 2015.

Huxley, Aldous. *Brave New World.* London: Harper Perennial Modern Classics, 2006. Print.

Kafka, Franz. *Letters to Friends, Family, and Editors.* Translated by Richard Winston and Clara Winston. New York: Schocken, 2013. Print.

Latour, Bruno. "Morality and Technology: The End of the Means." Translated by Couze Venn. *Theory, Culture & Society* 19, nos. 5–6 (2002): 247–60. Print.

McKeon, Richard. "The Uses of Rhetoric in a Technological Age: Architectonic Productive Arts." *The Prospect of Rhetoric,* edited by Lloyd F. Bitzer and Edwin Black, Englewood Cliffs: Prentice Hall 1971, 44–63. Print.

McLuhan, Marshall, and Eric McLuhan. *Laws of Media: The New Science.* Toronto: University of Toronto Press, 1992. Print.

Orwell, George. *1984.* New York: Signet Classics, 1961. Print.

Perec, Georges. "History of the Lipogram." *Oulipo: A Primer of Potential Literature,* edited and translated by Warren Motte. Champaign: Dalkey Archive Press, 1998, 97–108. Print.

Rhodes, Margaret. "Nextdoor Breaks a Sacred Design Rule to End Racial Profiling." *Wired* (31 Aug. 2016): 52–63. Web. 14 Nov. 2016.

Saffer, Dan. *Microinteractions: Designing with Details.* Sebastopol: O'Reilly Media, 2013. Print.

Virilio, Paul. *The Original Accident.* Translated by Julie Rose. Cambridge, Mass.: Polity Press, 2007. Print.

Virilio, Paul, and Claude Parent. "Architecture Principe: 1966 and 1996." Translated by Georges Collins. Paris: Les Editions de l'Imprimeur, 1997. Print.

Vonnegut, Kurt. "Harrison Bergeron." *Welcome to the Monkey House.* New York: Random House, 2007, 7–14. Print.

Contributors

Casey Boyle is an assistant professor of Rhetoric and Writing at the University of Texas–Austin, where he researches and teaches rhetorical theory, media studies, and posthumanism. In addition to articles and books (including a nearly finished book manuscript titled *Rhetoric as a Posthuman Practice*), Casey is the author of book reviews for Collin Brooke's *Lingua Fracta* (*Kairos*) and Jeff Pruchnic's "Rhetoric and Ethics in the Cybernetic Age" (*Philosophy & Rhetoric*). He is currently composing a review for Cynthia Haynes's *The Homesick Phonebook*.

Kristie S. Fleckenstein, professor of English and director of the Graduate Program in Rhetoric and Composition at Florida State University, teaches graduate and undergraduate courses in rhetoric and composition. Her research interests include feminism and race, especially as both intersect with material and visual rhetorics. She is the recipient of the 2005 CCCC Outstanding Book of the Year Award for *Embodied Literacies: Imageword and a Poetics of Teaching* (Southern Illinois University Press, 2003), and the 2009 W. Ross Winterowd Award for Best Book in Composition Theory for *Vision, Rhetoric, and Social Action in the Composition Classroom* (Southern Illinois University Press, 2009). Her current project explores photography as a resource for visual rhetoric in nineteenth-century debates about racial identities.

Nathan Gale is an assistant professor of Rhetoric and Composition at Utah Valley University. He currently serves as an associate writing program administrator and teaches courses in posthuman rhetorics, public rhetorics, and rhetorical theory.

Julie Jung is a professor of English at Illinois State University, where she teaches graduate and undergraduate courses in contemporary rhetorical theories and writing. She is the author of *Revisionary Rhetoric, Feminist Pedagogy, and Multigenre Texts* (Southern Illinois University Press, 2005). Her scholarship has appeared in edited collections and in journals, including *College English, Disability Studies, enculturation,* and *Rhetoric Review.*

Steven B. Katz is R. Roy and Marnie Pearce Professor of Professional Communication and a professor of English at Clemson University. He is the author of *The Epistemic Music of Rhetoric* (Southern Illinois University Press, 1996) and (with Ann Penrose) *Writing in the Sciences: Exploring Conventions of Scientific Discourse* (3rd ed., Longman 2010). He has published discussions of Kenneth Burke in *Rhetoric Society Quarterly* (1995), *Judaic Perspectives on Composition* (Hampton, 2008), and "Burke's New Body? The Problem of Virtual Material, and Motive, in Object Oriented Philosophy" in *KB Journal* (Summer 2015). His Burkean poem "Pentadic Leaves" also appeared in *KB Journal* (Spring 2017).

Steven LeMieux is a PhD candidate in English with a focus on rhetoric and writing at the University of Texas–Austin. His current research focuses on the interrelations between rhetorical theory, posthuman theory, and the environment through the logic of the parasite. He is also engaged in both digital and material production that inform practice-based composition research. He lives with his wife and their two cats in San Francisco.

Chris Mays is an assistant professor in the Department of English at the University of Nevada, Reno. His research focuses on stability and change in public rhetorics and writing, often in terms of the local and interdisciplinary applications of systems and complexity theory. His work can be found in a variety of academic journals, including *College Composition and Communication, enculturation, JAC,* and *Rhetoric Review.* He also plays in a local garage-rock band started by his colleagues at UNR.

Jodie Nicotra is an associate professor of English at the University of Idaho. She has published articles on digital rhetorics, rhetorical theory, and the thought of Kenneth Burke in *enculturation, Rhetoric Society Quarterly,* and *College Composition and Communication,* among other places. Her textbook *Becoming Rhetorical: A Toolbox for Analyzing and Creating Written, Visual, and Multimodal Compositions,* will be available in fall 2017 from Cengage. She is currently working on a book manuscript about rhetorics of microbiome science, tentatively titled *The Microbial Imaginary.*

Jeff Pruchnic is an associate professor and the director of composition in the Department of English at Wayne State University. He is the author of *Rhetoric and Ethics in the Cybernetic Age: The Transhuman Condition* (Routledge, 2014) and numerous essays about the intersections of rhetoric, critical theory, and science and technology.

Timothy Richardson is an associate professor of English at the University of Texas–Arlington, where he teaches courses in media, writing, and theory. He is the author of *Contingency, Immanence, and the Subject of Rhetoric* (Parlor Press, 2013), as well as essays and articles in such journals as *enculturation, JAC, Kairos,* and *Pre/Text.*

Thomas Rickert is a professor of English at Purdue University. He's published *Acts of Enjoyment: Rhetoric, Žižek, and the Return of the Subject* (2007), and *Ambient Rhetoric: The Attunements of Rhetorical Being* (2013), both published by the University of Pittsburgh Press. His recent publications include "Parmenides, Ontological Enaction, and the Prehistory of Rhetoric" in *Philosophy & Rhetoric* 47, no. 4 (2014) and "Rhetoric and the Paleolithic" in *Review of Communication* 16, no. 4 (2016). He is currently working on a book project investigating a prehistory of rhetoric.

Nathaniel A. Rivers is an associate professor in the Department of English at Saint Louis University. His current research addresses the posthuman's impact on public rhetorics such as environmentalism and locative media. Together with Paul Lynch, he has edited *Thinking with Bruno Latour in Rhetoric and Composition* (Southern Illinois University Press, 2015), which explores the impact of Bruno Latour on rhetoric and composition. His work has appeared in various journals, including *Rhetoric Society Quarterly, College Composition and Communication, Technical Communication Quarterly, Quarterly Journal of Speech, College English, enculturation,* and *Kairos.*

Kellie Sharp-Hoskins is an assistant professor of English at New Mexico State University, where she teaches graduate and undergraduate courses in rhetoric and writing. Her work theorizing methodologies to identify and multiply rhetorical imagination has been published in *enculturation, JAC,* and *Rhetoric Review.* She is currently working on a book project theorizing rhetorical debt.

Robert Wess was trained as a Neo-Aristotelian at the University of Chicago under *Critical Inquiry*'s founding editor, Sheldon Sacks; then, influenced by Richard McKeon's philosophizing of rhetoric, Wess turned to Kenneth Burke, which led to *Kenneth Burke: Rhetoric, Subjectivity, Postmodernism* (Cambridge, 1996) and, with Jack Selzer, *Kenneth Burke and His Circles* (Parlor Press, 2008). Other works are posted at academia.edu. Wess attended the 1984 formation of the Kenneth Burke Society, received the Society's Distinguished Service Award in 1999, and served as its president from 2005 to 2008. He now belongs to the Oregon State University emeritus faculty after teaching in its English department, later renamed the School of Writing, Literature, and Film.

Index